lev	Write at a level appropriate to your subject and audience. **57**		
logic	Check the logic of your writing. **8**		
mm	Misplaced modifier: place it elsewhere so that it clearly modifies the intended word. **52**		
mo	Use the mood required by your sentence. **24**		
ms	Follow conventional manuscript form. **43**		
¶ No ¶	Begin a new paragraph; do not begin a new paragraph. **9, 11**		
‖	Make these elements parallel. **55**		
p	Correct the punctuation		

[]	brackets **36**	( )	parentheses **35**
:	colon **33**	.	period **29**
,	comma **25-28**	?	question mark **30**
--	dash **34**	" "	quotation marks **36**
…	ellipsis **36**	;	semicolon **32**
!	exclamation point **31**		

pred	Make the subject and predicate of this sentence relate to each other logically. **53**
ps	Know the parts of speech and their uses. **15**
ref	Make this pronoun refer clearly to its antecedent. **51**
rep	Eliminate the obvious repetition. **68**
shift	Correct the shift in verb or pronoun use. **56**
sp	Proofread for proper spelling, and work on your spelling weaknesses. **44**
sub	Use subordination to relate secondary details to main ideas. **45**
t	Use the correct verb tense. **22**
trite	Replace this trite expression with fresher language. **65**
ts	Use a topic sentence to focus each paragraph on one point. **9**
u	Unify this paragraph by making all sentences relate to the topic sentence. **11**
vague	Use specific and concrete words. **60**
var	Vary the length and word order of your sentences. **50**
vb	Use the correct form of this verb. **23**
wdy	Tighten this wordy expression. **68**
ww	Wrong word: choose a more exact word. **61, 62**

SHORT ENGLISH HANDBOOK /2

David E. Fear

Valencia Community College

Gerald J. Schiffhorst

University of Central Florida

Scott, Foresman and Company
Glenview, Illinois

Dallas, Tex.   Tucker, Ga.
Oakland, N.J.   London, England
Palo Alto, Cal.

A Study Guide, Short English Workbook, 2nd Edition,
as well as an Instructor's Manual for Short English
Handbook, 2nd Edition, is available. It may be obtained
through a Scott, Foresman representative or by writing
to English Editor, College Division, Scott, Foresman
and Company, 1900 East Lake Avenue, Glenview,
Illinois 60025.

Library of Congress Cataloging in Publication Data

Fear, David E., 1941–
    Short English handbook

    Includes index.
    1. English language—Rhetoric. 2. English
language—Grammar—1950-   I. Schiffhorst,
Gerald J. II. Title.

PE1408.F38 1981   808'.042   81-9425

ISBN 0-673-15545-5   AACR2

ACKNOWLEDGMENTS

Carl Sagan, *Broca's Brain: Reflections on the Romance of Science*. New York: Random House, 1979, p. 205.

From "My Philosophy" in *Getting Even* by Woody Allen. Published by Random House, Inc., 1972.

From "The Grey Beginnings" in *The Sea Around Us*, Revised Edition, by Rachel L. Carson, p. 82. Published by Oxford University Press, Inc., 1962.

Thorstein Veblen, "The Limitations of Marginal Utility." *Journal of Political Economy*, 1909.

Excerpt from *Reporting Technical Information*, Third Edition, by Kenneth W. Houp and Thomas E. Persell. Copyright © 1977 by Benziger Bruce & Glencoe, Inc. Reprinted by permission of Macmillan Publishing Co, Inc.

From "The Coming Victory of the New Television" by Nicholas Johnson, *The Humanist*, July/August 1972. Copyright © 1972 by The Humanist. Reprinted by permission.

From "The Theory of Practical Joking—Its Relevance to Physics" by R. V. Jones, *Bulletin* of the Institute of Physics, June 1957, p. 193. Reprinted by permission.

From *Understanding Media: The Extensions of Man* by Marshall McLuhan, p. 84. Published by McGraw-Hill Book Company, 1964.

"They're Putting Lids on Enrollments" by Jack Magarrell from *The Chronicle of Higher Education*, November 3, 1979, p. 1. Reprinted by permission.

From "Topics: Reflections on the Death of a Library" by Philip Roth, *The New York Times*, 1 March 1969. © 1969 by The New York Times Company. Reprinted by permission.

From "One Way to Solve the Pollution Problem" by Larry E. Ruff, *St. Petersburg Times*, December 28, 1969. Reprinted by permission.

Preface

Our purpose in this second edition of the *Short English Handbook* is the same as in the first: to provide students and other writers with clear, concise answers to questions that arise during the composing process or to those that an instructor might pose in responding to an essay. Such writers neither want nor need to labor through detailed discussions of the many options available in English; but they do need explanations and examples which they can apply to their own work. And they must be able to find such information quickly: They need to spend their time writing rather than leafing through elaborate textbooks. In revising this book, we have again sought to fulfill these needs by providing a useful source of clear, brief answers to the major questions about writing.

As students write, they should see grammar and style as part of the writing process. For that reason, our text begins with chapters on planning whole essays and on developing essays through paragraphs. Though the book warns students of some common pitfalls in writing, it takes a predominantly positive tone, encouraging students to make choices that will express their ideas clearly and effectively. As students develop their writing skills, they will discover those areas of grammar and style on which they should concentrate when revising their essays.

Chapters 3 and 4 treat basic sentence structures and the conventions for punctuating those structures. Although we rely as little as possible on formal terminology, some terms are needed to explain sentence structure and these terms are usually defined both in the text and in the Glossary of Grammatical Terms. Chapter 5 turns from the merely correct sentence to the effective sentence, suggesting ways to make writing clearer and smoother. Chapter 6 extends this discussion to the choice of accurate, expressive words. The final two chapters emphasize common conventions as well as the processes involved in preparing research papers and other forms of college and job-related writing.

As a result of this practical, concise approach, the first edition of the Handbook met with considerable success. Thus we have retained most of the book's original features and have added several others to enhance its usefulness both as a classroom text and as an aid to students working on their own. First, we have supplied additional exercises in most sections to give students the fullest possible source of practice. Second, we have added a short section on sentence combining so that the chapter on sentences is more complete in its presentation of syntactical strategies. Third, we have expanded the Glossary of Usage. Finally, we have reworked the research paper chapter, which now follows the MLA format on documentation and includes a new sample student paper.

To keep individual entries brief and accessible, we maintain, whenever possible, a simple, easy-to-follow plan. We state a principle, explain it briefly, then present one or more pairs of examples marked with such designations as "weak/improved" or "incorrect/correct." For the most part, these examples come directly from student writing. Where necessary, the examples are followed by further discussion of refinements, variations, and special cases. Completing each entry is a set of exercises which test and reinforce the student's mastery of the principle.

Access to the entries is possible through the correction chart, printed on the inside front cover, which is keyed to entry numbers. The inside back cover presents a useful, brief checklist for writers which is also keyed to entry numbers. The complete index gives detailed listings of specific points discussed in the entries.

Like all such texts, this handbook is the product of more years of marking student papers than we care to count. But we are happy to acknowledge the work of many students at various institutions who have continually sharpened our critical skills and provided us with innumerable examples of enjoyable writing. We are also grateful to four consultants whose suggestions on the first edition helped make the text consistent in its purpose and in its representation of our complex language: Roy C. O'Donnell of the University of Georgia, Donald C. Freeman of Temple University, Wayne Harsh of the University of California at Davis, and Joseph Williams of the University of Chicago.

We had a great deal of help from reviewers for the first edition and would like to thank the following for their help on the revision: Marvin Austin, Columbia State Community College; David Barber, University of Idaho; Millard Dunn, Indiana University Southeast; Douglas Eason, Columbia State Community College; John Hutchens, Pitt Community College; Paul Kaser, Reedley College; Michael Miller, Long-view Community College; Carol Niederlander, St. Louis Community College at Forest Park; Joan Patrie, Jamestown Community College; Nancy Veglahn, South Dakota State University; Kristin Woolever, Allegheny College; and Joseph Yokelson, Bridgewater State College.

Of special value in revising the book were the helpful comments of May L. Ryburn of the College of DuPage, the guidance on sentence combining generously provided by Marian Price of the University of Central Florida, and the research assistance of Christine H. Young of UCF. In addition to our Valencia and UCF colleagues, we are also happy to acknowledge our indebtedness to those at Scott, Foresman who have made the project both possible and pleasant: our patient editors, Jane Steinmann and Anita Portugal, as well as Amanda Clark, Harriett Prentiss, Stan Stoga, Richard Welna, and John J. Miller.

David E. Fear
Gerald J. Schiffhorst

Contents

5 EFFECTIVE SENTENCES *135*

6 **WORDS** *175*

7 **THE RESEARCH PAPER** *217*

8 SPECIAL APPLICATIONS *299*

GLOSSARY OF GRAMMATICAL TERMS *315*

INDEX *321*

THE WHOLE COMPOSITION

Some Introductory Advice

Instead of reading this book straight through, you will probably refer to various chapters and entries as you need them. Even so, to put the individual entries in perspective and to help you get the most from the time you spend writing, we will begin with an overview of the whole subject of writing.

We are not going to present a simple, foolproof formula guaranteed to make you a competent writer. Unfortunately, there is no such formula. Writing is like playing tennis: you learn and improve by doing—by practicing, by listening to criticism, and by practicing some more. Good writing does not just avoid blunders. It holds the reader's interest. When you write well, you begin by thinking out what you want to say. Then you say it, in clear, logical sentences and carefully chosen words, expressing your thoughts and feelings so that your audience will understand them just as you want them to be understood.

Most writing—certainly all the writing we will be concerned with here—has a purpose and a method suited to it. Writers tell stories: they say what happened (narration). Or they argue: they speak for or against something (argument). Or they describe: they tell how something looks or sounds or moves (description). Or they explain: they tell how something works or why it does not work (exposition). As you plan what you want to say in a paper, you will also be deciding which of these four approaches you will use. This does not mean that you will choose one approach and leave the rest in storage. In college writing, you may be called on to explain, argue, describe, or narrate, or explain *and* argue, or describe *and* narrate, or do all four in one paper. Nevertheless, the assignment or your own purpose or a combination of your purpose and your material will usually make one approach predominant. For example, you may start out by describing ways in which consumers are deceived by television commercials, then end up arguing that there should be stricter regulation of such advertising. Since the emphasis in this case should fall on the argument, your purpose in describing commercials is to prepare your reader to believe as you do about regulation.

The writing most commonly required of college students is expository. In an essay on punk rock, for example, your main purpose might be to explain this style. In the process, you might compare punk rock with other kinds of rock; you might classify punk-rock groups in various ways; you might analyze different views of punk rock, using quotations from magazines and newspapers. But almost certainly you would also describe the dress of the performers and their fans, and you might very well include a narrative account of a visit to a punk-rock concert. Finally, you might conclude with your own opinion of the social implications of punk rock: should it be seen as a harmless diversion or as a corrupting influence? Still, the finished product would be mostly expository: here is punk rock as I know it from talking and reading about it, from listening to records and going to concerts.

To a certain degree, all such writing must be persuasive. It must persuade readers that it is worth their time and attention. What you have to say will get a fair hearing only if you make sure it deserves one. Writing that deserves to be read is the kind we will be concerned with throughout this book.

Find an interesting and manageable topic.   To convince others that what you write is worth reading, you must first be interested in the subject yourself. Picking a subject you know and feel something about will make planning and developing the paper easier and more pleasant. It will also give the finished paper an authenticity, authority, and enthusiasm that will capture and hold your reader's interest. When a topic is assigned, make sure you are comfortable with it before you start to write. You must understand just what is being asked of you, and you must know—or find out—enough about the subject so that you can handle it with some confidence.

In general, broad topics lead to shallow papers. If you are asked to write five hundred words on the energy problem, consider whether you can write on *some phase* of the problem. You could end up with a topic as manageable as "What the Tenants in Our Building Are Doing to Save Electricity." If you limit your topic, you will be able to develop your ideas fully and give your reader some useful, specific information. (See **1** and **2** on selecting and limiting topics.)

Consider your reader.   When you write, you should not be trying just to express yourself on paper; you should be addressing an audience. Try not to write solely for your instructor. Imagine yourself writing for some specific outside audience (if your instructor has not chosen one for you). Whenever possible, aim your paper at a person or a group you might actually want to communicate with. A record review or a book review, for example, might be addressed to your classmates. An editorial could be written with the readers of the campus newspaper in mind. A report or an abstract might be prepared for an employer. A proposal or a protest might be intended for your mayor or state representative.

Write a rough draft. If you scramble frantically to finish a paper the night before it is due, neither it nor your reader will benefit. Get the first draft on paper as soon as you have some ideas. Making a start is the first big hurdle. Scribble away until the ideas run out, and then stop writing. But keep on thinking. If possible, let a day or two pass before you read over what you have written. You may decide that you have to start all over again, or you may be able to add a few paragraphs and have a complete draft. Most likely, you will want to keep some of what you did, replace some, rearrange some. If you begin early enough, you will have time to do all this and then get on with the polishing.

Develop effective openings and closings. You need not imitate the student who started each of his essays with an obscenity in order to get the reader's attention, but you do need to get that attention. The effect of a good opening will carry over into the rest of the paper. And remember that a last impression is as important as a first impression: a weak ending can destroy the effect of even the most carefully composed paper. A strong ending reemphasizes key ideas, reinforces what you have been trying to do throughout, and leaves the reader satisfied. (See **13** and **14** for more on introductions and conclusions.)

Develop your own voice as a writer. Inexperienced writers often incorrectly assume that writing must sound "literary"—full of long words and complicated sentences. Although your written English is bound to be somewhat more formal than your spoken English, avoid striking a pretentious pose. Instead of trying to impress your readers with formal or unfamiliar language, impress them by expressing sound ideas in well-chosen words. That is the voice that will be expected of you in most college writing.

Read your work aloud. You can identify and replace many an awkward or otherwise ineffective expression because it does not *sound* right.

Revise, revise, revise. Before preparing your final draft, go over your paper with the greatest care, working from the largest elements—the parts and paragraphs—to the smallest—individual words and marks of punctuation. Revision includes such matters as reorganizing the paper and rewriting wordy and awkward sentences so that they say exactly what you want them to say. If time permits, type the final rough draft to see how the finished product will look. The final draft must be as clear and direct and as free from errors as you can make it.

Learn from criticism. Painful as it may be to have someone tear your work apart, you should study such criticism, make sure you understand it, and then rework your papers with that criticism in mind. That is the best way to improve your writing. Just as the greatest golfers return to instructors for help with their games, so you can learn from your instructor's criticism.

Read extensively. Read books by good writers, noticing how they choose words, shape sentences, organize para-

5

graphs, and create a flow of ideas that carries the reader along to a logical conclusion. Read newspapers and magazines, too, always with a critical eye, studying the writers' techniques and asking yourself what makes a piece of writing effective or ineffective.

Trust yourself. Since you are a unique human being, your papers should present your ideas, your reasoning, your words—uniquely yours even if the whole class writes on the same topic. As a writer, you will be working—sometimes struggling—to express those ideas and develop them so that others will find them worth reading. The purpose of this book is to help you achieve that goal.

1

Select a topic that fits the assignment, that interests you, and that is appropriate to your audience.

In preparing a paper for a class, begin by studying the broad assignment ("For your classmates, write a 500-word explanation of a process or a technique that you have found useful") and the specific suggestions ("Possibilities range from planting tomatoes to adjusting a carburetor to housebreaking a puppy"). Settle on a topic that interests you; that you know something about; and that you believe you can make interesting and useful to your audience.

Here are examples of topics students chose for papers addressed to an audience of classmates:

INAPPROPRIATE:	A Simple Method of Determining Chi Square with a Pocket Calculator
APPROPRIATE:	A Foolproof Method of Balancing a Checkbook with a Pocket Calculator
INAPPROPRIATE:	The Sources of the Fantasy and Myth in Tolkien's Fiction
APPROPRIATE:	Some Reasons for the Popularity of Tolkien's *Lord of the Rings*

The first inappropriate example assumes a stronger background in statistics than most students have. It would be appropriate for a group of students who use chi square in interpreting research data but not for students in the average writing class. The second inappropriate topic deals with a broad subject that most students could treat successfully only through extensive research. A good paper on that topic would require more time and space than the typical college essay permits.

The first appropriate topic has a broad appeal. Many of us know nothing about chi square, but almost all of us know about unbalanced checkbooks. The second appropriate topic is more sensible in scope than the overly ambitious topic on Tolkien's fiction as a whole, and it gives the writer more opportunity to present personal judgments.

EXERCISE 1 _____

Which of the proposed theme topics below are appropriate for an audience of nonspecialists, such as college students? Mark those that would be appropriate A, *inappropriate* X.

1. Chaucer's Ironic Treatment of the Courtly Love Tradition
2. The Effects of Laetrile on Cancer Patients
3. The Problems of Being a Student Athlete
4. Blocking Assignments on the Fullback Trap Play
5. The Differences Between AM & FM Radio Stations
6. G.E. Moore's Concept of the Naturalistic Fallacy

7. Year-round Daylight Saving Time as an
   Energy-conservation Measure
8. The Design of Heat-resistant Semi-conductors
9. The Reasons for Bilingual Education
10. Arguments Against the Grand Jury System

2

Limit your topic so that you can develop it fully in the space and time available.

Students too often try to cover in a short theme a topic
that they could treat adequately only in a term paper or
even in a book. Keeping in mind the time you have to
gather and arrange your information, limit your subject
so that you can give it the coverage it deserves—that is,
back up your general statements with particular facts
and details. The following examples show how you
might begin with a very broad subject and narrow it to
a topic which you can handle in a short paper:

FAR TOO BROAD:	The Serious Side of Science Fiction
STILL TOO BROAD:	Key Themes in the Science Fiction of Ray Bradbury
WELL LIMITED:	The Dehumanizing Effect of Machines in Ray Bradbury's "The Pedestrian"
FAR TOO BROAD:	Football Safety
STILL TOO BROAD:	Reasons for Football Injuries
WELL LIMITED:	The Role of Artificial Turf in Football Injuries
FAR TOO BROAD:	Modern Technology Harms the Environment
STILL TOO BROAD:	Industrial Chemicals Produce Water Pollution
WELL LIMITED:	Acid Rain, Caused Mostly by Coal-Burning Plants, Kills Lakes

EXERCISE 2 _____

Study the theme topics below. Mark those that are well limited for a 300–500-word paper L, *those that are too broad* X.

1. Victimless Crimes
2. Why Many Young People Distrust the Police
3. Capital Punishment Should Be Banned
4. Why the Marx Brothers' *Animal Crackers* Is Still Funny
5. Why I Am Majoring in Fresh Water Ecology
6. The Right of Teachers to Strike
7. The Feasibility of Electric Cars
8. Subliminal Advertising
9. Recent Changes in the Family Structure
10. How to Play Lacrosse

3

Explore your topic before starting to write.

Once you have chosen a well-limited topic on a subject that interests you and that can be made interesting to your readers, you can begin to locate and arrange material. In fact, the process of composing a paper begins as soon as you jot down whatever comes into your head about the topic. In this free flow of ideas known as prewriting, you probe what you know and feel about the topic. One or two key ideas should emerge, along with secondary ideas and examples that you can use or discard as the essay takes shape. When you scribble down ideas or take notes on something you read, you are literally prewriting because you have not begun your first draft. You are gathering material even before you know what your main point will be. You are not concerned with correct form or style but with exploring your topic as fully as you can.

Given a general subject, such as "How Television Contributes to Sexual Stereotypes," here are basic questions you should ask yourself before you begin to write:

1. What do key terms mean? (What are "sexual stereotypes"?)
2. What do I know about the subject? (What TV programs come to mind?)
3. What have I read or heard in class about the subject? (Can I find any notes or articles about stereotypes in the media?)
4. How should I approach the subject? (To limit the topic, should I consider only commercials? Should I argue a point of view or just describe stereotypes?)
5. What do I think about the topic? (What are my feelings about the stereotyping of sexual roles?)

When you answer these questions, you will discover what you know about the topic and what you need to learn. You can then look through your jotted notes for a central idea you want to develop (your answer to question 5 will be especially helpful) and for details to support your central idea.

EXERCISE 3 _____

Study the potential theme topics below. Choose two to explore further; then answer the five questions above about each topic.

1. Raising the Drinking Age to 21
2. Ways of Keeping Politics Out of the Olympics
3. Positive versus Negative Reinforcement in Disciplining Children
4. Using Sphagnum Moss to Air-Layer a Plant
5. Changes Needed in the Electoral College

4

Give your paper focus with a precise thesis statement.

Your central idea—your *thesis*—summarizes what you want to say about your topic. To make sure that your central idea will control your paper, construct a sentence that expresses the thesis as precisely as possible. This thesis statement does not simply announce what you are going to write *about* ("This paper will discuss the effect of removing the emission-control devices from Ford V-8 engines"). It specifies the main point that you are going to make. For example, you may want to say:

> Removing emission-control devices from a Ford V-8 can give you as many as five extra miles per gallon and improve performance.
>
> *Or:* Removing emission-control devices from a Ford V-8 can make the engine almost impossible to keep in tune and can seriously increase air pollution.
>
> *Or:* Despite saving the owner a small amount on gasoline bills, removing the emission-control devices from a Ford V-8 can make the engine almost impossible to tune and seriously increase air pollution.
>
> *Or:* Despite saving the owner a small amount on gasoline bills, removing the emission-control devices from Ford V-8 engines will cause more trouble than it is worth.

Each of these thesis statements serves three functions:

1. It identifies the limited subject and thus provides a test for what material should go into your paper.
2. It makes clear your attitude toward the subject.
3. It focuses the reader's attention on the specific features of the subject that you will discuss.

The inadequate thesis statements that follow perform only one or two of those three functions:

INADEQUATE: The allied health fields are very promising today.

IMPROVED: Many new, well-paying, challenging positions are opening up in medical technology.

INADEQUATE: Police officers today are different from the way they used to be.

IMPROVED: As increasing numbers of college-educated men and women join the police forces of our major cities, the old stereotype of the big, dumb cop is becoming as out-of-date as it is insulting.

Notice that the improved thesis statements point to the kind of material that should be presented in the paper. Such thesis statements make it much easier to put information together. For instance, if you were developing the paper on jobs in medical technology, you would know that you need data on recent developments in the field, on salaries, and on jobs that call for more than routine performance—and you would know that you should ignore information with no bearing on these matters.

Despite the importance of a thesis statement, you need not feel bound to the first one you write. If you come upon contradictory information or if your attitude changes as you think about the topic, you can always revise your thesis. You might, for example, decide to change your thesis statement on the new breed of police officers to something like this:

The change in big-city police forces today results not so much from college graduates entering police work as from policemen and policewomen taking advantage of opportunities for advanced education and specialized training.

EXERCISE 4 _____

Study the thesis statements below. A. Mark with W those that look as if they would work well for a paper of 300 to 500 words. Mark with X those that need to be more sharply focused—that is, more specific. B. Revise those you have marked X so that they are suitable for a short paper.

1. A Southerner who moves to a big city in the North must adjust to a different, faster-paced style of life.
2. Television shows give young viewers detailed information about committing crimes.
3. Despite their obvious differences, skiing on snow and skiing on water require the same basic skills and provide the same kind of thrills.
4. Professional athletes are overpaid.
5. The lyrics of songs by the Beatles, Bob Dylan, and other recording stars of the last twenty years are worthy of being compared to the "serious" poetry taught in English courses.
6. Euthanasia, or mercy killing, by its very name is murder and never should be legalized.
7. Abortion should be a woman's prerogative since she alone should have control over her own body.
8. Mopeds, although they offer cheap transportation, are too dangerous both to their drivers and others.
9. Ray Charles's lyrics and style result from his early life.
10. A home can be altered to accommodate the physically handicapped.

5

Use a rough outline to organize your ideas.

To organize your material and get started on a first draft, list the major points you will use to develop your thesis. You need not construct a formal outline with major and minor headings. Just set down your three or four major points in the order in which you plan to take them up. Then you can sort the information you accumulate about your topic under the different headings in your list, discarding whatever does not fit. You may, of course, turn up so much information on a new point that you will decide to add it to your outline or substitute it for a point already there or combine it with one of the old ones. Go right ahead. The rough outline is merely a tool.

Below is a sample thesis statement with two rough outlines—one unsuccessful, one more effective—for an essay explaining the popularity of a television program.

THESIS: Largely because of poor governmental coordination, bilingual education often fails to help young non-native speakers of English cope with American society.

UNSUCCESSFUL:
1. Students' inability to read English
2. Governmental red tape
3. More than 500,000 children involved
4. $700 million a year spent by taxpayers
5. Hispanics not only group involved

SUCCESSFUL:
1. Local and state programs with different goals
2. Legal action by U.S. Supreme Court and Department of Education
3. Insufficient funds for needed teachers
4. Some schools forced to teach biculturalism rather than English
5. Children in some cities remain in native-language classes for years

The second rough outline is superior because each of the five points is distinct. In the first outline, points three and four are almost the same. But the primary difference is that the second outline picks up the key points in the thesis statement. It should work nicely to help develop the thesis.

EXERCISE 5 _____

Study the thesis statements and rough outlines below. Mark each outline that would be helpful with H, *unhelpful with* X.

1. *Thesis:* Most students find that living on campus is preferable to living at home.

   rough outline:
   1. cafeteria food is one drawback
   2. opportunities to make more friends
   3. developing independence
   4. proximity to classes and libraries
   5. learning to live on a budget

2. *Thesis:* There are many types of prejudice other than religious and racial.

   rough outline:
   1. small-town roots vs. urban sophistication
   2. big-name schools vs. lesser known ones
   3. physically handicapped people vs. non-handicapped
   4. Southern accents vs. Northern accents
   5. wealthy families vs. middle-class families

3. *Thesis:* Alcoholism has become a major health problem.

   rough outline:
   1. nearly 40 million Americans cannot control their drinking
   2. teenage drinking rises
   3. cost of alcohol strains family budgets
   4. alcohol-related crimes increase
   5. brain cells and liver damaged

4. *Thesis:* The coming of Walt Disney World to Florida has brought happiness to tourists, riches to promoters, and problems to most area natives.

   rough outline:
   1. joys of the "magic kingdom"
   2. more restaurants, theaters, and shopping centers
   3. overnight millionaires
   4. higher taxes and prices
   5. congested streets and highways

5. *Thesis:* Americans' Sunday habits have changed substantially over the past thirty years.

   rough outline:
   1. no more Sunday drives
   2. no more Sunday clothes

3. Sunday sports on TV
4. fewer, if any, Sunday dinners
5. family members living farther apart

6

Build a topic outline or a sentence outline with a major division for each section of your paper.

A thorough topic outline can provide a complete, point-by-point layout of your entire paper. A sentence outline can do even more. It can give topic sentences for all of your points. Detailed topic or sentence outlines are excellent guides to organization and can be especially helpful in preparing a long paper.

To develop a good topic outline, start by using the points on your rough outline as the major divisions (I, II, III, etc.). Then develop subdivisions (A, B, C) for each. Although two levels may be enough for a short paper, a third level (1, 2, 3) will help you organize details in longer projects. Sometimes even a fourth level is useful.

The following diagram shows the various levels of the conventional outline. In outlining most college papers, you will probably use numbers or letters in parentheses rarely, if at all.

I. _____
  A. _____
  B. _____
    1. _____
    2. _____
      a. _____
        (1) _____
          (a) _____
          (b) _____
        (2) _____
      b. _____

The topic outline presented below is followed by a sentence outline of the same material.

TOPIC OUTLINE

Title: The Value of *Sesame Street*

Thesis: *Sesame Street* has proved that television programming can be both educational and entertaining.

    I. The program's appeal to young audiences
       A. Music and the Muppets
       B. Animation and fast-paced style
    II. The serious purpose: to improve the learning skills of preschool children
       A. Parental concern about need for early education and impact of TV on children
         1. Research on the influence of TV on young viewers
         2. Demands for nonviolent programs
       B. Idea of a nonviolent educational program
         1. Funds and staff sought
         2. Ambitious goals outlined
         3. Creative format conceived
   III. Success despite some criticism
       A. High ratings and faithful audiences
       B. Some criticism by educators
         1. Help for the disadvantaged questioned
         2. Help for children to solve problems to learn actively questioned
       C. Much irrelevant criticism
    IV. Television's ability to teach certain skills and to show that some parts of education can be entertaining

SENTENCE OUTLINE

Title: The Value of *Sesame Street*

Thesis: *Sesame Street* has proved that television programming can be both educational and entertaining.

    I. The program has an obvious appeal to young audiences.
       A. Music and the Muppets are typical of its entertaining features.

     B. Animation and a fast-paced style hold young
        viewers' attention.

II. Behind the lighthearted surface, *Sesame Street* has a
    serious purpose: to improve the learning skills of
    preschool children.
     A. When the program was developed, Americans
        were becoming increasingly aware of the need for
        early education and concerned about the impact of
        television on children.
        1. Research revealed the influence of television
           on children.
        2. Parents demanded nonviolent programs.
     B. The Children's Television Workshop created the
        idea for a nonviolent educational program.
        1. The producers sought a large grant and
           assembled a talented staff.
        2. The staff outlined an ambitious set of goals for
           the show.
        3. The staff conceived a creative format for
           presenting the educational material.

III. The show was a success despite the criticism
    it generated.
     A. The Nielsen ratings were high and the audiences
        faithful.
     B. Educators became critical of the program.
        1. They asked whether *Sesame Street* reached
           the disadvantaged.
        2. They asked if the program helped children
           solve problems and if it encouraged children to
           learn passively.
     C. Much of the criticism misses the point of the show.

IV. *Sesame Street* has proved that educational television can
    effectively teach certain skills to children and that
    some parts of education can be entertaining.

7

Follow the conventions in drawing up a formal outline.

If your instructor has you draw up a formal outline to be handed in with your paper, you should be aware of certain established conventions for outlining. The purpose of these conventions is to make the organization of your material clear and logical.

Make your outline either a topic outline or a sentence outline, not a mixture of the two. If it is a topic outline, then make *all* the divisions and subdivisions phrases. If it is a sentence outline, then make *all* the divisions and subdivisions full sentences.

Make your subdivisions logically consistent. If your main division is "I. Students in four-year colleges," and your first two subdivisions are "A. Freshmen" and "B. Sophomores," then you should logically continue with "C. Juniors" and "D. Seniors." If, instead, you switch to "C. History majors" and "D. Students on athletic scholarships," you are obviously changing your approach in mid-theme.

Always use at least two subdivisions. If you have "I.A," you must have "I.B," and if you have "A.1," you must have "A.2." It makes no sense to "divide" something into one part. If you have "A. Folk Rock," followed only by "A.1. Bob Dylan," think over what you are actually going to say in your paper. Are you going to talk about other kinds of folk rock than Dylan's? Then add subdivisions A.2, A.3, and so on. Is it only Dylan's folk rock that you are going to discuss? Then make your A. heading "Bob Dylan's Folk Rock," and have no subdivisions.

Do not subdivide unnecessarily. As a general rule, sub-divisions should stand for blocks of material, not single sentences and certainly not single words. For example, in a paper on automobile sales in the United States, you may have the division "III. Foreign Compact Cars," and you may plan to refer to nine specific makes. If you plan to give equal coverage to each—say, a full paragraph— then you would need nine subdivisions: III.A., III.B., III.C., and so on. But unless you are writing a very long paper, you will probably do no more than list some of the makes, and might need only the four headings "German," "Japanese," "Swedish," and "French," or simply the two categories "European" and "Japanese."

EXERCISE 7 _____

Study the outline below. Rearrange entries, add new entries, and change the wording of entries where needed to make the outline follow the standard conventions.

Thesis: Many Americans refuse to worry about the numerous problems our cities face.

    I. Most people believe that solutions are unlikely.
       A. Many now realize the complexity of the problems.
       B. Cynicism about ability of political leaders
          1. Effects of Watergate
       C. Others just assume that the problems will solve themselves.
       D. Media blamed for creating or exaggerating problems
    II. Many serious problems
       A. High crime rates
       B. Declining neighborhoods
       C. Rising costs of police & fire protection
       D. Rising costs of public housing
       E. Declining downtown shopping is due to newer suburban malls.
       F. Inflation affects schools
       G. Welfare costs soar
       H. Slow state & federal aid to cities

III. For many, problems seem far away
   A. Urban riots in sixties
   B. Gleaming new skyscrapers distract urban visitors
   C. Problems ignored by those unaffected
      1. Need for safe streets
      2. Is white exodus to suburbs over?
      3. Decaying schools
      4. Declining tax base

8   logic

Check the logic of your writing.

Successful writing is convincing as well as interesting. Before completing your final copy, check your reasoning to make sure that it is logical, free from those errors known as *fallacies*. Expect others to be as skeptical about what you write as you are—or should be—about what you read. For example, statistics will be convincing only if your reader knows how reliable they are. In any persuasive writing, anticipate objections to your opinions. Admit that there are other views. In refuting opinions you disagree with, do not attack those who hold the opposing views but instead give your reader good reasons to reject those views. If you cannot show logically why your opinions are preferable to others, you need to do more thinking and reading or consider changing your thesis.

Logic is concerned with the way thought moves from assumptions to conclusions. It does so in two ways, by induction and by deduction. *Induction* begins with specific facts and proceeds to general statements: "Every tree that has been examined throughout history has had roots; therefore, I conclude that all trees have roots." The other kind of reasoning, *deduction*, proceeds from the general to the specific: "Since all trees have roots, the maple tree in my yard must have roots."

8 logic

Hasty generalization. The chief fallacy in inductive reasoning is the hasty generalization, a conclusion based on insufficient evidence. When you hear such generalizations as "Women are no good at math" or "Drinking is responsible for most fatal car crashes," you must ask yourself, "Is there sufficient evidence to justify the statement? Are no women competent mathematicians? Do most fatal car crashes result from a single cause—drunkenness—or from a combination of causes?"

The most common hasty generalizations include absolute terms such as *all, none,* and *every* rather than such terms as *some, few,* or *many.* A sweeping statement such as "Service stations along interstate highways overcharge for parts and labor" (a statement which implies *all*) becomes more defensible if it is reduced to established fact: "According to *Consumer Reports,* there were more than one hundred complaints of overcharging by interstate service stations in New York and New Jersey last year."

Non sequitur. The chief fallacy in deductive reasoning is called the non sequitur (meaning "it does not follow"), a conclusion that does not follow from the preceding statement(s). A typical non sequitur is Chris Evert Lloyd uses Ultra Brite toothpaste; therefore, using Ultra Brite will make me more attractive to men." You could just as logically claim that using it would improve your tennis game. The crucial word in this fallacy is *therefore* (or *thus, so,* and related words). It should indicate that you are making a logical deduction.

The way to avoid non sequiturs is to test the logic of your statements. The non sequitur about the toothpaste actually says that (1) Chris Evert Lloyd uses the toothpaste, (2) she is attractive to men, (3) therefore, by using the toothpaste, I will be more attractive to men. For this chain of reasoning to make sense, it would have to be established that Mrs. Lloyd's attractiveness depended entirely on the whiteness of her teeth—a dubious proposition. Often, you will have to fill in even more of the chain of reasoning to get at what you have actually said. If you find that you have written, "Hawkes must be a Southerner; he's full of prejudice," your thinking must have run something like this: Southerners are full of prejudice; Hawkes is full of prejudice; therefore, Hawkes is a Southerner. In fact, your "reasoning" offers no evidence at all of Hawkes' place of origin, since you have not tried to suggest that *only* Southerners are "full of prejudice."

Post hoc.   Just because one event preceded another, do not assume that the first caused the second. For example, "Since I started dating Maria, my grades have improved" may be true; but to convince anyone that dating Maria is the *cause* of the improvement, you must show some more direct evidence. Did Maria tutor you? Did she insist that you study? Similarly, "Reelect me; Louisville has grown by fifteen percent since I've been mayor" represents *post hoc, ergo propter hoc* reasoning ("after this, therefore because of this") unless the mayor can show that he actually brought about the high growth rate.

Begging the question.   This common fallacy assumes as true something that needs to be proved. A question such as "Why do we let them cheat us this way?" begs the question "Are they in fact cheating us?" Similarly, a statement such as "Only union bargaining can stop the company's unfair labor practices" calls for proof that the company's labor practices are unfair.

Faulty dilemma.   This is the either-or fallacy: "The university must either persuade more students to take Spanish or eliminate the Spanish department." Such statements are not accurate when there are other alternatives. (The size of the Spanish department might be reduced.)

8 logic

False analogy. Analogies (comparing items that are similar in one or more respects but dissimilar in others) provide an effective way to clarify a point and can even be persuasive, but they are not acceptable as logical proof. For instance, the United States today resembles in some ways the ancient Roman Empire, but arguing that the United States is therefore doomed to collapse is illogical.

Arguing to the man (ad hominem). Trying to discredit an argument by attacking someone who upholds it or trying to win an argument by praising someone who shares your view is illogical. For example, "Don't vote for the mayor's tax proposal; he neglects his wife and children." Ideas should finally be judged on their own merits, not on the merits of those who support them.

Argument to ignorance. This fallacy is found in several forms. One common form is the assertion that something is true because it has not been proved wrong. No one has proved that UFOs do not come from other planets, but that does not prove that they do. The burden of any argument is on the writer to support an assertion, not on others to disprove it. In another form of this fallacy, a writer overwhelms the readers with statistics or technical language that they cannot understand or with appeals to authorities with whom they are unfamiliar. Unscrupulous political writers often refer to mysterious "reliable sources," of whom the readers have never heard but who they often assume must be genuine.

Ignoring the question. Sometimes called a "diversion" or "red herring," an argument that exhibits this fallacy introduces material that has little if anything to do with the point in question and so serves only to distract the reader. In a discussion of Jimmy Carter's record as

logic **8**

President, an attack on the activities of Billy Carter would be ignoring the question. Always be sure that your material is directly relevant to your thesis.

EXERCISE 8 _____

Identify and explain the error in reasoning in each of the following assertions.

1. Fifty percent of the doctors interviewed recommended aspirin for colds.
2. This country will never get off dead center until more members of our party are elected.
3. You can't trust state legislators; five of them were arrested for crimes last year.
4. Since hunters oppose gun control, Brown, who voted for gun control, cannot be a hunter.
5. Everyone is wild about the new Woody Allen movie.
6. Though I haven't met Trevor, I know he will be polite since he is English.
7. Since young men can be drafted at 18, they should be allowed to drink at that age.
8. Should the police stop the investigation and just wait for the next murder?
9. Abolishing capital punishment will mean an increase in crime.
10. The traffic is moving so slowly that there must be an accident up ahead.
11. Since Catholics oppose abortion and since Susan favors it, she is not a Catholic.
12. Tests show that the more education a person has, the more likely he is to fall asleep at the wheel; so college graduates should not be allowed to drive.
13. The President is the captain of our ship of state, steering our country toward peace. To vote him out of office would be a mutiny.
14. Crime rose during Governor Smith's term and fell just after he left; he was obviously soft on crime.
15. Experts are divided as to the harmful effects of television violence.

16. Opponents of equal rights for women have little
    credibility since the notorious Nora Jones is their leader.
17. The fact that the Bermuda Triangle mysteries have not
    been conclusively solved shows that they have a
    supernatural origin.
18. Mr. Roby, the attorney, must be affluent; income in his
    profession averages $60,000 a year.
19. Just like a lighthouse throwing its beams out to sea, the
    death penalty is a much-needed warning.
20. Since more women than men are attending college now,
    women will soon be replacing men in leadership positions.

2

PARAGRAPHS

Writers use paragraphs to build sentences into blocks of thought which can then join with other paragraphs to develop the main idea of an essay or other piece of writing. A paragraph can introduce a thesis (the main idea of a paper), develop one of the points supporting the thesis, conclude the discussion, or supply a transition between parts of a fairly long paper. The paragraphs which support the thesis often correspond to the points in a rough outline (**5**) or to the main sections of a detailed outline (**6**). For example, you might begin a short film review with a paragraph describing the movie as amusing and well-acted but easily forgettable. Then, in three longer paragraphs, you might take up in turn the amusing plot, the skill of the actors, and the lack of originality that kept the movie from being memorable.

A good paragraph presents enough facts and examples to satisfy the reader that its topic has been properly developed; and it does so in sentences that fit together, or cohere, to form a single unit. The following sections examine the main qualities of an effective expository paragraph.

9 ts

Use a topic sentence to focus each paragraph on one point.

The topic sentence of a paragraph states the central idea that the rest of the paragraph clarifies, exemplifies, or otherwise supports. A good topic sentence is therefore useful to both writer and reader. The writer can use it to guide the development of the rest of the paragraph; the reader uses it as a clue to what lies ahead. Though a topic sentence is often the first sentence in a paragraph, it sometimes follows a transitional opening sentence. It may even appear at the end of a paragraph that leads the reader to a climactic conclusion. Experienced writers often do not give every paragraph a topic sentence, but beginning writers are usually well advised to use topic sentences consistently and to make them easily recognizable.

A good topic sentence identifies the subject of the paragraph and the specific issue to be developed. When the focus is blurred, the topic sentence offers no sense of direction to the reader, who may suspect that the writer himself was not sure where the paragraph was heading. In the following examples, note how the sharpened topic sentences point to the supporting sentences:

NOT FOCUSED: Television does more than present entertainment and advertising.

SHARPENED: *Television not only distributes programs and sells products but also preaches a general philosophy of life.* Television tells us, hour after gruesome hour, that the primary measure of an individual's worth is his consumption of products, his measuring up to the ideals that are found in packages mass produced and distributed by corporate America. Many products (and even programs), but especially the drug commercials, sell the gospel that there are instant solutions to life's most pressing personal problems. You don't need to think about your own emotional maturity and development of individuality, your discipline, training, and education, your perception of the world, your willingness to cooperate and compromise and work with other people; you don't need to think about developing meaningful human relationships and trying to keep them in repair. "Better living through chemisty" is not just duPont's slogan—it's a commandment of our consumer society.

— Nicholas Johnson, "The Coming Victory of the New Television"

NOT FOCUSED: Almost all jokes have some sort of gimmick that appeals to the reader's or listener's sense of humor.

SHARPENED: *The crux of the simplest form of joke seems to be the production of an incongruity in the normal order of events.* We hear the story, for example, of Maxwell showing Kelvin some optical experiment, and inviting Kelvin to look through the eyepiece. Kelvin was surprised to find that, while the phenomenon described by Maxwell was undoubtedly there, so was a little human figure, the incongruity, dancing about. Kelvin could not help asking "Maxwell—but what is the little man there for?" "Have another look, Thomson," said Maxwell, "and you should see." Kelvin had another look, but was no wiser. "Tell me, Maxwell," he said impatiently, "What *is* he there for?" "Just for *fun,* Thomson," replied Maxwell. When we consider a simple incongruity of this type, we can see why this form of humor is sometimes described as "nonsense"; for "sense" implies the normal order of things, and in this order an incongruity makes "nonsense." A simple incongruity in the literature of physics is R. W. Wood's recording of the fact that he cleaned out an optical instrument by pushing his cat through it.

— R. V. Jones, "The Theory of Practical Joking—Its Relevance to Physics"

In a first draft, begin every paragraph with a topic sentence. If you write down the topic sentence, it will help you make sure that the paragraph accomplishes its purpose. When you revise your early draft, you may want to move the topic sentence to another position or get rid of it entirely. Placing the topic sentence at the end can give it special emphasis, saying to the reader, "Here's what I've been leading up to." But if you overuse that arrangement, you may make your reader wonder if you know what you are trying to do.

EXERCISE 9 _____

A. Examine the following topic sentences, marking with E *those that would effectively develop the following central idea (thesis statement) of a whole essay: "Adolescent suicide is an alarming problem which cries out for solutions."*

1. There are thousands of attempted suicides each year among teenagers.
2. Understanding what causes teenagers to consider suicide may help prevent it.
3. The quest for escape from pressures and fears is a common cause of adolescent suicide.
4. Suicidal personalities develop as the result of several factors.
5. Though many young people use suicide as a threat, it should be seen as a call for help.

B. Rewrite the following topic sentences to give each a sharper focus. Then choose one as the basis of a paragraph of your own.

1. Americans generally regard jury duty as a small-scale version of the draft.
2. Traffic lights in low traffic areas are more than a nuisance.
3. When the "real" Bicentennial is celebrated in 1987, will it be a repetition of 1976?
4. Steve Allen said that television is "junk food for the mind."
5. Many citizens oppose the production and sale of cheap handguns.

10 dev

Use enough detail to support and explain your topic sentence.

To be interesting and convincing, paragraphs must present relevant, specific details to clarify or support the topic sentence. Failure to include such details is a common weakness in college writing. Many students think it sufficient merely to assert a point: they fail to develop it with facts and examples. Though it is possible to give readers more details than they want or need, bad writing usually suffers from too little detail rather than too much. Short paragraphs often indicate lack of thought or effort. If your paragraphs are frequently less than a hundred words long, you are probably not giving them the development they deserve.

> **WEAK DEVELOPMENT**: *The 1980 men's final match at Wimbledon did as much to enhance the prestige of the loser, John McEnroe, as it did that of the winner, Björn Borg.* Borg won an unprecedented fifth consecutive title, marking him as unquestionably the greatest champion. McEnroe played what has to be considered the best tennis ever played by a loser.

> **IMPROVED**: *The 1980 men's final match at Wimbledon did as much to enhance the prestige of the loser, John McEnroe, as it did that of the winner, Björn Borg.* Borg won an unprecedented fifth consecutive title, marking him as unquestionably the greatest champion. He lost the first set and was behind in the second to McEnroe, who played what has to be considered the best tennis ever played by a loser. Then, as he has done so often before, Borg reached back and found a little extra, winning that second set. He took the third set easily. Starting the fourth set, he was once again his invincible self; but McEnroe somehow rallied and forced a tie-breaker. John appeared ready to sweep the final set; but, no, Bjorn once again rallied, and won.

> **WEAK DEVELOPMENT**: *The magnificent Monterey coast of California is often called Steinbeck country.* Even though sardines have not

been processed at Cannery Row since 1942, it lives as a tourist attraction because Steinbeck's fiction has been known to millions of readers. Thanks to his fictional re-creation of the rugged coastal area, Cannery Row has become a literary shrine. It is also, because of what Steinbeck wrote, a recognized piece of Western history.

IMPROVED: *The magnificent Monterey coast of California is often called Steinbeck country.* If it had not been for the late author of *Cannery Row* and *Tortilla Flat,* the area around the old Cannery Row might be a depressed series of run-down factories. But, even though sardines have not been processed there since 1942, it lives as a tourist attraction because Steinbeck's unforgettable world of fishworkers and bums has been known to millions of readers. Thanks to his fictional re-creation of the rugged coastal area, Cannery Row has become a literary shrine of art galleries, elegant restaurants, and antique shops. It is also, because of what Steinbeck wrote, a recognized piece of Western history. To walk along Monterey's "Path of History," past the Old Custom House and the novelist's old adobe, is to follow in the path of adventure.

EXERCISE 10 _____

Study the three pairs of short paragraphs below. Mark the paragraphs that are well developed with W and those that are poorly developed with X.

1A. *Ray Bradbury's science fiction story "The Pedestrian" satirizes several features of our present society, including our addiction to television as a substitute for activity and conversation.* The author suggests that man is becoming a zombie-like viewer of useless trash. More broadly, Bradbury satirizes the way in which technological progress can lead people into conformity. By showing that there is no crime in the year 2053 because the citizens cannot choose to commit crimes, Bradbury reveals the lack of individuality in his future city. And he may also be alerting us to government intrusion in our lives since his fictional state has complete control over what people think, see, and read. In essence, Bradbury, in criticizing our conformity, is writing as much about the present as about the future.

1B. *Ray Bradbury's science fiction story, "The Pedestrian" satirizes several features of our present society, including television.* The author suggests that man is becoming a viewer of trash. However, the author is also satirizing the way in which technological progress can lead people into conformity. Bradbury clearly shows the lack of individuality and creativity in his future city. And he may be alerting us to the role of the state today, when government intrudes more and more into our lives, since in the story the state has complete control. In essence, Bradbury is writing as much about the present as about the future. It is a thought-provoking story which shows that "science fiction" can truly be fact.

2A. *A New York City taxi seems designed to test the endurance of the most patient rider.* The experience of travelling in one of these legendary conveyances is often irritating to the passengers, whether they be Manhattan natives or tourists. The drivers are often insulting, ill-informed, and unhelpful. What is worse, they drive too fast in heavy traffic and jolt the hapless rider along countless potholes in cabs which almost always seem to lack shock absorbers. The result is discomforting and nerve-wracking. Similar conditions exist in other major cities; but, for sheer violence, no taxi ride can compare with one in New York.

2B. *A New York City taxi seems designed to test the endurance of the most patient rider.* The drivers are known for their ability to insult the passenger in colorful language, to refuse to open doors or help with luggage, and to know little about landmarks or shortcuts. More distressing to the hapless victim is their tendency to speed into the most heavily-trafficked streets while either bearing down on the accelerator or snapping on the brakes as they thump over roads so full of potholes that they resemble moonscapes. While the passenger reaches for a tranquilizer, wondering what happened to the shock absorbers, he is forced to sit like a nervous yogi—eyes shut, fists and teeth clenched, knees taut. Though similar conditions exist in other major cities, for sheer violence no taxi ride can compare with one in New York.

3A. *The handshake as a form of greeting has changed in the past decade.* A generation ago, a firm handshake between men was seen as a sign of masculinity. The paternal advice of old—to extend a strong hand for a simple clasp—is now at odds with at least two more recent handshaking styles. One, the slap downward on the palm-upward hand, probably grew up in black ghettos during the 1960's and moved into sports events, where such a fast, casual greeting seems more appropriate. The other addition to the ritual of grasping hands is a vertical gesture, which resembles a position in hand wrestling. This handshake is a far cry from the once limp-wristed shakes of some men and indicates, if nothing else, that extending a man a friendly hand can no longer guarantee the expected response.

3B. *The handshake as a form of greeting has changed in the past decade.* A generation ago, a firm handshake between men was seen as a sign of masculinity, an indication of male character. Many a father would tell his son, "Never give a man a limp hand, boy." Such paternal advice, like the simple clasp it advocated, is now at odds with at least two more recent handshaking styles. One, the slap downward on the palm-upward hand, probably grew up in black ghettos during the 1960's and moved into the televised world of big-league sports. When a baseball player is greeted at home plate by his teammates after a home run, such a fast, casual exchange seems more appropriate. The other addition to the ritual of grasping hands is a vertical gesture, which resembles the beginning position for hand wrestling. This handshake, which seems to have ancient Roman as well as modern political overtones, is a far cry from the old-fashioned clasp. It seems, among men at least, that extending a friendly hand can no longer guarantee the expected response.

11 u

Make all other sentences relate to the topic sentence.

If a paragraph is to perform its function, it must meet two principal criteria: unity and coherence (see also **12**). In a unified paragraph, every sentence contributes to the central idea. Every detail supports the topic sentence to produce a single, unfolding idea.

Examine each sentence in your paragraphs to make certain that it follows from and develops the topic sentence. Details not directly relevant to the central point do not belong in the paragraph. For instance, if your topic sentence were "I support our university's policy of recruiting student athletes because it benefits the students academically and the school economically," your supporting sentences would deal with the advantages to student athletes and to the university budget for recruitment. Sentences about the problems raised by the policy of building winning teams would violate the unity of the paragraph. To deal with these problems, you would need a new paragraph.

The first step toward paragraph unity is to construct a clear, specific topic sentence. The next step is to develop the idea that the topic sentence expresses throughout the rest of the paragraph. When you revise your rough draft, eliminate all irrelevant points, no matter how interesting or well stated they are. In the first example below, two sentences in the first paragraph violate unity. Note how the second paragraph is improved when we delete those sentences.

LACKING UNITY: *The presidential press conference is a relatively recent phenomenon.* Herbert Hoover, like some of his predecessors, would answer only written questions submitted by reporters in advance, contending, like most European monarchs, that the chief executive should not be interrogated like a common criminal by people he did not even know. A victim of the Great Depression, Hoover was overwhelmingly defeated by Franklin D. Roosevelt in 1932. The modern tendency for reporters to question the president directly evolved under Presidents Roosevelt and Truman but emerged into a powerful device under Dwight Eisenhower during the 1950's, when television found its way into the American living room. Eisenhower's rambling style confused many reporters but bothered few others. The televised news conference was raised to an art by John Kennedy, who used it to display his ready wit, and became a tool of confrontation and persuasion under Lyndon Johnson and Richard Nixon. Since then, presidents have continued to use the press conference as a political tool of persuasion.

UNIFIED: *The presidential press conference is a relatively recent phenomenon.* Herbert Hoover, like some of his predecessors, would answer only written questions submitted by reporters in advance, contending, like most European monarchs, that the chief executive should not be interrogated like a common criminal by people he did not even know. The modern tendency for reporters to question the president directly evolved under Presidents Roosevelt and Truman but emerged into a powerful device under Dwight Eisenhower during the 1950's, when television found its way into the American living room. The televised news conference was raised to an art by John Kennedy, who used it to display his ready wit, and became a tool of confrontation and persuasion under Lyndon Johnson and Richard Nixon. Since then, presidents have continued to use the press conference as a political tool of persuasion.

EXERCISE 11 _____

In paragraphs below, underline the sentences that violate paragraph unity. The topic sentences are in italics.

1. In all the years of Russian-American wrestling competition, a United States team has never been able to defeat a Soviet international wrestling team. America, even though it has done well in recent years, has never been

able to dominate the Olympic wrestling games by taking more gold medals than all other single teams. In fact, nationalism and international rivalries often replace competition as the Olympic games have become increasingly political. The point is not that America's wrestlers are bad; in fact, the United States probably has the best wrestlers in the world. Both nations have many skilled and talented athletes, fully capable of winning gold medals. *But what has kept the United States from dominating the international competition is that a different style of wrestling is used in American high schools and colleges than that used in international tournaments.* This use of one style at home and another in competition has put American wrestlers at a disadvantage in Olympic and other international competitions.

2. *Newspapers have often written about American Indians in a condescending and, at times, derogatory manner.* The press would certainly not refer to a black child as a *pickaninny*, yet demeaning words referring to Indians have been commonplace. Political activism among Indian groups may have reduced the problem, but old habits die hard. Some expressions are silly clichés, such as *paleface, heap big chief, redskin,* and *warpaint*; others, like *Injun*, are intended to be humorous, yet they offend many native Americans and others who believe that such unthinking words help to perpetuate stereotyped Hollywood images of the Indians as objects of ridicule. In decades of Western films and television shows, they were depicted as little more than grunting savages. A few years ago a caption in a Washington, D.C. newspaper article about Indian dancers at the White House read: "Indian braves whoop it up at White House powwow." Surely if the visitors had been Israelis, Africans, or Irish, no similarly demeaning or trivializing words would have been even considered.

3. By repeatedly and unjustly exempting itself from the laws it enacts, Congress remains immune from the impact of its own fair employment legislation. For example, Congress is exempt from the provisions of the 1964 Civil Rights Act and the 1972 Equal Opportunity Act aimed at protecting workers against discrimination. The Equal Pay Act, the Occupational Safety and Health Act, and the Fair Labor

Standards Act are some other examples of laws which do not—but should—apply to members of Congress and their staffs. Many major corporations have been required to pay large sums for their failure to promote or hire women, blacks, and other minorities. But Congress is even immune from Social Security tax increases. Not surprisingly, the public's dissatisfaction with the "imperial Congress" has been growing. Members of Congress respond that, as elected officials, they are a special case; and constitutional lawyers do not agree that a clear double standard exists. *Still, federal legislators should find some way to live under the same fair hiring rules as ordinary people.*

4. *The method of teaching undergraduates at Oxford University is sharply different from that of almost any American college.* Whereas American students attend classes and are graded according to their mastery of the course, their counterparts at England's oldest university have no classes as such. They meet with faculty, called tutors, in groups of one or two and discuss a given reading list in depth. Tutors once lived and ate with the students, too, but this tradition has waned. In addition, seminars on specific topics, for a half dozen or more students, are often helpful in preparing for comprehensive examinations. There is thus more individualization and specialization than in American undergraduate education. Students also attend formal lectures, which are often seen as optional or secondary to the tutorials. Surprisingly, the riches of an Oxford education are largely free: students can have all of their fees paid by the state.

12 coh

Provide coherence within and between paragraphs.

Good writing must be coherent: its parts must fit together. In your essays, the paragraphs should lead the reader from beginning to end according to a logical plan.

When you have covered the topic of one paragraph, proceed to a related topic, providing signals that your reader can follow. These signals are transitional devices to indicate, for example, that you are moving from an introductory paragraph which states a problem to supporting paragraphs that cite causes and effects, offer solutions, or provide examples.

In a paragraph, coherence is the natural flow from one sentence to the next. The sentences interlock so that the first idea leads to the second, the second to the third, and so on. You cannot write a succession of isolated sentences and expect your reader to supply the words and phrases that tie them together. You must make the reader feel that by the end of the paragraph you have made your point clearly and smoothly.

12a   Achieve coherence by keeping thoughts in order.

The first step in achieving coherence is to follow a clear, logical order. That is, point A might precede point B because A happened before B, or because A led to B or caused B, or because B illustrates A. Or your purpose might determine the order: you might put A first to give it special prominence; you might lead up to point G, leaving it till last for emphasis. Always try to find a pattern that will seem sensible both to you and to your reader.

12b   Use transitional devices to improve coherence.

On reading over your rough draft, you may find that, logical as your pattern is, the sentences do not flow from one to the next. Sentence A ends with a thump. Then sentence B starts up. And so on. You may need transitional devices to bridge the gaps. These devices connect the sentences and bind the paragraph into a single, coherent unit. The most common transitional devices are presented here.

Pronouns. Since each pronoun refers to an antecedent, a pronoun and its antecedent form a link. You can often make a paragraph cohere merely by using pronouns properly. On the other hand, incorrectly used pronouns can weaken coherence. See **19–20**. In the following examples, notice how pronouns in the second sentence of each pair provide coherence by referring to antecedents in the first:

> *Daily receipts* are taken to the central office. *They* are then tallied and posted with those from the other shops.

> *Patients* must fast for twelve hours before the test. *They* should also avoid red meats for seventy-two hours before coming in.

Repetition. Substituting a pronoun for a noun is actually a kind of repetition. Direct repetition of a word or expression will give a similar effect:

> Our new plans allow for a total of twenty-six *elevations*.

> Each *elevation* can be built in a three-, four-, or five-bedroom model.

Use direct repetition with care. Overdoing it will give an awkward, immature ring to your writing ("*Daily receipts* are taken to the central office. *Daily receipts* are then tallied . . ."). You can get much the same transitional effect by using synonyms or slightly altered forms of the repeated expressions:

> *Richard Nixon* rarely meets the press. Since leaving office, *the former President* has appeared on television fewer than a dozen times.

Transitional terms. Transitional terms make a paragraph coherent by relating ideas. Like pronouns, many of these terms come to mind automatically, but the thoughtful writer carefully chooses among them. Here is a partial list of common transitional terms:

1. *Time words:* next, then, after, before, during, while, following, shortly, thereafter, later on, the next day, secondly, finally.
2. *Place words:* over, above, inside, to the left, just behind, beyond.
3. *Contrast words:* however, but, nevertheless, on the other hand, nonetheless, notwithstanding, on the contrary, conversely.
4. *Cause-effect words:* so, therefore, thus, accordingly, consequently, as a result, hence, because of this.
5. *Addition words:* and, furthermore, moreover, likewise, similarly, in a like manner, too, also.
6. *Emphasis words:* indeed, in fact.
7. *Summary words:* in other words, in short, to sum up, in conclusion, that is.
8. *Example words:* for instance, for example.

The following sequences of sentences illustrate the use of transitional terms:

> Ten years hadn't aged Leo a bit. *In fact,* he looked as though he still belonged on the surfboard that had been his trademark in high school.

> We were allowed to send only two voting delegates. *Furthermore,* we were prevented from bringing our other members as unofficial observers.

> A major, yet often ignored, contribution to the settlement of the American West was made by Spanish missionary priests. Junipero Serra, *for example,* was the first of these idealistic pioneers.

Transitional sentences and paragraphs. Pronouns, repetition, and transitional terms can provide coherence within paragraphs and can even link consecutive paragraphs; but to link two paragraphs that differ significantly in content, you occasionally will need a complete sentence or even a short paragraph. If, for instance, you have devoted three or four paragraphs to the theories of one authority and are ready to shift to those of another, you will probably need a sentence to help the reader make the transition. For example: "A critic who approaches Shakespeare's plays differently, however, is Maynard Mack, who. . . . " The following transitional sentence links a short section on Florida orange production with a section on grapefruit production: "While Florida has not done well in exporting oranges, its exports of grapefruits are much more substantial."

Between major sections of a long paper, you may even need a short paragraph for smooth transition. Here, a transitional paragraph from the paper on citrus-fruit production introduces a section on the industry in Brazil:

> Israel, Cyprus, and South Africa dominate the European citrus market. Mexico can be seen as a strong competitor in some areas, but the most threatening potential force in the world citrus market is Brazil. In fact, if Japanese and Arab investments continue to grow, Brazilian production could easily triple or quadruple in the next few years.

In the following paragraph by Carl Sagan, notice the simple but effective repetition of *it* to link the sentences to the first (topic) sentence. Sagan is careful, however, not to overdo this transition and bore the reader; sentences which begin the same way are varied in length.

> Planetary exploration has many virtues. *It* permits us to refine insights derived from such Earth-bound sciences as meteorology, climatology, geology and biology, to broaden their powers and improve their practical applications here on Earth. *It* provides cautionary tales on the alternative fates of worlds. *It* is an aperture to future high technologies important for life here on Earth. *It* provides an outlet for the traditional human zest for exploration and discovery, our passion to find out, which has been to a very large degree responsible for our success as a species. *And it* permits us, for the first time in history, to approach with rigor, with a significant chance of finding out the true

answers, questions on the origins and destinies of worlds, the beginnings and ends of life, and the possibility of other beings who live in the skies—questions as basic to the human enterprise as thinking is, as natural as breathing.

Here are two versions of a paragraph from a student paper. In the first, transitional devices are omitted. In the second, they have been inserted and italicized.

LESS EFFECTIVE: The stars shone brilliantly through the plane's clear, small windows. There was no time for me to notice these bright, tiny dots in the darkness above me. Getting accustomed to the darkness in front of me was difficult as I slipped into the small, hard, cold seat, aware only of the instrument panel's dull redness and of a maze of straps and wires. Reaching forward, my fingers gripped a smooth, bowl-like object. It was my helmet. After placing it over my head, I felt more secure. I pulled the two thin chin straps taut and fastened their buckles. I locked my tinted visor in the "up" position since there was no sun to glare in my eyes. Anxiety concerning the outcome of the next two hours began to make me feel uncomfortable. This was only the beginning of my experience; desire dictated that I was to continue, even though I was not quite sure of my immediate future.

EFFECTIVE: The stars shone brilliantly through the plane's clear, small windows. *But* there was no time for me to notice these bright, tiny dots in the darkness above me. Getting accustomed to the darkness in front of me was difficult as I slipped into the small, hard, cold seat, aware only of the instrument panel's dull redness and of a maze of straps and wires. Reaching forward, my fingers gripped a smooth, bowl-like object. It was my helmet. After placing it over my head, I felt more secure. I *then* pulled the two thin chin straps taut and fastened their buckles. *And* I locked my tinted visor in the "up" position since there was no sun to glare in my eyes. *At this point* anxiety concerning the outcome of the next two hours began to make me feel uncomfortable. *However,* this was only the beginning of my experience; *for* desire dictated that I was to continue, even though I was not quite sure of my immediate future.

EXERCISE 12 _____

A. Add appropriate transitions to make these paragraphs more explicitly coherent.

A. The benefits of shale oil production are more numerous than the drawbacks. Oil shale has been found to produce an effective fuel, in both liquid and gaseous forms. Shale oil represents a potential, long-range source of fairly secure oil and gas. An abundance of by-products can be derived from oil shale processing. There are some disadvantages, particularly for the environment. These negative features concern socioeconomic impact, surface disturbance, pollution, and water supply. There are some legal questions concerning government control of shale oil processing. Experts believe that the future is bright for the oil shale industry.

B. There is no Nobel Prize for mathematics, and mathematicians rarely make the headlines. It is not a glamorous profession. There are no exotic, expensive pieces of equipment—no cyclotrons, body scanners, or electron microscopes—for the public to identify with. Research tools are plain. Pencil, paper, chalk, and a calculator are about all one needs. In a time when some scientists' names—Einstein, Jung, Freud, and others—have become household words, few people could name even one great modern mathematician. Mathematics is so basic to most scientific disciplines that it has been called the language of all experimental dialogue.

13

Your introductory paragraph should focus the reader's interest on your thesis.

A good introduction serves two important functions: it attracts the reader's interest and focuses that interest on the thesis. Therefore, to write a good introduction you need to know what your thesis is and why your reader might care about what you have to say. If you can be sure that your reader is already interested in your topic, and if your paper is short, then you hardly need an introduction at all. You can just start with the thesis statement and move right into the first point:

> Anyone who earns over $10,000 a year should be aware of three simple techniques for saving money on income taxes. The first and most obvious of these . . .

To treat the same subject in a longer paper, in more than a few paragraphs, you might need to mention all three techniques in the introduction so that the reader would know what to expect. Then the next paragraph could begin discussing the first technique.

If your reader needs background information to understand why your topic is significant, provide that information in your introductory paragraph. If, for example, you were going to report on new techniques for catching shoplifters at the store where you work, you could first discuss what shoplifting costs the average consumer, then lead your reader to the specific case of your store and finally to your thesis statement.

The pattern just discussed for the introductory paragraph on shoplifting is the most reliable way of introducing college papers:

> General statements related to topic and to reader's interests
>
> ↓
>
> Any necessary background material
>
> ↓
>
> Thesis statement

Jokes, clever quotations, and other dramatic openings can capture attention; but they can also fall flat. It is safer to begin with an interesting example or anecdote, then show how the example leads to your main point:

Somewhere in the boonies near West Palm Beach, forty thousand people are jammed into a small racetrack designed to hold five thousand spectators. Despite voracious mosquitoes, croaking frogs, and six inches of mud, all forty thousand remain because they have paid fifteen dollars apiece to see Eric Clapton. And this miserable slop festival is typical of rock performances today. The bands and their promoters are so concerned about earning quick money that they readily violate health standards, safety regulations, and common sense in order to squeeze as many paid customers as possible into the audience.

Unlike the more common general-to-specific introductory paragraph, the one just shown moves from a specific instance (one concert) to a general comment on rock concerts. But there is a basic pattern behind all successful introductions: they begin with something that will interest the reader, then move smoothly to the thesis statement.

EXERCISE 13 _____

A. A student's essay on violence in sports begins with the following paragraph. Suggest ways to rearrange some of the more interesting points to provide a more colorful introduction.

Violence in sports is not new, nor is it restricted to the United States. It is probably as old as competitive athletics itself. In ancient Rome, enslaved men fought each other to the death in order to satisfy the citizens' thirst for blood. In our own century, the sport which Teddy Roosevelt almost banned in 1905—football—continues to kill more than 25 players and injure another 1200 a year at all levels of competition. Just recently, a London newspaper headline read: "Cricket, Ugly Cricket—Violence Must Be Stamped Out." Laugh if you wish, but on playing fields all over the world, athletic competition has become a deadly serious business, of which violence is a major part. On the grass, in the mud, on the hardwood, or on the ice, players are spilling blood in search of victories. Why has violence become such an integral part of sporting events?

*B. Here are a thesis statement and topic sentences for the three
main paragraphs of a short essay. Write an introduction.*

Thesis: For many young people, telling jokes is seen as trite
and old fashioned.

First topic sentence: Ethnic jokes have worn thin and are usually
tasteless.

Second topic sentence: A joke often suggests a "dirty story."

Third topic sentence: Tastes in comedy, reflected in recent films
and television shows, have changed.

14

Use your final paragraph to reemphasize your key points and provide a strong conclusion.

Just as the introductory paragraph should lead smoothly
into the paper, the concluding paragraph should lead
smoothly out. It should remind readers of how they
began and where they have been. It should vividly
reassert your thesis. In a short essay, summarizing main
points is unnecessary and tedious, but in more substantial compositions, you may wish to reemphasize both
the overall thesis and the main points you used to
develop it.

Whether you cover all of your main points or just
your thesis, follow these guidelines in writing concluding paragraphs: 1) Do not introduce new topics; everything you present should emphasize points you have
already made; 2) Do not repeat the same words and
examples you have used earlier; 3) Make your writing
forceful; do not overestimate the importance of what
you have said, but do not hesitate or apologize, either.

The paragraph below ended a newspaper editorial
that presented a specific plan for attacking air and water
pollution. Notice how this short paragraph calls the

reader's attention to the plan, emphasizes its necessity, and, in the last sentence, closes quietly but powerfully.

> **EFFECTIVE**: The price system outlined here is no magic formula. But it is the only system that attacks the pollution problem at its roots and that can provide a long-term realistic solution. The sooner it is understood, the sooner we all will be able to breathe more easily.
> — Larry E. Ruff, "One Way to Solve the Pollution Problem"

Consider this final paragraph of a student's analysis of an Aerosmith album:

> **EFFECTIVE**: "Rocks" is, in short, a vibrant album, not one for the timid but for the spirited. Leaving the listener with a feeling of raging rowdiness, it is full of that energizing force that has made Aerosmith one of the decade's top rock groups. If you are not yet an Aerosmith fan, "Rocks" will soon make you one.

Notice how the student has concisely summed up his view of the album and ended the essay on a positive, forceful note.

EXERCISE 14 _____

Write a concluding paragraph for the essay suggested in Exercise 13B.

BASIC GRAMMAR

The principles of grammar are means to an end: effective communication. They express the conventional practices followed by experienced speakers and writers of Standard English. Not following these conventions often results in writing that is not only technically *incorrect* but also confusing or misleading. Most of the time we follow the conventions of English without thinking about them. But some errors are almost inevitable, and knowing the rules makes correcting those errors much easier.

15 ps

Know the parts of speech and their uses.

The parts of speech are the words of English classified according to their forms and their uses in sentences: verbs, nouns, pronouns, adjectives, adverbs, prepositions, conjunctions, and interjections. Many words can serve as more than one part of speech. *Round,* for example, can be a noun (we won the round), a verb (they rounded the corner), or an adjective (they have a round table). Being able to recognize parts of speech will help you analyze and discuss the sentences you write.

15a   Verbs show action, process, or existence.

The verb is an essential part of every sentence (see **15g**). Most verbs show some kind of action or process:

Barry *resigned.*   The lady *screamed.*   The water *boiled.*

Other verbs, known as linking verbs, introduce a state of being. They include *be (am, is, are, was, were), become, remain, grow, seem, appear, look, sound, feel, taste,* and *smell:*

Dean *is* a brilliant attorney.   The meat *smelled* rancid.

Tense. Most verbs change form to show tense. Different tense forms usually indicate differences in time: Dean *writes;* Dean *wrote;* Dean *will write.* See **22**.

Voice. Voice indicates whether the subject of the sentence acts or receives an action (see **24**):

ACTIVE VOICE: The reviewer condemned the film's violence.
                (subject [reviewer] acts)
PASSIVE VOICE: The film's violence was condemned by the
                reviewer. (subject [violence] receives action)

Forms. The English verb has a limited number of forms. Verbs may be regular (*walk*) or irregular (*see*):

Infinitive: to walk, to see
Present: walk, walks; see, sees
Past: walked, saw
Past participle: walked, seen
Present participle: walking, seeing

The infinitive, the past, and the past participle are known as the *principal parts* of a verb. Most verbs are regular: they just add *-ed* to form the past and past participle. Irregular verbs may change spelling: *go, went, gone; see, saw, seen.* See **23**. The present participle is always the infinitive stem plus *-ing*. For the addition of *-s* in the present tense, see **18**.

Verb phrases. A verb phrase is made up of a main verb preceded by one or more auxiliary verbs: *shall have been going.* The most commonly used auxiliaries are *have (has, had), be (am, is, are, was, were, been), do (does, did), will, would, shall, should, can, could, may, might, must,* and *ought.*

The first auxiliary verb in a verb phrase is the one which shows tense or agrees with the subject: she *has* gone; she *had* gone; they *have* gone; they *had* gone.

In identifying verb phrases, note that other words may come between the first auxiliary and the rest of the phrase:

His writing *has* never *made* sense to me.

Most children *have*, at least once in their lives, *dreamed* of riding on a fire engine or in a police car.

Verbals. The infinitive, the two participles, and the gerund (which has the same form as the present participle) may function as nouns, adjectives, or adverbs. When they do, they are called *verbals,* and they may combine with other words in *verbal phrases: Waiting for the train every day* is not my idea of happiness. See **15g**.

15b   Nouns name things.

Also essential to grammatical sentences are nouns—the names given to things real or imagined, tangible or intangible:

trees   endurance   Colorado   woman   physics

In sentences, nouns can be used as subjects, objects, complements, and appositives (see Glossary for definitions):

				OBJECT OF		INDIRECT
SUBJECT	APPOSITIVE			PREPOSITION		OBJECT
John Nolan,	*assistant*	to	the	*mayor,*	gave	*reporters*

DIRECT	
OBJECT	
a written	*statement.*

Nouns can also function as modifiers, as in *stone* wall, *television* news.

Almost all nouns take an *-s* or *-es* ending or change spelling to refer to more than one of the thing named (see **44**). They also take an apostrophe and *s* or apostrophe alone to show possession: *women's* rights, *prospectors'* hunches (see **38**).

15c Pronouns take the place of nouns.

The noun which a pronoun refers to is called the antecedent:

> The men rushed in. *They* were angry. (The antecedent of *they* is *men*.)

There are different kinds of pronouns:

Personal pronouns (*I, he, she, it, they,* etc.) take different forms according to their function in a sentence. See **20**.

Relative pronouns (*who, whom, whose, which, that*) join a dependent clause to a noun. See **15g**.

Interrogative pronouns (*who, whom, whose, which, what*) are used in questions.

Demonstrative pronouns (*this, that, these, those*) point to nouns. They may be used as adjectives or pronouns: *This* amplifier is more powerful than *that*.

Indefinite pronouns refer to indefinite persons or things. Examples are *someone, everyone, anything, another*.

For verb agreement with indefinite pronouns as subjects, see **18**.

15d   Adjectives and adverbs are modifiers.

To modify is to describe, qualify, or limit the meaning of a word. Adjectives modify nouns; adverbs modify verbs, adjectives, and other adverbs:

> The salesman approached the *reluctant* customer.
>   (adjective modifying noun *customer*)
>
> The program progressed *quite rapidly.* (adverb *quite*
>   modifying adverb *rapidly*)
>
> We faced *extremely* serious problems. (adverb modifying
>   adjective *serious*)

Most adjectives and adverbs can be compared: *happy, happier, happiest; angrily, more angrily, most angrily.* See **21**.

15e   Prepositions and conjunctions are structure words that work with the major parts of speech.

Verbs, nouns, adjectives, and adverbs express most of the information in sentences, but the meaning of a whole sentence also depends on structure words that show relationships among those major words. Two main groups of structure words are prepositions and conjunctions.

Prepositions relate a noun to another word; examples are *on, into, at, to, for, after, with, in spite of, with regard to, aside from.* Prepositions join with nouns and pronouns to form **prepositional phrases:** *near the property, in the neighborhood.* Prepositional phrases can function as adjectives or adverbs. See **15g**.

Conjunctions connect words or word groups. The coordinating conjunctions *and, but, or, nor,* and *yet* join words, phrases, or clauses of the same grammatical type:

The *camera* and the *lens* must be purchased separately.
(nouns)

He *lied* and *stole* but never *killed*. (verbs)

The hunter was *old* yet *strong*. (adjectives)

Neither *on land* nor *on sea* did they meet any resistance.
(prepositional phrases)

I know *what I like* and *what I dislike*. (dependent clauses)

He looked, but *he did not see.* (independent clauses)

For and *so* are used only between independent clauses:

He used the wrong film, so *the pictures did not turn out.*

Adverbial subordinating conjunctions join dependent clauses to independent cluases; examples are *since, because, after, while, when, if, as soon as:* We will leave *as soon as* he arrives. See **15h**, **45**.

15f   Interjections express emotion.

Interjections such as *oh, hey,* and *phooey* show emotion. They may be punctuated as sentences (Oh!) or included in sentences (Oh, I wish you would say something), but they are not grammatically related to other words in sentences.

15g   A phrase is a word group without a complete subject and verb that functions as a noun, verb, adjective, or adverb.

Often the function of a single word can be filled by a group of words. Such a group of words that work together but lack a complete subject and verb is called a *phrase:*

NOUN:	I enjoy *art*.
PHRASE AS NOUN:	I enjoy *visiting museums*.
VERB:	He *went*.
VERB PHRASE:	He *should have been going*.
ADJECTIVE:	The *tall* man is my uncle.
PHRASE AS ADJECTIVE:	The man *towering over the others* is my uncle.
ADVERB:	She tried *hard*.
PHRASE AS ADVERB:	She tried *with all her strength*.

Other than verb phrases (see **15a**), the major types of phrases and their principal uses are illustrated here:

Prepositional phrase (see **15e**):

ADJECTIVE:	The clock *on the mantel* belonged to my grandfather.
ADVERB:	He drove the truck *around the block*.

Infinitive phrase:

NOUN:	He wants *to fight with everyone*.
ADJECTIVE:	There must be another way *to settle this problem*.
ADVERB:	The plumber came *to fix the sink*.

Gerund phrase:

NOUN:	*Playing on a winning team* adds to the fun of baseball.

Participial phrase:

ADJECTIVE:	The smoke *rising from the house* alerted the neighbors.
	A house *built on a rock* will endure.

15h   An independent clause can be punctuated as an independent sentence; a subordinate clause functions as a noun, adjective, or adverb, and so cannot be set off as an independent sentence.

Unless it is a command having no expressed subject *(come here)*, a clause contains a subject (a noun or equivalent) and a predicate. The predicate usually follows the subject and contains a verb that expresses something about the subject:

SUBJECT	PREDICATE
The *file*	*was taken* from the drawer.
The *secretary*	*took* the file from the drawer.

If the verb is in its infinitive form (shown by the sign *to*: *to take*) or in its participle form *(taking, taken)*, it must be combined with an auxiliary verb (see **15a**). A word group containing an infinitive or participle without an auxiliary verb must be included in a sentence as a phrase:

The mayor *spoke* last night. (clause properly punctuated as sentence)
The mayor *spoken* last night. (ungrammatical)
The mayor *has spoken* many times. (clause)
The words *spoken last night* will be remembered.
    (participial phrase as adjective modifying *words*)

An **independent clause** can stand by itself as a sentence. Two or more independent sentences may be combined in a compound sentence (see **17**, **46**):

SIMPLE SENTENCES: Mildred read the entire poem.
                       Tom did not listen.
COMPOUND SENTENCE: Mildred read the entire poem, but
                       Tom did not listen.

A **subordinate clause** usually begins with a subordinating conjunction (*after* Mildred read the poem; *because* Mildred read the poem) or a relative pronoun (*who* read the poem; *that* she read). A subordinate clause functions as a noun, adjective, or adverb:

NOUN: They do not know *who wrote the threatening letter.*
            (object of *know*)
            What he actually wrote could not be printed.
            (subject)
ADJECTIVE: People *who exercise* live longer than those *who do not.*
ADVERB: I ate the cake *because I was hungry.*

See **45** for a fuller discussion and a list of subordinating conjunctions.

A sentence that contains an independent clause and at least one subordinate clause (as in the examples just given) is called a *complex sentence*. A *compound-complex sentence* contains at least two independent clauses and at least one subordinate clause:

> They do not know who wrote the threatening letter, but they do have a theory about the case.

16 frag

Use grammatically complete sentences.

A group of words that is punctuated as a sentence but that is not a grammatically complete sentence is called a *fragment* or a *sentence fragment*. Although experienced writers sometimes use fragments intentionally, fragments are usually unacceptable in college writing. Unintentional fragments can create misunderstanding and distract your readers. A fragment is usually either a *phrase* (a group of words that lacks the complete subject-predicate combination needed for a clause) or a *subordinate clause* (see **15f**).

COMPLETE SENTENCE:	David is a talented artist. (independent clause)
FRAGMENT:	Because David is a talented artist. (subordinate clause)
FRAGMENT:	Like a talented artist. (prepositional phrase)

Most fragments result from chopping a phrase or clause from the end of an adjoining complete sentence. It is usually a simple matter to correct them. You can reconnect the fragment to the previous or following complete sentence, or you can add the necessary elements to make the fragment a grammatically complete sentence. Subordinating conjunctions such as *although, because, if,* and *when* introduce subordinate (dependent) clauses, and such clauses cannot stand alone as sentences. The following examples show the most common types of clauses or phrases used incorrectly as fragments, followed by corrections:

INCORRECT: Although the fashion designers keep skirt lengths well below the knee. Many American women insist on wearing their skirts higher. (subordinate clause introduced by *although* as fragment)

CORRECT: Although the fashion designers keep skirt lengths well below the knee, many American women insist on wearing their skirts higher. (subordinate clause connected to following independent clause)

INCORRECT: After pressures from all sides, including personal phone calls from the governor, the county board finally selected as county attorneys the local firm of Cullom and Cullom. A very successful father and daughter team. (noun phrase as fragment)

CORRECT: After pressures from all sides, including personal phone calls from the governor, the county board finally selected as county attorneys the local firm of Cullom and Cullom, a very successful father and daughter team. (noun phrase as appositive connected to previous sentence)

INCORRECT: The Delta Sigs were disappointed once more. Having finished second in the Greek sing for the fifth year in a row. (participial phrase as fragment)

CORRECT: The Delta Sigs were disappointed once more, having finished second in the Greek sing for the fifth year in a row. (phrase connected to preceding sentence)

CORRECT: The Delta Sigs were disappointed once more.
                 This was the fifth year in a row that they had
                 finished second in the Greek sing.
                 (phrase expanded to independent clause)

INCORRECT: Collectively they vowed to combine their efforts
                 toward one goal. To win first place next year.
                 (infinitive phrase as fragment)

CORRECT: Collectively they vowed to combine their efforts
                 toward one goal: to win first place next year.
                 (infinitive phrase connected to previous sentence)

INCORRECT: Practice sessions will begin immediately and will
                 be held weekly for the whole year. After each
                 business meeting.
                 (prepositional phrase as fragment)

CORRECT: Practice sessions will begin immediately and will
                 be held after each weekly business meeting for
                 the whole year.
                 (prepositional phrase inserted in previous
                 sentence)

EXERCISE 16 _____

Read the word groups below. A. Mark with S *those that are
grammatically complete sentences; use* X *for fragments. B. Rewrite
the fragments as sentences.*

1. Hoping to write more skillfully.
2. Getting up thirty minutes earlier than normal so I can
   eat in the cafeteria.
3. A new feeling of hope was present among the victims
   of the hijacking.
4. Absolutely the best course I have ever taken.
5. The first chapter dealing with freedom, the second with
   poverty, and described in an unforgettably moving way.
6. Although oil supplies kept increasing while prices
   stayed high.
7. Although oil supplies kept increasing, prices stayed high.
8. Oil supplies kept increasing while prices stayed high.
9. His department's attempts to determine the extent
   of damage.
10. His department attempts to determine the extent
    of damage.

17   fs cs

Separate two independent clauses with a period, semicolon, or comma and coordinating conjunction.

If you fail to separate independent clauses adequately, you will create one of two structural problems: a *fused sentence* (or *run-on*) or a *comma splice.*

An independent clause is a group of words which can be punctuated as a complete sentence (see **15h**). Whenever a sentence contains two independent clauses, those clauses must be separated by a semicolon or by one of the coordinating conjunctions *(and, or, nor, for, but, yet,* or *so)* plus a comma. A comma alone is not adequate punctuation, even if it is followed by a conjunctive adverb such as *furthermore, however,* or *moreover.*

FUSED SENTENCE:	The prosecution could not present reliable witnesses the case was dismissed.
COMMA SPLICE:	The prosecution could not present reliable witnesses, the case was dismissed.

Once you learn to identify fused sentences and comma splices, you can easily avoid them. Some of the most common ways are shown here:

1. Make each clause a separate sentence:

    The prosecution could not present reliable witnesses. The case was dismissed.

2. Place a semicolon between the clauses:

    The prosecution could not present reliable witnesses; the case was dismissed.

3. Insert a conjunctive adverb between the clauses. The adverb should be preceded by a semicolon and followed by a comma:

The prosecution could not present reliable witnesses;
therefore, the case was dismissed.

4. Place a comma and coordinating conjunction between
the clauses:

The prosecution could not present reliable witnesses**,**
so the case was dismissed.

5. Convert one clause into a dependent clause by beginning it with a relative pronoun *(who, whom, whose,
that, which, whoever, whomever, whichever, whatever)* or with
a subordinating conjunction such as *because, after, since,*
or *while:*

Because the prosecution could not present reliable
witnesses, the case was dismissed.

6. Recast the entire sentence into another pattern:

The case was dismissed for lack of reliable witnesses.

All of these revisions are grammatically correct. Choosing the best correction is a matter of style (see Chapter
5, "Effective Sentences"). Each of the following fused
sentences and comma splices can be corrected in ways
other than the one shown:

FAULTY: Last week was unbelievably hectic, this week I
will get some rest. (comma splice)

CORRECTED: Last week was unbelievably hectic; however,
this week I will get some rest. (semicolon plus
conjunctive adverb)

FAULTY: Joe Tisch won the first annual Big Mac
Munchoff he ate twenty-three hamburgers in
only six minutes. (fused sentence)

CORRECTED: Joe Tisch won the first annual Big Mac Munchoff when he ate twenty-three hamburgers in
only six minutes. (the second clause made subordinate by introducing it with *when*)

FAULTY: There is one major difference between men and
boys, it is the cost of their toys. (comma splice)

CORRECTED: There is one major difference between men and
boys; it is the cost of their toys. (semicolon)

FAULTY: Ninety-three-year-old Mr. Kozelko has fallen out of bed three times while trying to climb over the rail, he will have to be restrained for his own protection. (comma splice)

CORRECTED: Ninety-three-year-old Mr. Kozelko has fallen out of bed three times trying to climb over the rail, so he will have to be restrained for his own protection. (comma plus coordinating conjunction)

FAULTY: Sam borrowed my car twice last week he and three friends used the CB to help the sheriff's department patrol the golf course for vandals. (fused sentence)

CORRECTED: Sam borrowed my car twice last week. He and three friends used the CB to help the sheriff's department patrol the golf course for vandals. (punctuated as two sentences)

FAULTY: Many citizens believe that they should not become involved in others' problems this attitude contributes to the crime problem. (fused sentence)

CORRECTED: Many citizens believe that they should not become involved in others' problems, a belief that contributes to the crime problem. (sentence recast)

EXERCISE 17 _____

Some of the word groups below are grammatically correct sentences, some fused sentences, some comma splices. A. Mark C for the grammatical sentences, X for the comma splices or fused sentences. B. Correct those marked X.

1. The exit sign at the north end of the parking lot must be replaced, it was run over by the groundskeeper's tractor.
2. Jackson Browne will never get the recognition he deserves he's too quiet and modest.
3. Unlike some rock stars, who are obnoxious and abusive to almost everyone, he minds his own business and treats everyone kindly.

4. I enjoy reading contemporary literature *Bullet Park* and *The Bell Jar* are two of my favorite novels.
5. Piers Paul Read, an English writer, is the author of seven novels, they have not received as much attention as they deserve.
6. Read is best known for *Alive*, a nonfiction book involving cannibalism his fiction is less sensational.
7. Working while attending college is demanding setting priorities is especially difficult.
8. Unscheduled overtime often conflicts with a major examination, but work comes first in the eyes of management.
9. Most instructors are understanding but a student can only expect a certain amount of special consideration.
10. Working while studying is often frustrating, but perseverance pays millions make it every year.

18 agr

Make each verb and its subject agree in number.

Use the singular form of a verb with a singular subject and the plural form of a verb with a plural subject:

Singular	*Plural*
She watches.	They watch.
The watch runs fast.	The watches run fast.
The team is playing.	The teams are playing.
The plan has changed.	The plans have changed.
He was especially kind.	They were especially kind.

Notice that the *-s* or *-es* ending makes nouns plural but makes present-tense verbs singular.

Making subjects and verbs agree is usually easy in short sentences, but it can be more difficult in longer, more complicated sentences. Be careful to identify the subjects so that your verbs agree with the correct words:

INCORRECT:	Felix's attention to time, efficiency, and savings deserve favorable consideration.
CORRECT:	Felix's attention [subject] to time, efficiency, and savings *deserves* favorable consideration.
INCORRECT:	My supervisor's first priority in cutting departmental expenses are reducing overtime and sick pay.
CORRECT:	My supervisor's first priority [subject] in cutting departmental expenses *is* reducing overtime and sick pay.

In a sentence beginning with *there,* the subject follows the verb:

CORRECT:	There *is* an extra pair [subject] of shoes in the hall closet.
CORRECT:	There *are* no good concerts [subject] at the Sports Stadium anymore.

Forms of the verb *to be* agree with the subject of the sentence, not the complement, even when the subject is plural and the complement is singular, or vice versa:

CORRECT:	Unsafe working conditions [subject] *were* the primary cause [complement] of the wildcat strike.

18a   With compound subjects joined by *and,* use a plural verb.

INCORRECT:	The plot and the acting is inane, but somehow the film held my interest.
CORRECT:	The plot and the acting *are* inane, but somehow the film held my interest.

But when *each* or *every* precedes the compound subject, use a singular verb:

INCORRECT:	Every man, woman, and child risk drowning by swimming alone.
CORRECT:	Every man, woman, and child *risks* drowning by swimming alone.

18b   With compound subjects joined by *or* or *nor*, make the verb agree with the nearer subject.

Use a singular verb when two singular subjects are joined by *or* or *nor:*

INCORRECT: Either *Hamlet* or *Othello,* rather than the usual *Macbeth,* are going to be performed this year.

CORRECT: Either *Hamlet* or *Othello,* rather than the usual *Macbeth,* is going to be performed this year.

Use a plural verb when two plural subjects are joined by *or* or *nor:*

INCORRECT: Neither John Hawkes' novels nor those of Djuna Barnes is as well known as they should be.

CORRECT: Neither John Hawkes' novels nor those of Djuna Barnes *are* as well known as they should be.

When *or* or *nor* joins a singular subject and a plural subject, the verb usually agrees with the nearer subject:

INCORRECT: Dawn could not remember whether the novel *The Godfather* or the two *Godfather* movies was more violent.

CORRECT: Dawn could not remember whether the novel *The Godfather* or the two *Godfather* movies *were* more violent.

ALSO CORRECT: Dawn could not remember whether the two *Godfather* movies or the novel *was* more violent.

INCORRECT: Neither the clerks nor the assistant manager were watching the register.

CORRECT: Neither the clerks nor the assistant manager *was* watching the register.

ALSO CORRECT: Neither the assistant manager nor the clerks *were* watching the register.

18c   *Each, either, neither, one, everybody, somebody, nobody,* and *anyone* require singular verbs.

INCORRECT: Each of the team's twelve members were given a small replica of the championship trophy.

CORRECT: Each of the team's twelve members *was* given a small replica of the championship trophy.

INCORRECT: Nobody from inside the company *are* ever given serious consideration for the top positions.

CORRECT: Nobody from inside the company *is* ever given serious consideration for the top positions.

18d Quantitative words such as *some*, *half*, *all*, *part*, *most*, and *more* are singular or plural depending on the nouns they refer to.

CORRECT: All of the members *were* notified, and most *have* arrived.

CORRECT: Most of the committee's time *was* wasted in senseless wrangling.

CORRECT: One third of all meals eaten in this country *are* purchased in restaurants and fast-food stops.

CORRECT: Two thirds of his diet *is* starch.

None usually obeys the same rule, though some writers consider the word's origin ("not one") and treat it consistently as singular: I left messages for all of the members, but none *has* returned my call.

18e A collective noun that refers to a group as a unit takes a singular verb.

Nouns such as *class, committee, team, family, crew, jury, faculty, majority,* and *company* take singular verbs when they refer to a group as a whole:

CORRECT: The company *has* tried to diversify its investments.

CORRECT: If a majority *votes* in favor of adjournment, no further motions are allowed.

Occasionally you may need a plural verb to show that you are treating a group as individuals:

INCORRECT: If a majority votes according to their consciences, these amendments will be defeated.
CORRECT: If a majority *vote* according to their consciences, these amendments will be defeated.

In the incorrect sentence, the writer has been forced to shift from a singular verb *(votes)* to a plural pronoun *(their)*. Once you have decided whether a collective noun is singular or plural, treat it consistently as one or the other. Another example:

CORRECT: The jury votes by secret ballot, with twelve votes required for indictment. (*jury* treated as a whole)
CORRECT: The jury have taken their seats. (*jury* treated as individuals)
INCORRECT: The jury has taken their seats.

Many writers of American English avoid using collective nouns in the plural. They say "members of the jury" when they treat the jury as individuals acting separately, or they use the singular: The jury *is* seated.

18f Some singular subjects may look like plurals.

Certain nouns look like plurals but function as singulars and require singular verbs. *News, economics, politics, physics,* and *mathematics* are common examples.

INCORRECT: Politics, unfortunately, often enter into decisions of campus committees.
CORRECT: Politics, unfortunately, often *enters* into decisions of campus committees.

EXERCISE 18 _____

Study the sentences below for verb-subject agreement. A. Mark those that are correct with C, *those that have faulty agreement with* X. *B. Correct those marked* X.

1. Even with modern medicine, measles are still a serious problem in many countries.

2. Roger Kahn's *The Boys of Summer* and Dan Jenkins' *Semi-Tough* are two sports books that sold well even among those who are not sports fans.
3. Neither weight lifting nor isometrics are as good for building up injured muscles as is the Nautilus.
4. Either pasta dishes or Mexican food are being served at the opening of the new student union.
5. Everybody who attended the grand opening were given free souvenirs.
6. Neither the food nor the souvenirs were any good.
7. There are, said the campus chaplain in one of his lectures, every reason to be careful.
8. The newspaper staff are composed almost entirely of journalism students.
9. Nobody could figure out why a pair of sneakers were hung from the flagpole.
10. A wide variety of petroleum products is derived from shale oil.

19 agr

Use singular pronouns to refer to singular nouns, plural pronouns to refer to plural nouns.

Make each pronoun agree in number (singular or plural) with its antecedent: The flight instructor finished *his* lecture, but the pilots remained in *their* seats. Agreement is normally a simple matter, but you may need to take extra care when the antecedent is a collective noun or an indefinite pronoun and when the antecedent is compound.

19a Collective nouns such as *team, committee, chorus,* and *class* can be either singular or plural depending on how they are used.

Avoid treating a collective noun as both singular and plural:

INCORRECT: The interview committee *is* going to finish *their* deliberations tomorrow.

CORRECT: The interview committee *is* going to finish *its* deliberations tomorrow.

INCORRECT: Our rugby team *has* not won yet, but Saturday *they* will be doing *their* best.

CORRECT: Our rugby team *has* not won yet, but Saturday *it* will be doing *its* best.

See **18e** for a fuller discussion of collective nouns.

19b Indefinite antecedents such as *a person*, *each*, *neither*, *either*, *someone*, *anyone*, *no one*, *one*, and *everybody* almost always take singular pronouns.

INCORRECT: There are too many animals for officials to give each one the attention they deserve.

CORRECT: There are too many animals for officials to give each one the attention *it* deserves.

INCORRECT: When a person is confused, they should ask questions.

CORRECT: When a person is confused, *he* should ask questions.

Although *a person* could as easily refer to a female as to a male, traditional usage requires the masculine pronoun form. But many writers now avoid such usage. In very informal business situations, they often use the plural form *they* for *he*, or, in formal situations, use both the masculine and feminine forms *(he or she)*. Perhaps the safest method is to recast the sentence.

CORRECT: When confused, a person should ask questions.

See **18c** and **18d** for more on indefinite pronouns.

19c Compound antecedents with *and* take plural pronouns.

CORRECT: Sven and Eric—neither a polished typist—typed *their* own papers.

19d If a compound antecedent is joined by *or* or *nor*, the pronoun usually agrees with the nearer antecedent.

If the antecedents are singular, use a singular pronoun:

INCORRECT: Neither the television station nor its radio
             affiliate ever had their license revoked.
CORRECT: Neither the television station nor its radio
             affiliate ever had *its* license revoked.

If both antecedents are plural, use a plural pronoun:

CORRECT: It was impossible to blame either the reporters or
           the editors. *They* did all *they* could to verify
           the story.

If one antecedent is singular and one plural, make the pronoun agree with the closer antecedent:

CORRECT: Either the teacher or the students are responsible
           for turning off *their* classroom lights and air
           conditioner.

Do not waste time puzzling over intricate agreement problems with subjects or antecedents joined by *or* or *nor*. If following the rules in this section and in **18b** results in an absurd or awkward sentence, simply rewrite. You may be able to join the subjects or antecedents with *and:*

AWKWARD: Neither Amanda nor Bob will be in [his? her?
            their?] office this afternoon.
REWRITTEN: Both Amanda and Bob will be out of their
            offices this afternoon.

EXERCISE 19 _____

A. Mark with X those pronouns which are used inappropriately in the sentences below. If the sentence is correct, use C. B. Revise correctly those marked X.

   1. Either the coach or one of the assistants is always in the
      weight room working on their own conditioning.

2. The Phil Jones Combo will have their first concert here next Saturday at 8:00.
3. Every student writing on sexism in popular music used Florence King's article as their source.
4. The Subcommittee on Aging will issue its report next week.
5. Either the union or the workers will have to change its position.
6. The Brainert, Brainert, and Ridilla law firm is noted for their work in pain-and-suffering suits.
7. Find any piece of news you can and print it.
8. Neither Hemingway nor bullfighters respect cowardice in their work.
9. Industry has become aware of pollution and of the part they play in causing it.
10. Every great golfer spends endless hours perfecting their game.

20 **ca**

Determine the correct case of a pronoun by the word's function in the sentence.

The personal pronouns (*I, we, you, he, she, it, they*) appear in different case forms depending on their function in the sentence: *I* liked *her*, but *she* hated *me*.

	Nominative	Objective	Possessive*
First Person	I, we	me, us	my, mine, our, ours
Second Person	you	you	your, yours
Third Person	he, she, it, they	him, her, it, them	his, her, hers, its, their, theirs

*Note that no apostrophe is used for the possessives.

The **nominative** (also called **subjective**) case forms are used for the subject and predicate nominative functions:

> *We* were turned away. (subject)
>
> This is *she*. (predicate nominative)

The **objective** case forms are used for direct objects, indirect objects, and objects of prepositons:

> The sound system gave *us* trouble all night. (indirect object)
>
> The Cougars beat *us* badly in both games. (direct object)
>
> Next year we will be ready for *them*. (object of preposition)

The **possessive** case forms are used to show possession:

> *Their* system was no better than *ours*. (possessives)

Be especially careful of pronoun case in compound structures. Note the following:

INCORRECT:　Him and his older brothers learned to play "Duelling Banjos."

CORRECT:　He and his older brother learned to play "Duelling Banjos." (compound subject)

INCORRECT:　She may try to get you and I in trouble.

CORRECT:　She may try to get you and me in trouble. (object of *get*)

INCORRECT:　The nurse was unsympathetic to my mother and I.

CORRECT:　The nurse was unsympathetic to my mother and me. (object of *to*)

A pronoun used as an appositive (an explanatory word, phrase, or clause which clarifies a noun) should be in the same case as the noun or pronoun it refers to:

CORRECT:　The culprits, Harvey and I, were caught at midnight.

CORRECT:　The police quickly apprehended the culprits, Harvey and me.

INCORRECT:　Three finalists were chosen: Mary Lazenby, Mary McNulty, and me.

CORRECT:　Three finalists were chosen: Mary Lazenby, Mary McNulty, and I.

Use the possessive form immediately before a gerund:

INCORRECT: My parents are concerned about me working
while carrying fifteen credit hours.

CORRECT: My parents are concerned about *my working*
while carrying fifteen credit hours.

But you can generally use a non-possessive common
noun before a gerund, especially if the noun is plural:

CORRECT: The officials attributed the rise in unemployment
to *women entering* the job market.

Use the nominative case for the subject of an implied
verb form:

INCORRECT: No one on their team is as tall as me.

CORRECT: No one on their team is as tall as *I*.
(understood "am tall")

Use the nominative form as the subject of a clause
regardless of the function of the clause:

INCORRECT: Most Americans still show great respect for
whomever is President.

CORRECT: Most Americans still show great respect for
whoever is President. (*Whoever* is the subject
of *is* in the final clause.)

In formal writing, such as theses and research papers,
always use *whom* as you would *me* or any other objective
form. Many people have stopped using *whom,* especially
in speech and informal writing; but the safest course in
most college writing is to use *whom* whenever it is
called for:

INCORRECT: Whom did you say was calling?

CORRECT: Who did you say was calling? (*Who* is the subject
of *was.*)

CORRECT: Whom did you call? (*Whom* is the object of *call.*)

CORRECT: To whom was that call made? (*Whom* is the
object of the preposition *to.*)

A quick way to determine the case is to rephrase such
questions as statements: "You did call whom."

As a relative pronoun, *whom* is often dropped from the sentence:

CORRECT: Alderman Fischer is the only one [whom] we should reelect. (*Whom* is the direct object of *reelect*.)

EXERCISE 20 _____

Study the following sentences. A. Mark X for those with improper pronoun case, C *for those sentences that are correct. B. Correct those marked* X.

1. Simone Weil is worth reading; few writers are as original as her.
2. She is the thinker who Camus called "The only great spirit of our time."
3. My friend's parents are upset over him seeing me so much.
4. The credit manager is the one to whom Stan complained.
5. The oddsmakers are listing you and I as the team to beat.
6. Last year's champions, Bill and I, were not allowed to play together this year.
7. Jackson does not remember me paying the rent.
8. Who did Mr. Gold think the manager was?
9. Few could believe that the only victims were Josie and she.
10. Whom did you say was playing at the Bach concert next week?

21 adj/adv

Use adjectives to modify nouns; adverbs to modify verbs, adjectives, or other adverbs.

Both adjectives and adverbs are modifiers; they limit or describe other words.

ADJECTIVES: The *radical* changes of personnel were *unpleasant* but *necessary*.

ADVERBS: The *highly* complex steering mechanism turned the glider *smoothly*.

Adverbs are usually distinguished by their -ly endings (rapidly, formally), but many adjectives, such as *ghastly* and *heavenly,* also end in -ly, and many adverbs, such as *often* and *well,* do not. If you are in doubt whether a word is an adjective or adverb, check your dictionary.

In very informal writing and speaking certain adjectives, such as *sure, real,* and *good,* are often used in place of the adverbs *surely, really,* and *well;* but in more formal writing, the safer practice is to use the adverb forms to modify verbs, adjectives, and other adverbs and use adjectives only to modify nouns or pronouns:

VERY INFORMAL: I did so *bad* on my first calculus test that I never regained my confidence.

MORE FORMAL: I did so *badly* on my first calculus test that I never regained my confidence.

Use adjectives for subjective complements after verbs such as *feel, look, smell, sound,* and *taste,* which function like forms of the verb *to be;* use adverbs to modify these verbs. A quick test to make sure that the complement is correct is to substitute *is, was,* or other appropriate form of the verb *to be.*

PREDICATE ADJECTIVE: He was obviously upset, but he did not look *angry.* (Substitute *was* for *did look*)

ADVERB MODIFYING VERB: He looked *angrily* at us, then stalked off.

PREDICATE ADJECTIVE: I felt *nervous* as I approached the dark building. (Substitute *was* for *felt*)

ADVERB MODIFYING VERB: I felt *nervously* in my pocket for a match.

21a Use the correct comparative and superlative forms for adverbs and adjectives.

Most short adjectives add -er for the comparative and -est for the superlative. Longer adjectives and most adverbs use *more* and *most*. A few have irregular comparative and superlative forms. Check your dictionary when you are in doubt.

Positive	Comparative	Superlative
strong	stronger	strongest
happy	happier	happiest
surprising	more surprising	most surprising
happily	more happily	most happily
good	better	best
well	better	best
bad	worse	worst

Use the comparative form when comparing two items, the superlative for three or more:

INCORRECT: Marlowe and Jonson are both excellent play-wrights, but Jonson is the best craftsman.

CORRECT: Marlowe and Jonson are both excellent play-wrights, but Johson is the *better* craftsman.

INCORRECT: *M.A.S.H.* is the more entertaining of the three Robert Altman films I have seen.

CORRECT: *M.A.S.H.* is the *most* entertaining of the three Robert Altman films I have seen.

EXERCISE 21 _____

A. Mark the following sentences with C *if they are correct; mark with* X *those containing incorrectly used adjective or adverb forms. B. Correct those marked* X.

1. Sandra and Traci were both bright girls, but Traci was the best physics student of the two.
2. Be sure that the job is done proper and fast.
3. Roxanne had fasted for three days but didn't even feel hungrily when she could finally eat.
4. Arnold, an excellent graphic artist, came through with very good work on the special edition, even though he didn't feel very good.
5. The special edition left the editorial staff tired, but we in production were even more exhausted.

6. Oxford is the oldest of England's two original, prestigious universities.
7. Many public speakers act nervously, yet they talk eloquently in small groups.
8. Barry always looks well even though he usually feels ill.
9. Claire always looks well even when she is too busy to be well groomed.
10. Walker Percy is one of the more gifted of today's American novelists.

22   t

Use the verb tense appropriate to the time of an action or situation.

Although English relies heavily on adverbs and adverbial phrases and clauses to refer to time *(now, tomorrow, yesterday morning, after the play had already started)*, it also indicates time by changes in the verb. By using verb tenses accurately, you can help your reader keep track of time relationships in your writing.

English verbs have only two primary tenses, present and past; but by using auxiliary verbs we can create complex verb forms. Thus we can list three simple tenses, three perfect tenses, and progressive forms for all six.

Simple tenses. The **simple present tense** is far from simple in the ways it is used:

Present time: I *hear* you calling. He *looks* anxious.

Habitual time: I *hear* the train go by every morning. He *repairs* his old Volkswagen himself.

Historical present: Brutus *hears* the mob hailing Caesar.

Literary present: In "The Man That Corrupted Hadleyburg," Twain *exposes* the power of money to corrupt us.

Future action: The case *goes* to court next week. When the defense attorney *finishes* her remarks, the jury will retire.

In the present tense, third-person singular subjects require an -*s* ending on the verb (see **18**).

The **past tense** is formed by adding -*ed* to regular verbs or by changing the spelling of most irregular verbs (see **23**). The **future tense** uses the auxiliary *shall* or *will.* Traditionally, *shall* has been reserved for use with first-person subjects *(I shall go), will* with second- and third-person subjects *(you will go; she will go),* except when the writer reverses the usage to show strong emphasis: I *will* win; you *shall* obey me. Today, only the most formal writing observes that distinction, and *will* is regularly used with all persons.

The following list shows the forms for a regular verb *(play),* and for the most irregular and most often used English verb, *be:*

	Regular verb	*To be*
Present:	I play	I am
	you play	you are
	he, she, it plays	he, she, it is
	we, you, they play	we, you, they are
Past:	I played	I was
	you played	you were
	he, she, it played	he, she, it was
	we, you, they played	we, you, they were
Future:	I will (shall) play	I will (shall) be
	you will play	you will be
	he, she, it will play	he, she, it will be

Perfect tenses. The perfect tenses indicate the relation of two times. The **present perfect** refers to an indefinite time in the recent past or to a time beginning in the past and continuing to the present:

Congressman Green *has voted* with the conservatives
  more often than with the liberals.

This ten-dollar watch *has kept* perfect time for two years.

The **past perfect** indicates a time before some other
specified or implied time in the past:

The teams *had met* twice before the playoffs.

Similarly, the **future perfect** may be used to indicate
a time before some other stated or implied time in
the future:

Before they return, the astronauts *will have broken* the
  record for time spent in space.

Note that *return* in the previous example is a typical case
of the present used for future time. This use of the
present is very common in dependent clauses.

The perfect tenses combine a form of the auxiliary
have with the past participle of the main verb:

Present perfect:	I have played	I have been
	you have played	you have been
	he, she, it has played	he, she, it has been
	we, you, they have played	we, you, they have been
Past perfect:	I had played	I had been
	you had played	you had been
	he, she, it had played	he, she, it had been
	we, you, they had played	we, you, they had been
Future perfect:	I will (shall) have played	I will (shall) have been
	you will have played	you will have been
	he, she, it will have played	he, she, it will have been
	we, you, they will have played	we, you, they have been

Progressive tenses. Progressive forms of verbs indicate continuous actions:

> The candidates *are waiting* for the results of the election.
>
> I *was running* toward the stop when the bus pulled away.
>
> I *shall be working* on my tax return all day tomorrow.
>
> Mr. Velkoff told me last week that I *had been using* the wrong forms for at least six months.

There are progressive forms for all six tenses:

Present progressive:
I am playing
he, she, it is playing
we, you, they are playing

Past progressive:
I was playing
he, she, it was playing
we, you, they were playing

Future progressive:
I, he, she, it will (shall) be playing
we, you, they will (shall) playing

Present perfect progressive:
I have been playing
he, she, it has been playing
we, you, they have been playing

Past perfect progressive:
I, he, she, it had been playing
we, you, they had been playing

Future perfect progressive:
I, he, she, it will (shall have been playing
we, you, they will (shall) have been playing

Tenses of verbals. Verbals (infinitives, gerunds, and participles) have present and present-perfect forms. The participle also has a past form.

> *Present infinitive:* to sink, to be sinking
> *Perfect infinitive:* to have sunk
>
> *Present gerund:* sinking
> *Perfect gerund:* having sunk

Present participle: sinking
Perfect participle: having sunk, having been sinking
Past participle: sunk

Use the past or perfect form of a verbal to indicate a time before the main verb in the clause:

Emily would like [now] *to have played* in last night's concert.

He could not get over *having failed* his teammates.

Having signed all the letters, she went home early.

But: The woman *addressing* the assembly will retire next month. (The present participle here indicates the same time as the speaking or writing of the sentence.)

Use the past participle to indicate a time before that of the main verb or to describe a condition that began before the time of the main verb in the clause:

Angered by the story, the apartment owner sued both the newspaper and the reporter.

In most other cases, use the present forms of verbals:

Emily decided *to play* Chopin. (The playing follows the deciding.)

Emily enjoys *playing* Chopin. (The playing and the enjoying take place at the same time.)

Writing about *Bonnie and Clyde,* Pauline Kael remarked. . . . (The writing and the remarking take place together.)

Voice. English verbs also show active voice (the butler *committed* the crime) or passive voice (the crime *was committed* by the butler). The forms presented in this section have all been in the active voice. Verbs in the passive voice combine a form of *be* with the past participle of the main verb:

	Active	*Passive*
Present:	I know	I am known
Past	I knew	I was known
Future	I will know	I will be known

Present perfect:	I have known	I have been known
Past perfect:	I had known	I had been known
Future perfect:	I will have known	I will have been known

Progressive verbs are sometimes used in the passive voice: I *am being watched.* For a discussion of voice and style, see **48e**.

EXERCISE 22 _____

A. Mark the following sentences with C *if they are correct, with* X *if they contain errors in verb tense. B. Correct those sentences marked* X.

1. As of next month, the dean will be at the university twenty-five years.
2. Since many orchestra conductors lead long lives, many people believe that conducting will be increasing one's longevity.
3. Talese, having received great publicity before his recent book was published, had disappointed many eager readers.
4. The Equal Rights Amendment was ratified by twenty-two states in 1972, and sixteen others had been expected soon to follow suit.
5. But fewer states took positive action, however, and several even changed their positions.
6. Having approved the amendment in 1972, Congress narrowly gave the ERA thirty-nine more months to have gathered sufficient approval.
7. In June, 1980, when Illinois voted no, it seems that the amendment was virtually dead.
8. The Davis Cup competition has become such a political event that it loses its appeal to tennis enthusiasts.
9. Bill decided to have opposed a tax reduction.
10. Anderson had been president of our chess club for the past three years and will probably be re-elected.

23 vb

Use the correct principal parts of irregular verbs.

The principal parts of verbs are the forms you must know in order to form all the tenses correctly. English verbs have three principal parts: the infinitive (or present stem), the past tense, and the past participle. For regular verbs, the past tense and past participle are formed by adding -d or -ed to the infinitive: *walk, walked, walked; close, closed, closed.* Other verbs—the irregular verbs—form the past tense and past participle by various means, usually by changing a vowel in the infinitive *(win, won).* The list below includes the principal parts of the most common irregular verbs and a few regular verbs often mistakenly treated as irregular. Your college dictionary also gives the principal parts of irregular verbs. If it does not list the past tense and past participle forms, you can assume that the verb is regular.

Infinitive	*Past Tense*	*Past Participle*
awake	awaked (awoke)	awaked (awoke)
beat	beat	beaten
become	became	become
begin	began	begun
bend	bent	bent
bite	bit	bitten
bleed	bled	bled
blow	blew	blown
break	broke	broken
bring	brought	brought
build	built	built
burst	burst	burst
buy	bought	bought
catch	caught	caught
choose	chose	chosen
come	came	come

Infinitive	Past Tense	Past Participle
cut	cut	cut
deal	dealt	dealt
dig	dug	dug
dive	dived (dove)	dived
do	did	done
drag	dragged	dragged
draw	drew	drawn
drink	drank	drunk
drive	drove	driven
drown	drowned	drowned
eat	ate	eaten
fall	fell	fallen
fight	fought	fought
fly	flew	flown
forget	forgot	forgotten (forgot)
freeze	froze	frozen
get	got	got (gotten)
give	gave	given
go	went	gone
grow	grew	grown
have	had	had
hide	hid	hidden
hold	held	held
keep	kept	kept
know	knew	known
lead	led	led
leave	left	left
lend	lent	lent
let	let	let
lose	lost	lost
mean	meant	meant
prove	proved	proved (proven)
read	read	read
ride	rode	ridden
ring	rang	rung
rise	rose	risen
run	ran	run
say	said	said
see	saw	seen
sell	sold	sold

Infinitive	Past Tense	Past Participle
send	sent	sent
sew	sewed	sewed (sewn)
shake	shook	shaken
shave	shaved	shaved (shaven)
shrink	shrank (shrunk)	shrunk
show	showed	showed (shown)
sink	sank (sunk)	sunk
speak	spoke	spoken
swear	swore	sworn
swim	swam	swum
take	took	taken
teach	taught	taught
tell	told	told
think	thought	thought
throw	threw	thrown
wear	wore	worn
win	won	won
write	wrote	written

A few verbs that have two distinct meanings have different principal parts in each meaning:

bid (a price)	bid	bid
bid (an order)	bade (bid)	bidden (bid)
hang (execute)	hanged	hanged
hang (suspend)	hung	hung
shine (emit light)	shone	shone
shine (polish)	shined	shined

Three pairs of verbs are easily confused, especially in their past-tense and past-participle forms. The key distinction is that one of each pair is transitive (it takes an object) but the other is intransitive (no object).

Transitive

lay (place)	laid	laid
set (place)	set	set
raise (lift)	raised	raised

Intransitive

lie (recline)	lay	lain
lie (falsehood)	lied	lied
sit (be seated)	sit	sit
rise (rise up)	rose	risen

He *laid* his head on a rock and *lay* in the sun for an hour.

She *set* her pen on the desk and *sat* waiting for others to finish.

He *rose* from the bed and *raised* the window.

EXERCISE 23 _____

Circle the correct verb forms in the following sentences.

1. The brothers have *forgot/forgotten* how many times they have *dived/dove* for treasure.
2. They have *swam/swum* professionally for five years, not long enough to have *grown/grew* careless.
3. Joe's telephone *rung/rang* eight times before I finally *hung/hanged* up.
4. The men *rose/rised* at dawn to *rise/raise* the flag.
5. Lucille has *broke/broken* the necklace which she *lay/laid* on the table.
6. Joan's sister *lent/lended* her the money, which had *laid/lain* in a savings account for a year.
7. Mark has *run/ran* to the baseball field as soon as the last bell has *rang/rung* every day.
8. My arm *bled/bleeded* profusely after our mascot had *bit/bitten* it.
9. "I do not *chose/choose* to run," Coolidge tersely announced.
10. Helen would have *spoke/spoken* more clearly if she had not *drank/drunk* the champagne.

24 **mo**

Use the mood required by your sentence.

English has three moods: *indicative* for statements of fact and questions about facts, *imperative* for commands, and *subjunctive* for wishes or statements either possible or contrary to fact.

> *Indicative:* I *know* who he *is.*
>
> *Imperative: Be* yourself.
>
> *Subjunctive:* If I *were* you, I would avoid that subject.

The subjunctive is used far less now than earlier in the history of the language, but there are some situations in which the subjunctive is still the usual choice:

CORRECT: He demanded that Maria *finish* the work.
(Desired action. Less formally, this might be expressed, "He told Maria to finish the work.")

CORRECT: It is essential that I *be seen* at the party.

CORRECT: Mario drank as if Prohibition *were* being reintroduced. (contrary to fact)

CORRECT: Eve wishes that she *were* more talented. (contrary to fact)

Only a few forms of the subjunctive are different from the indicative forms given in **22**. Those forms are shown here in bold type:

Present:	that I walk	that I **be**
	that he, she, it **walk** (no -*s*)	that he, she, it **be**
	that we, you, they walk	that we, you they **be**
Past:	that I walked	that I **were**
	that he, she, it walked	that he, she, it **were**
	that we, you, they walked	that we, you, they were
Present perfect:	that I have walked	that I have been
	that he, she, it **have** walked	that he, she, it **have** been
	that we, you, they have walked	that we, you, they have been

EXERCISE 24 _____

Study the sentences below. A. Mark with C those that are correct, with X those that have errors in mood. B. Correct those marked X.

1. He laughed as though the accident were the greatest joke on record.
2. Your Honor, I demand that this evidence is ruled inadmissible.
3. If the customer look at all suspect, the employee is supposed to call security.
4. The doctor insisted that more tests are run.
5. If writing a great many novels was the key to fame, Bulwer-Lytton's name would be known to us all.
6. I would be surprised if his name was known by five percent of our undergraduates.
7. Angus requested that he be given the recognition he deserves.
8. "Holmes will be able to determine if the letter was forged," Dr. Watson said.
9. In 1951, President Truman demanded that General MacArthur be relieved of his command.
10. Ms. Stochan, if I was in your position, I'd call the police.

4

PUNCTUATION AND MECHANICS

Punctuation marks represent much of the information we convey in speaking when we pause and raise or lower our voices, information such as where a sentence ends and whether the sentence is a question or a statement. They also signal things that we cannot communicate easily in speech, such as quoting someone directly, for example. Although we can often "hear" when we need a punctuation mark, as where we need commas in this sentence, we cannot always tell which mark to use. The only sure way to punctuate correctly is to know the conventions.

25 ,

Use commas to separate certain elements of a sentence.

The comma is the most widely used—and misused—mark of punctuation. One of its most common uses is

to separate clauses and phrases. Use it with a coordinating conjunction to join two independent clauses, to
separate introductory clauses and long introductory
phrases from the rest of the sentence, and to separate
items in a series.

25a Place a comma before a coordinating conjunction joining two independent clauses.

Use a comma before coordinating conjunctions *(and, but,
or, nor, for, yet,* or *so)* when they join two independent
clauses. A comma without a coordinating conjunction
between such clauses is not enough (see **17**).

INCORRECT: The poor are legally first-class citizens but they
    can afford only second-class protection.
CORRECT: The poor are legally first-class citizens **,** but they
    can afford only second-class protection.

INCORRECT: Jack read innumerable warnings about smoking
    so he gave up reading.
CORRECT: Jack read innumerable warnings about smoking **,**
    so he gave up reading.

If the clauses are very short and closely related, you may
omit the comma, but it is generally safer to include it.

CORRECT: It is dark and I am alone.
CORRECT: The facts are important **,** but the truth is essential.

Note the difference between a compound sentence (one
with two independent clauses) and a sentence containing a compound predicate (double verb):

CORRECT: The counselors *listen to and help* dozens of students
    each week. (No comma is used before this *and* since
    it does not join two independent clauses.)

25b Place a comma after an introductory subordinate clause or a long introductory phrase.

INCORRECT: Although there are many trial marriages there is no such thing as a trial child.

CORRECT: Although there are many trial marriages **,** there is no such thing as a trial child.

—Garry Wills

INCORRECT: Paying close attention to Louisa's reactions the psychologist made careful notes during each session.

CORRECT: Paying close attention to Louisa's reactions **,** the psychologist made careful notes during each session.

INCORRECT: When Fred's company adopted flexible work hours no one imagined that so many employees would come in late.

CORRECT: When Fred's company adopted flexible work hours **,** no one imagined that so many employees would come in late.

INCORRECT: Though it was hard to believe the story was true.

CORRECT: Though it was hard to believe **,** the story was true.

A short introductory phrase often does not require a comma:

CORRECT: Every evening we met at Jimmy's to discuss politics and baseball.

Use a comma to separate a subordinate clause or long phrase *following* the main clause only if the subordinate clause or phrase is very loosely related to the main clause or adds a contrasting idea:

COMMA NEEDED: The supervisor decided to use the new C.P.M. calculator in determining next year's budget **,** although she had never tried it on even a small job.

NO COMMA NEEDED: No one imagined that so many employees would come in late when Fred's company adopted flexible work hours.

25c Place commas between items in a series.

Place a comma after each item except the last in a series of words, phrases, or clauses unless all items are joined by conjunctions. In a series with the last two items joined by a conjunction (a, b, *and* c), place a comma before the conjunction to prevent a possible misreading. Some writers omit this comma, but the safer practice is to use it.

INCORRECT: Dr. Lovekin found that the roll omitted students named Allen Brady Welch and Zellers.

CORRECT: Dr. Lovekin found that the roll omitted students named Allen, Brady, Welch, and Zellers.

INCORRECT: Mankind looks for a way to escape his planet to search for intelligent beings to seek some assurance that he is not alone in the universe.

CORRECT: Mankind looks for a way to escape his planet, to search for intelligent beings, to seek some assurance that he is not alone in the universe.
—Jacques-Yves Cousteau

INCORRECT: Make up and label drawers for each of the following items: washers mollies wing nuts nuts and bolts.

CORRECT: Make up and label drawers for each of the following items: washers, mollies, wing nuts, nuts, and bolts.
Or: Make up and label drawers for each of the following items: washers, mollies, wing nuts, and nuts and bolts. (The first correct sentence asks for five drawers, the second for four drawers; the incorrect sentence is unclear.)

25d Use commas to separate coordinate adjectives.

Coordinate adjectives modify a noun equally:

long, windy speech   cold, dark, muddy waters

You can identify coordinate adjectives by placing *and* between them or by reversing their order:

Long and windy speech   muddy, dark, cold waters

Do not place commas between cumulative adjectives, those in which one adjective modifies the rest of the expression:

severe economic difficulties

In the above example, *severe* modifies not just *difficulties* but *economic difficulties*. *And* could not be inserted between *severe* and *economic*, nor could the adjectives be reversed. Therefore, no comma is used.

INCORRECT: The class presidency was a mentally challenging physically tiring and psychologically demanding position.

CORRECT: The class presidency was a mentally challenging, physically tiring, and psychologically demanding position.

INCORRECT: We replaced our old, manual typewriter.
CORRECT: We replaced our old manual typewriter.

EXERCISE 25 _____

Correct any errors in comma usage in the following sentences.

1. Dostoyevski wrote many outstanding novels but *The Brothers Karamazov* stands above all others.
2. Other important works are *The Idiot, Crime and Punishment,* and *Notes from Underground.*

3. Although he was a contemporary of Dostoyevski Leo Tolstoi wrote entirely different types of novels.
4. Tolstoi supposedly wrote much better Russian than Dostoyevski who translates well into English.
5. Even though he lived a century ago, Dostoyevski seems to speak to the inner suffering and torment and even the the insanity of modern man.
6. When my father retired, he received the usual shiny, gold watch.
7. Jason, my stockbroker, did not recommend the inexpensive new utility stocks because of the uncertain, political climate.
8. Our drama class was assigned plays by Marlowe, Webster, Middleton, and other Renaissance playwrights.
9. Being inexperienced as a salesman, Dennis approached each customer unsure whether to speak or be spoken to.
10. My brother wants to marry a tall blonde beautiful girl who owns a Cadillac dealership and a chain of liquor stores.

26 ,

Use commas to set interrupting elements apart from the rest of the sentence.

Commas set apart groups of words that interrupt the normal flow of a sentence. Four such interrupters are especially common: nonrestrictive modifiers, appositives, parenthetical expressions, and transitional adverbs or phrases.

26a Use commas to separate a nonrestrictive modifier from the rest of the sentence.

A **restrictive modifier** limits or restricts the noun or pronoun it modifies. The noun *candidate*, for example, can refer to any of those people seeking office, but *candidate who supports higher taxes* refers to someone from a much more limited group. In the sentence, "A candidate who supports higher taxes cannot get elected in this state," the modifier *(who supports higher taxes)* is needed to restrict the noun *(candidate)* so that it refers to someone in the smaller group. Take out the modifier and the sentence is no longer accurate: "A candidate cannot get elected in this state."

A **nonrestrictive modifier,** on the other hand, is not needed to restrict the noun or pronoun it modifies: "Phil Spender, *who supports higher taxes,* cannot get elected in this state." Here the subject already refers to just one person, and the modifier simply adds information. Thus the modifier is nonrestrictive.

Enclose a nonrestrictive modifier in commas:

INCORRECT: Houdini who triumphed over obscurity in his lifetime continues to fascinate people.

CORRECT: Houdini, who triumphed over obscurity in his lifetime, continues to fascinate people. (nonrestrictive)

INCORRECT: The Robie House which was designed by Frank Lloyd Wright is open to visitors on Mondays and Wednesdays.

CORRECT: The Robie House, which was designed by Frank Lloyd Wright, is open to visitors on Mondays and Wednesdays. (nonrestrictive)

Do not set off a restrictive modifier with commas:

INCORRECT: Other houses, designed by Frank Lloyd Wright, can be seen in Oak Park.

CORRECT: Other houses designed by Frank Lloyd Wright can be seen in Oak Park. (restrictive)

INCORRECT: Stores, which honor credit cards, have noticed an increase in sales.

CORRECT: Stores which honor credit cards have noticed an increase in sales. (restrictive)

CORRECT: Fairway Stores, which honor all major credit cards, have noticed an increase in sales. (nonrestrictive)

It is often difficult to determine whether a modifier is restrictive or nonrestrictive. Study the sentence both with and without the modifier. If the meanings are substantially different, the expression is restrictive and no commas are needed. You can also read it aloud: if you pause noticeably before and after the expression, you need commas.

CORRECT: For the majority of immigrants who do not know English **,** language is the chief problem. (restrictive)

ALSO CORRECT: For the majority of immigrants **,** who do not know English **,** language is the chief problem. (nonrestrictive)

Note: Be careful to place a comma at both ends of a nonrestrictive element (unless, of course, the clause ends the sentence).

26b   Use commas to separate an appositive from the rest of the sentence.

An appositive is a noun or a noun phrase that restates, explains, or supplements a preceding noun:

> The newcomer **,** *a friend of Rita's* **,** is from Venezuela.

Most appositives are nonrestrictive (see **26a**) and can be dropped from the sentence without changing its meaning. Enclose them in commas:

INCORRECT: Flannery O'Connor the great American writer who lived in Georgia died at age 39 in 1964.

CORRECT: Flannery O'Connor **,** the great American writer who lived in Georgia **,** died at age 39 in 1964.

INCORRECT: When I graduate in June, I will begin work at Rio Piñar a local country club.

CORRECT: When I graduate in June, I will begin work at Rio Piñar **,** a local country club.

A restrictive appositive, like a restrictive modifier, clarifies the meaning of the sentence and so should not be set off with commas:

CORRECT: My friend *Jamie* always avoids using the word *dumb.*

26c   Use commas to separate a parenthetical element from the rest of the sentence.

Parenthetical elements are words, phrases, or clauses inserted into a sentence to clarify or emphasize a point or to give extra information. They interrupt the basic sentence structure and so should be set off with commas:

CORRECT: Economics is **,** as Carlyle put it **,** "the Dismal Science."

CORRECT; The family was upset **,** of course **,** by Aunt Leah's eccentric behavior.

Use commas to set off nouns in direct address (nouns which name the reader or listener):

CORRECT; Genevieve **,** you will have to send her to a nursing home.

CORRECT: Those of you who think that the examples I have just cited are isolated cases of suburban crime **,** consider the following statistics.

Use commas, too, for mild interjections:

CORRECT: Well **,** I guess I have no choice in the matter.

Commas also prevent misreadings:

CORRECT: Unless Joe calls **,** his grandmother will not be expecting him.

26d   Use commas to set off transitional expressions.

Words like *however, moreover, nevertheless,* and *in fact* are parenthetical expressions that provide transition between sentences or paragraphs. (See **12b** for a brief list.) Set them off with commas:

CORRECT: Hemingway's Americans sound more like Hemingway than Americans. *On the other hand,* they could not be anything other than Hemingway Americans.

CORRECT: *Therefore,* many readers find Hemingway's style American in a special way.

The comma in the last sentence is optional, and many writers would omit it. The best way to tell whether to use a comma with a short transitional expression is to read the sentence aloud. If you pause between the transition and the rest of the sentence, use a comma.

EXERCISE 26 _____

Correct any errors in comma usage in the following sentences.

1. David Albert Corbin a well-known medium will appear at the Great Southern Music Hall next week.
2. The quarter system, which we abandoned last year, is less efficient than the present semester system.
3. I was surprised that S. I. Hayakawa who wrote my Freshman English book is also a prominent politician.
4. Our Clayton store as a matter of fact has the best selection of records.
5. Oh, I don't know about that.
6. However *The Tempest* does not resemble most comedies.
7. The girl wearing the red shoes is in my typing class.
8. My wife wearing the red shoes is standing by the information booth.
9. Well, I am not an atheist.
10. A bore moreover is one who lights up a room by leaving it.

27 ,

Use commas in numbers, addresses, titles, and quotations.

Separate the day of the month from the year with commas:

October 24, 1957   December 23, 1981

When only a month and year are given the comma is optional:

February, 1941 *or* February 1941

The military form, 1 December 1981, requires no commas.

Commas also separate numbers into thousands, millions, and so on:

3,916 *or* 3916   4,816,317,212

Commas also separate items in addresses:

Toledo, Ohio
400 7th Street, New Kensington, Pennsylvania 15068
121 87th Street, Brooklyn, New York 11209

Notice that no comma appears between the state name and the ZIP code.

In sentences, the final item of an address or a date is also followed by a comma:

Working in Palm Springs, California, has many
   compensations.
March 12, 1922, was a day he never forgot.

Use commas to separate titles and degrees from proper names:

Ronald B. Nelson, Ed.D.   Robert J. Heidenry, M.D.
Robert Pew, Ph.D., C.D.P., C.D.E.
Albert M. Johnston, Jr., took over as chief clerk.

Use commas to introduce direct quotations and to separate quoted material from non-quoted material:

> Dr. Guber asked **,** "When is her test scheduled?"
> "I'm not sure **,**" I answered **,** "that I really want to go."

When a quotation ends in a period, change the period to a comma when the quotation is followed by non-quoted material:

> "Psychology involves pulling habits out of rats **,**" Douglas
>   Bush said.

EXERCISE 27 _____

Add or delete commas as needed in the following sentences. If a sentence is correct, mark it with **C**.

1. Josephine Canteras was born on May 26, 1934 in New Kensington, Pennsylvania.
2. She was married in Quantico, Virginia, in September 1955.
3. Pearl Harbor was attacked on 7 December, 1941.
4. 3726 Overdone Drive, Rockford, Illinois, 62521.
5. She received an inheritance of $3,814,211.19 before taxes.
6. Her new title is Cheryl Johnson C.P.S.
7. "You have to arrange a time trade," ruled Chief LaCorte "if you want to take courses."
8. Richard S. Grove Ph.D. spoke to the graduates on June 1 1978.
9. My seminar was held in San Francisco, 28 December 1975.
10. "Well," I said "a fit audience though few."

28 no ,

Omit all unnecessary commas.

Unnecessary commas will make your reader pause needlessly or look for relationships that are not there.

Use a comma only when any of the guidelines above calls for one or when you are certain that a comma is necessary to prevent misreading.

Do not separate a subject from its verb:

INCORRECT: Their daily problems in getting their car started**,** were bothering the whole neighborhood.

CORRECT: Their daily problems in getting their car started were bothering the whole neighborhood.

Do not separate a verb from its object:

INCORRECT: Chief Kaiser always says**,** that we must be going to a fire when we arrive early.

CORRECT: Chief Kaiser always says that we must be going to a fire when we arrive early.

Do not use a comma before a coordinating conjunction *(and, but, for, or, yet)* except when the conjunction ends a series or joins two independent clauses:

INCORRECT: Reading modern novels**,** and writing papers about them are not equally appealing activities.

CORRECT: Reading modern novels and writing papers about them are not equally appealing activities.

CORRECT: Father Smith both knows and respects my beliefs. (compound predicate, no comma)

Do not separate a restrictive modifier from the rest of the sentence (see **26a**):

INCORRECT: The access roads**,** that were built before the construction of SR 427**,** already need repair.

CORRECT: The access roads that were built before the construction of SR 427 already need repair.

Do not use a comma before the first item or after the last item of a series:

INCORRECT: Private offices, shower rooms, and a large lounge**,** are included in the new wing.

CORRECT: Private offices, shower rooms, and a large lounge are included in the new wing.

EXERCISE 28 _____

A. Circle any unnecessary commas in the following sentences.

1. A man is not honest, merely because he does not steal.
2. I would remind you, that Plato was the first censor.
3. Everyone, Kierkegaard said, is an exception.
4. Rollo May's *Love and Will* includes chapters entitled "Love and Death," "The Will in Crisis," and "Communion of Consciousness."
5. Frances FitzGerald has written a book, on twentieth-century history textbooks entitled, *America Revised.*

B. Add commas as needed in the following sentences.

1. Jean-Paul Sartre the philosopher and playwright who died in 1980 left an indelible mark on modern thought.
2. Often overlooked are Sartre's short stories such as "The Wall" which offers a chilling picture of men who are about to die.
3. Jack Nicklaus, considered the greatest golfer of his time had probably his greatest day in the game on June 15, 1980.
4. He proved his prowess by winning his fourth U.S. Open tournament which was played at Balstural Country Club in New Jersey.
5. Louis Mitchell Jr. cannot decide whether to take a Ph.D. or an Ed.D. and whether to go to Ohio State or to Michigan State his alma mater.

29 .

Use periods after statements or commands and in abbreviations and decimals.

The period ranks second to the comma as the most common mark of punctuation. It is also one of the easiest to use properly, serving three basic functions: to end sentences, to end abbreviations, and to separate decimals.

29a   Use a period after a sentence that is not a direct question or exclamation.

The examples below show three types of sentences ended by periods:

> *Direct statement:* The occult sciences are alive and flourishing.
>
> *Indirect question:* I wonder why Chris walks so slowly.
>
> *Instruction or command:* Turn it down, please.

29b   Use periods according to conventions in abbreviations and decimals.

Periods are required after most abbreviations, as shown below. See **41** for help in using abbreviations.

> Ms.   Mrs.   Mr.   Jr.   Dec.   a.m.   e.g.

Do not use periods in acronyms (abbreviations pronounced as words) and abbreviations of company names and governmental agencies:

> NATO   CORE   ITT   FBI   CIA   NOW

Use a period as a decimal point preceding a decimal fraction, between a whole number and decimals, and between dollars and cents:

> .007   .95   98.6°   3.1416 $.19 $36,500.00

See Exercise 31.

30   **?**

Use a question mark to indicate a direct question.

Question marks are end stops for direct questions; they can also be used within sentences, as shown below:

CORRECT: Why has *The Hobbit* remained so popular❓

CORRECT: I want to go, but how can I❓

CORRECT: "When will we get there❓" she asked.

CORRECT: Mr. Walsh called in three backup units (who knows why❓) when none were needed.

CORRECT: You actually like Sean❓ (Notice that the question mark here shows the reader how to read the sentence; a period would produce an entirely different meaning.)

Use a period after an indirect question:

CORRECT: Brad asked if he could be seated without a tie❗

See Exercise 31.

31 ❗

Use an exclamation point to show extreme emphasis.

An exclamation point shows extreme emotion or disbelief and can end a sentence, an interjection, or a clause or phrase. Do not overuse the exclamation point. Try to achieve emphasis through your choice of appropriate words.

CORRECT: What a night we've had❗

CORRECT: Get out of my way❗ Now❗

CORRECT: No, you can't be serious❗

EXERCISE 31 ⸻⸻⸻⸻⸻⸻⸻⸻⸻⸻⸻⸻

Correct any errors in end punctuation in the following sentences.

1. Why! Many local jails are worse than state penitentiaries!

2. I ask why people being held for trial are often treated like convicts?
3. "Why do you always procrastinate," I inquired?
4. Would you please pay attention?
5. You must be kidding!
6. You must be kidding?
7. You must be kidding.
8. That certainly is a strange choice of words!
9. Did he really tell her to shut up?
10. I have long wondered why he didn't do it sooner.

32   ;

Use semicolons to separate independent clauses and punctuated items in a series.

The semicolon is an intermediate mark, stronger than a comma but weaker than a period. It is used only between grammatically equal units—two or more independent clauses or two or more items in a series.

32a   Use a semicolon to connect two independent clauses not joined by a coordinating conjunction.

In compound sentences (two or more independent clauses that could stand alone as sentences), join the clauses with a semicolon unless you use a coordinating conjunction *(and, or, nor, for, but, yet* or *so)* and a comma (see **17**):

INCORRECT: Our courts need a better definition of insanity, the standard definitions are inadequate. (comma splice)

CORRECT: Our courts need a better definition of insanity; the standard definitions are inadequate.

INCORRECT: The student parking lot is half empty at 3:15 p.m. this must be a commuter campus. (fused sentence)

CORRECT: The student parking lot is half empty at 3:15 p.m.; this must be a commuter campus.

Use a semicolon before a conjunctive adverb *(however, hence, therefore,* etc.) or transitional phrase that introduces an independent clause:

INCORRECT: The skill of big-name athletes is indisputable, however, their greed is threatening to destroy professional sports.

CORRECT: The skill of big-name athletes is indisputable; however, their greed is threatening to destroy professional sports.

INCORRECT: Their music is not a chaotic mishmash, as the casual listener often thinks, on the contrary, it is as carefully contrived as the work of any so-called serious composer.

CORRECT: Their music is not a chaotic mishmash, as the casual listener often thinks; on the contrary, it is as carefully contrived as the work of any so-called serious composer.

Before a coordinating conjunction joining two long independent clauses that contain internal punctuation, use a semicolon rather than a comma:

PREFERRED: My father never mentioned Louis Armstrong, except to forbid us to play his records; but there was a picture of him on our wall for a long time.
      —James Baldwin, *Notes of a Native Son*

Do not use semicolons between a main clause and a subordinate clause:

INCORRECT: Although the skies looked threatening; the game began on time. (dependent clause with independent clause)

CORRECT: The skies looked threatening; the game nevertheless began on time. (both independent clauses)

32b   Use semicolons to separate the items in a series when the items themselves contain commas.

When punctuating a series of items that contain commas, such as dates or cities and states, use semicolons between the items to avoid confusion with the internal commas:

INCORRECT: Bonnie has already attended colleges in Fort Collins, Colorado, Tempe, Arizona, and Galesburg, Illinois.

CORRECT: Bonnie has already attended colleges in Fort Collins, Colorado; Tempe, Arizona; and Galesburg, Illinois.

INCORRECT: Murray met three uninvited guests at the door: Bruno, his older brother, Max, his former roommate, and Maria, his secretary.

CORRECT: Murray met three uninvited guests at the door: Bruno, his older brother; Max, his former roommate; and Maria, his secretary.

EXERCISE 32 _____

In the following sentences, change incorrectly used commas to semicolons and incorrectly used semicolons to commas where needed.

1. My boss, if he wished to be considerate, could let me off by 3:00 p.m., but, mainly to assert his authority, he insists that I remain at my desk until at least 4:00.
2. I ran into several complications: Stephanie, my sister-in-law, was hospitalized, Ginger, my Doberman, escaped three times this week, and my car was demolished.
3. Professor Langley will not tolerate absences, furthermore, she insists that everyone arrive at least five minutes early for class.
4. The important dates to remember are June 21, 1978, September 10, 1979, and February 13, 1981.
5. Also riding in the van were Billy, his stepson, his stepdaughter, Polly, his sister-in-law, Debra, and his best friend, Joe Poole.

6. It is not that he does not recognize the problems of the disadvantaged; he just does not care about them.
7. Everyone was convinced that the bad weather would prevent the series from beginning on time, on the contrary, not one game was postponed or even delayed.
8. Mr. Chubb reluctantly left the board, however, as he made clear, he would be available as a consultant.
9. Despite the endless street noises; we slept soundly.
10. We slept through the din of fire engines, trucks, and trains, in fact, silence would have startled us.

33 **:**

Use a colon to call attention to what comes next or to follow certain mechanical conventions.

The colon is a rather formal mark which indicates that something will follow. It also has special uses in titles, scriptural references, time references, and formal letters. Do not confuse it with the semicolon, which separates coordinate expressions.

33a Use a colon to introduce a list, an explanation or intensification, an example, or (in certain cases) a quotation.

Place a colon at the end of an otherwise grammatically complete sentence to introduce a list of items, an explanation of the first part of the sentence, or an example. A complete sentence following a colon may begin with either a capital or a lowercase letter:

CORRECT: As project coordinator, my boss always followed the same policy: Do what is right today; justify it later.

CORRECT: In my old neighborhood we lived lives of plenty: plenty of relatives, boarders, landlords, cats, fights, and cockroaches.

INCORRECT: Peter is interested only in: his stereo outfit, his motorcycle, and his girlfriend. (The words before the colon are not a grammatically complete sentence.)

CORRECT: Peter is interested only in his stereo outfit, his motorcycle, and his girlfriend.

Colons may substitute for semicolons to separate two independent clauses, but use them only when the clauses are very closely related and the second explains or intensifies the first:

CORRECT: Miguel couldn't decide what to do or where to turn: he was stymied.

CORRECT: Yesterday I realized my age: my son asked if I remembered an old-time singer named Bob Dylan. (The second part of the sentence explains the first part; the colon = *that is.*)

Use a colon to introduce a long quotation (more than one sentence) or a shorter quotation not introduced by a word such as *said, remarked,* or *replied:*

CORRECT: I remember my reaction to a typically luminous observation of Kierkegaard's: "Such a relation which relates itself to its own self (that is to say, a self) must either have constituted itself or have been constituted by another."
                                    —Woody Allen, "My Philosophy"

CORRECT: Consider the words of John Donne: "No man is an island entire of itself. . . ."

33b   Use a colon between title and subtitle, between Bible chapter and verse, between hours and minutes, and after the salutation of a formal letter.

Scripture: Genesis 1:7   John 3:16
Time references: 3:00   1:17 p.m.

Salutations: Dear Ms. Jones**:**   Dear Sir or Madam**:**
*Subtitles: Greek Tragedy***:** *A Literary Study*
          *The Fields of Light***:** *An Experiment in Critical*
          Reading

EXERCISE 33 _____

Add or delete colons where necessary in the following sentences.

1. She and Travis have one characteristic in common, they are both alone.
2. The old proverb still has value "He who hesitates is lost."
3. He read from Proverbs 3, 17.
4. Services lasted until 1:15.
5. My report was entitled: "Music to Our Ears—the Effect of High-Volume Sound on Human Hearing."

34 --

Use dashes to signal sharp changes or to set apart emphatic parenthetical elements.

The dash is a strong, dramatic mark that has several important uses. Unfortunately, it is often misused and overused. In college- and job-related writing, it should be used sparingly, not overused as a substitute for other punctuation.

34a Use a dash to signal a sharp change in thought or tone.

CORRECT: "There is a simple solution to every complex problem **--** the wrong one."

                           —H. L. Mencken

CORRECT: Kendricks' treatment of urban health problems is
poorly researched, inaccurately documented, badly
written--but why go on?

34b   Use dashes to separate and emphasize a parenthetical element or to set off a parenthetical element that contains commas.

As a stronger mark than the comma, indicating a longer
pause in reading, the dash gives extra emphasis to
parenthetical elements. It is also useful when parenthetical elements themselves contain commas:

CORRECT: The first step in literary analysis--reading the
work carefully--is often ignored.

CORRECT: We have assigned our most reliable team of
illustrators--Bert Weldy, Sue Cawly, and Ray
Phillips--to take over the project.

In printed material, the dash is shown as a continuous
line. In typing, however, form a dash by using two
hyphens together with no space before or after. For
hyphens, see **39**. See also Exercise 35.

35   ( )

Use parentheses to set off parenthetical material that is long or strictly supplementary.

Unlike dashes, which emphasize parenthetical material,
and commas, which relate the material closely to the
rest of the sentence, parentheses set such material apart
from the rest of the sentence but deemphasize it. Use
parentheses for material that is not essential to the
meaning of the sentence, material that could as well

appear in footnotes. Notice in the first example below that the period is inside the parentheses: The parenthetical material is a complete sentence and is not included in another sentence. Otherwise, put end punctuation after the final parenthesis.

CORRECT: One good way to save money would be to get rid of that big gas guzzler and get a smaller car. (The Ford Fairmont looks good.)

CORRECT: Only one of the thirteen tests (see Appendix A) showed even minor irregularities.

CORRECT: Scholars and critics (Leo Marx and Lionel Trilling among them) are still debating the meaning of the final five chapters of *Huckleberry Finn,* but they all agree on the novel's excellence.

EXERCISE 35 _____

Correct any of the following sentences that have parentheses or dashes omitted or used improperly.

1. Jeff found a job through CETA (Comprehensive Educational Training Act).
2. My brother-in-law the wild one I told you about finally got a job last week.
3. My wife Dan's baby sister thinks he is just misunderstood and mistreated.
4. The other sisters (Beth, Darlene, and Wanda) all recognize him for the lazy person he is.
5. Dan can be completely charming (if he stays sober).

36 " "

Use quotation marks to indicate direct quotations.

Quotation marks enclose words quoted directly from another source. Use them only when you quote the exact words of your source. Indirect quotations, which report only the gist of a message but not the exact words, do not need quotation marks.

36a   Enclose direct quotations in double quotation marks.

Put double quotation marks around the exact words spoken or written by your source; do not enclose introductory or interrupting information, such as *she said.*

CORRECT: According to Samuel Kaplan, " The social and economic segregation of suburbs also is resulting in the political segregation of suburbs. "

CORRECT: " I'll bet you can't catch me, " Martha retorted, jumping back quickly.

Do not enclose an indirect quotation in quotation marks:

DIRECT: According to *Robert's Rules of Order,* " The subsidiary motion to Amend . . . requires only a majority vote, even in cases where the question to be amended takes a two-thirds vote for adoption. "

INDIRECT: *Robert's Rules of Order* says that an amendment needs only a simple majority, even when the main motion needs a two-thirds vote.

COMBINED: *Robert's Rules of Order* says that an amendment needs only a simple majority, " even in cases where the question to be amended takes a two-thirds vote for adoption. "

Single-space and indent quotations of four or more lines; do not use quotation marks:

CORRECT: Roger Taylor comments on women writers:

The Equal Rights Amendment has stimulated community interest in the issues of women's rights. Both men and women are taking a second look at the roles and expectations of women in society. The subject of women and "women writers," therefore, moves to the forefront of what should be offered to the community.

Single-space and center quoted poetry between the left and right margins:

CORRECT: But at my back I always hear
Time's winged chariot hurrying near;
And yonder all before us lie
Deserts of vast eternity.
—Andrew Marvell

36b Use single quotation marks to enclose a quotation within a quotation.

CORRECT: As John Ehrlichman wrote, "Nixon is the 'Man of a Thousand Facets' to me."

36c Place other punctuation marks inside or outside closing quotes, according to standard conventions.

Place all periods and commas inside closing quotation marks.

CORRECT: "No," she replied, "I'm not interested in your proposition in the least."

CORRECT: His favorite poem is Matthew Arnold's "Dover Beach."

Place question marks and exclamation points inside closing quotation marks if the quoted material is a direct question or an exclamation.

CORRECT: My mother asked her favorite question, "Where do you think you're going, young lady?"

CORRECT: My only response was, "Oh, no!"

Place question marks and exclamation points outside closing quotation marks if the sentence is a direct question or exclamation but the quoted material is not. If both the sentence and the quoted material are questions or exclamations, use only the question mark or exclamation point inside the quotation marks:

CORRECT: Was it Pete Seeger or Woody Guthrie who wrote, "This Land Is Your Land"?

CORRECT: It was Guthrie, but wasn't Seeger the one who wrote "Where Have all the Flowers Gone?"

CORRECT: Why did Jim Hubbard submit a theme with the title, "An Immodest Proposal"?

Place all colons and semicolons outside closing quotation marks.

CORRECT: In his first conference he stated emphatically, "We will finish by July 30"; in the second conference he hedged a bit.

CORRECT: His first pronouncement was, "I am not yet ready to quit": he quit the next day.

36d   Use an ellipsis (. . .) to indicate material omitted from a quotation.

An ellipsis consists of three spaced periods. Use a full line of periods, though, when a full paragraph or more has been omitted. An ellipsis can appear at the beginning, middle, or end of a quotation; other punctuation may be placed before or after the three dots. At the end of a sentence, use four dots (period plus ellipsis), with no space before the first:

CORRECT: Herbert J. Gans in *New Generation* has this to say about young workers: " . . . many have embraced the expectation, common in the middle class, that the job itself should provide some satisfaction. . . . "

CORRECT: "As soon as sensible birth control devices became widely available, women . . . began to use the new methods—when the front office allowed them to."
—Richard Cornuelle, *De-Managing America*

36e   Use brackets ([ ]) to mark an insertion into a quotation.

Brackets have only one commonly accepted function in prose: to enclose editorial comments or other information inserted into a direct quotation. Do not confuse parentheses with brackets. Parentheses appear within quotations only when they are part of the quotation itself.

CORRECT: His response was a mild, "Well, I do the best I can [debatable], but sometimes that isn't good enough."

CORRECT: "They [the staff] are all conscientious, honest people."

Always quote your original exactly, including errors. Insert *sic* in brackets [*sic*] after the error to indicate that the error appears in the original:

CORRECT: "The civil rights movement picked up steam after President Kennedy's assassination in 1964 [*sic*]."

EXERCISE 36 _____

Correct any errors in punctuation in the following sentences.

1. "Architecture has its political uses . . . it establishes a nation, draws people and commerce, and makes the people love their country."
2. Christman defines general aviation as "all flying done other than by scheduled carriers [airlines] and defense agencies [military]".
3. Did Marilyn really ask, "Who the devil is George Bush?"
4. "Oh, heaven forbid!"
5. Jacobson said, "yes;" Johanson said, "no."
6. "President Nixon was inaugurated in 1968 [sic] and reelected in 1972."
7. When did you say, "I do?"
8. We said the words right after the minister asked, "Who objects?"
9. T. S. Eliot wrote that "The greatest treason [is] to do the right deed for the wrong reason".
10. "Art is a lie", Picasso said, "which makes us realize the truth."

37 ital

Use underlining (italics) or quotation marks to designate titles and certain types of words.

Enclose titles of articles, chapters, poems, short stories, musical compositions, or paintings in quotation marks:

CORRECT: Stanley thinks that Updike's best short story is "A&P."

CORRECT: I just read a helpful article entitled "Theftproof Your CB Radio."

CORRECT: The best poem in the magazine is "The Sandpiper."

Use underlining (italics) to designate the title of a book, newspaper, periodical, play, motion picture, or television series. In handwritten or typed materials, use underlining to indicate italic print.

CORRECT: Reston's column is featured in such papers as the *St. Louis Post-Dispatch.*

CORRECT: He always kept *The American Heritage Dictionary* and the *Information Please Almanac* close at hand.

CORRECT: After becoming popular in the television series *Rawhide,* Clint Eastwood starred in such movies as *Dirty Harry* and *A Fistful of Dollars.*

Never use both italics and quotation marks to indicate a title:

INCORRECT: One of my favorite paintings is *"The Naked Maja."*

CORRECT: One of my favorite paintings is "The Naked Maja."

Do not use italics or quotation marks to refer to the Bible or parts of the Bible:

CORRECT: Genesis is the first book of the Bible, Revelation the last.

Use underlining (italic) to indicate a foreign word that is not yet a standard part of English; a scientific name of a plant, animal, disease, etc.; a word mentioned as a word; or letters or numbers used as examples:

CORRECT: The word *liberal* comes from Latin *liber,* meaning free.

CORRECT: *Gauge* is now spelled *gage* in some professional journals.

CORRECT: *Dracaena marginata* is an easy plant to propagate by mound layering.

CORRECT: Social security numbers beginning with *3* come generally from the Midwest.

Some writers use underlining or quotation marks to give a word or phrase special emphasis, but you should do so very sparingly. Avoid enclosing slang in quotation marks as a form of apology. Emphatic wording is much more effective.

EXERCISE 37 _____

Correct any sentences in which italics or quotation marks are improperly used.

1. My oldest brother always carries a copy of the "New Testament."
2. Joel's capital F's and T's are almost impossible to distinguish.
3. *Apocalypse Now* is a film based on Conrad's novel "Heart of Darkness."
4. *Preludes* is one of the initial poems in the volume "The Complete Poetry of T. S. Eliot."
5. Richard enjoys baseball biographies such as "Mr. Cub," the story of Ernie Banks.
6. The new coach called his fast-moving attack a blitzkreig.
7. The medium told Pierre that his lucky number was 2.
8. "The Celebrated Jumping Frog of Calaveras County," one of Twain's earliest short stories, features a dog with no hind legs and a frog loaded with buckshot.
9. Was it a faux pas to ask for a legal conference "in camera"?
10. Some writers use "per se" and "ipso facto" unnecessarily.

38 '

Use apostrophes to form contractions, certain plurals, and the possessive form of nouns and indefinite pronouns.

38a   Use an apostrophe to indicate the possessive of nouns and indefinite pronouns.

Add an apostrophe and *s* to form the possessive of indefinite pronouns (*everyone, someone, somebody,* etc.) and of most singular nouns:

Sally's coat Ms. Cullom's office
anybody's game one's chances
a day's pay a cat's life

Add either an apostrophe and *s* or only the apostrophe to singular nouns ending in *-s:*

Lois' *or* Lois's
Countess' *or* Countess's

Add an apostrophe and *s* to plurals not ending in *-s*. Add only the apostrophe to plurals ending in *-s:*

girls' jumpers cats' lives
ladies' shoes two months' work
children's clothes mice's cages

Add an apostrophe and *s* to the last word of a word group or compound:

The editor-in-chief's office the chief of staff's car

Add an apostrophe and *s* to each name to indicate individual ownership; add the apostrophe and *s* only to the last name to show joint ownership:

Jo's and Arnie's cars David and Linda's apartment

38b Use an apostrophe to indicate the omitted letters in a contraction. Use it also to indicate omitted parts of dates or other numerals.

they'll (they will) it's (it is) can't (cannot) class of '65

Note that the apostrophe goes where letters are left out, not necessarily between words joined in a contraction:

wouldn't

38c   Use an apostrophe to form the plural of lowercase letters and of abbreviations followed by periods. Use it also to prevent confusion in forming plurals of other abbreviations, of capital letters, of symbols, and of words used or singled out as words:

M.S.'s   *i*'s   *miss*'s
J's or *J*s   UFO's or UFOs   @'s or @s

Note that the *s* is not italicized.

Never use an apostrophe to form a simple plural:

INCORRECT: Three dog's barked. Broiled steak's were served.

EXERCISE 38 _____
Where needed, correct the use of apostrophes in the following sentences.

1. Its function is to cool the room whenever its too humid.
2. Mississippi contains four *s*'s, four *i*'s, two *p*'s, and one *M*.
3. The pet store has cat's in cages piled three deep.
4. Each cats' cage is kept immaculately clean, though.
5. The Secretary of State's job is one of the most crucial in the world.
6. My mother-in-law's taste in art is provincial.
7. The Johnson's always send Christmas cards.
8. Mens' clothes are sold on the sixth floor of Boyd's.
9. Its true that many good books are unread.
10. The lives of the Adamses' were eventful.

39 -

Use a hyphen to join two words into a single adjective, to join a root word to a prefix or suffix, and to write out a fraction or compound number.

Compound words are sometimes written separately, sometimes hyphenated, and sometimes written together as one word. When in doubt, consult your college dictionary.

39a   Use a hyphen to join two or more words serving as a single adjective before a noun.

up-to-date information
seventeen-year-old son
well-intentioned actions

But do not hyphenate such adjectives following the noun:

The information was clearly not up to date.
His son was seventeen years old.
The agency's actions were well intentioned.

Do not use a hyphen between an adverb ending in -*ly* and an adjective:

unusually fine wine
carefully developed plot

39b   Use hyphens to write out fractions and compound numbers between twenty and one hundred.

But do not hyphenate a fraction used as a noun:

twenty-two	sixty-one
a two-thirds majority	two thirds of the members
one-fourth complete	one fourth of a day

39c   Use hyphens to join root words to certain prefixes and suffixes.

The suffix -*elect* and the prefixes *pro-, anti-, ex-, self-,* and *great-* are normally joined with hyphens to root words.

122

Check your dictionary when you are uncertain whether to use a hyphen with a prefix or suffix.

ex-convict   self-confessed   great-grandmother
anti-abortionist   pro-abolitionist   congressman-elect

39d   Use a hyphen to avoid a confusing combination of letters or syllables.

small-children's shop   re-creation *(not* recreation)
small children's-shop   steel-like *(but* froglike, etc.)

39e   Use a hyphen to divide a word at the end of a line.

Do not divide a one-syllable word:

dined   tenth   strength

Divide only between syllables. Consult your dictionary. Most dictionaries indicate syllabication with dots:

in · ti · mi · date   wis · dom   a · ni · mal

Do not put a single letter at the beginning or ending of a line; do not put a two-letter ending at the beginning of a line:

IMPROPER: thick- ly   ax- es   a- brupt   fox- y

EXERCISE 39 _____

Correct any misuses or omissions of hyphens in the following sentences.

1. Twenty-one freedom seeking refugees crossed the border.
2. Her dress was a light rosy-beige.
3. Oakwood Village's recreation of the Nativity scene is a tradition.
4. Mr. Stevenson, ex-district attorney and self-made man, is our new judge-elect.
5. Thirty-seven units were completed in one-half of the usual time.

40 cap

Always capitalize the first word of a sentence and the word *I*; capitalize proper nouns and important words in titles according to conventional practice.

Appropriate capitalization is a matter of convention. This section will show you basic conventions, but conventions vary, and careful writers often disagree on what should be capitalized. Consult your college dictionary for specific problems; words commonly capitalized will be capitalized in the dictionary entry.

40a Capitalize the first word of a sentence and *I*.

CORRECT: He advised our club on energy-saving devices.

CORRECT: I do not know whether I should use styrofoam or vermiculite insulation in the exterior walls.

40b Capitalize the names of persons, races, and nationalities.

Also capitalize derivatives of such words:

English	Maxwell R. Folger	Ms. Tucker
Chicano	Americanize	Cuban
Caucasian	Russian	Michigander

Neither *black* (Afro-American) nor *white* (Caucasian) is capitalized.

40c   Capitalize place names.

Puerto Rico	Amazon River	Orange County
Zaire	Nile Valley	North Carolina

40d   Capitalize the names of organizations, historical events, holidays, days of the week, and months.

World War II	Xerox	Thursday
Chrysler Corporation	Yom Kippur	Thanksgiving
Easter	NCAA	July

40e   Capitalize titles preceding a name.

Similar titles following a name are capitalized in addresses and typed signatures of letters, but not in text:

Professor Elizabeth Kirk	Elizabeth Kirk, Professor of English
Chairman Dick Fischer	Dick Fischer, Chairman of the Board

The chairman of the board called the meeting to order.

40f   Capitalize common nouns such as *street, company, river,* or *aunt* only when they are part of a proper noun. Capitalize *north, south, east,* and *west* only when they refer to specific regions.

Huskey Company	my brother's company
Kirkman Road	on the road
Roosevelt University	at a university
Atlantic Ocean	at the ocean
American Airlines	a major airline
Uncle George	my favorite uncle
Oak Ridge High School	my old high school
The Midwest	go west
East Texas	toward the east

40g Capitalize the first word and all important words of the title of a book, periodical, article, report, or other document. Also capitalize the titles of chapters and other major divisions.

The Scarlet Letter	*Macbeth*	*Newsweek*
"Chapter Six: Projected Revenue"	*Writers on Writing*	"Methods Used"

A, an, the, conjunctions, and prepositions of fewer than five letters should not be capitalized unless they are the first or last word in a title or subtitle.

EXERCISE 40 _____

Correct any errors in capitalization in the following sentences.

1. After graduating from Shimer College, Scott went to work for the Devex corporation in Chicago.
2. Jon is not going home for the Holidays.
3. Cyril's Welsh ancestry was not apparent in his singing voice.
4. The Colorado river flows through much of the west.
5. Awilda Orta is director of New York city's office of bilingual education.
6. In 1980, Bilingual Education was offered in seventy Languages, including Chinese, Hungarian, Russian, and Vietnamese.
7. Hugo graduated from Newark Community high school, in Newark, Illinois, a small town Southwest of Chicago.
8. For cultural reasons, many people consider south Florida as Northern and North Florida as southern.
9. When Peter the Great died in 1725, he had moved Russia out of the oriental middle ages and into the mainstream of modern western civilization.
10. The poet Milton was an official in the government of Cromwell, the English puritan leader who overthrew the monarchy of king Charles I in 1642.

41 ab

Capitalize and punctuate abbreviations according to conventional practice.

Abbreviations and figures are widely used in technical reports, tables, footnotes, and bibliographies; but only a few abbreviations and figures are commonly used in the text of college writing.

41a Use only conventionally accepted abbreviations in college and general writing.

The following abbreviations are recommended:

Mr. (Smith)	M.D.	Rev. (Smith)
Mrs. (Smith)	M.S.	Col. (Smith) and other
Ms. (Smith)	S.P.A.	military titles
Dr. (Smith)	A.D. or B.C.	Ph.D. and other degrees
St. (Saint)	a.m. or p.m.	CIA, IBM, NAACP, and
Jr.	no.	other groups commonly
Sr.	D.C.	known by initials

41b Spell out the following in college writing:

Units of measure: pounds, feet

Place names: Arkansas, New York

Parts of addresses: Street, Avenue, Road

Company   Incorporated (except in official titles)
page   chapter   volume
first names   names of courses

Check your college dictionary for the proper spelling, punctuation, and capitalization of abbreviations.

EXERCISE 41 _____

Correct any improper abbreviations or supply abbreviations as needed in the following sentences.

1. The Rev. came by this afternoon.
2. She was born in Texarkana, Ark., on a Tues. morn.
3. India is described on p. 367 in vol. 12.
4. The package weighed three pounds.
5. Washington, District of Columbia, is our nation's capital.
6. We took David Anthony to his Dr., Stephen Albert, M.D., for his annual physical.
7. Geo. Wm.'s new corp. is Steinberger Enterprises, Inc.
8. Oscar had wanted to be an R.N. ever since he could remember.
9. Terry moved from Chi. to L.A. then to N.Y.
10. Robt. Louis Stevenson is best known for his children's classic *Treasure Island.*

42

Spell out one- and two-word numbers except to follow certain conventions.

Use figures for page numbers, numbers with units of measure, time followed by *a.m.* or *p.m.*, percentages, decimals, identification numbers, and numbers that cannot be written in one or two words. Otherwise write out numbers in the text of your papers:

Use figures		*Write out*
428	5,687,414	eleven twenty-two
		seventeen thousand
3¾		three-quarters
		one third of the population
East 181st Street		East Eighty-first Street

Use figures	*Write out*
page 17	seventeen-page report
85°F 12 meters	eighty-five cadets
6:30 p.m.	six-thirty that afternoon
38%	
3.1416 .005	
U.S. 66 I-84 Channel 3	
4 B.C. 1984	

Write out numbers beginning sentences:

Four-hundred twenty-eight people attended the opening ceremonies.

In a series, if one number must be written in figures, write all the numbers in figures:

INCORRECT: Of the students who responded to the questionnaire, thirty had never used the pass-fail option, twelve had used it once, and 123 had used it more than once.

CORRECT: Of the students who responded to the questionnaire, 30 had never used the pass-fail option, 12 had used it once, and 123 had used it more than once.

EXERCISE 42 _____

Correct any errors in number usage in the following sentences.

1. The 30,000 BTU model needs 220 volt wiring, but the smaller models can use ordinary 110 voltage.
2. My ex-boyfriend lives on 81st Street near Interstate seventy-five.
3. 351 people attended the first performance.
4. Only twenty percent of my serves were good, by far my worst performance ever.
5. Pierre's lucky number is 3.
6. Sue counted 456 words on page seventy-five of Volume 3.
7. Only a third of my high school graduation class entered college immediately but another ¼ entered within a year.

8. Cable Channel Thirteen picks up many shows not shown by local network affiliates, channels 2, 6, and 9.
9. Temperatures in West Texas averaged over one hundred degrees throughout much of June 1980.
10. His 16-page term paper was thirteen days late.

43   ms

Use proper materials and follow conventional manuscript form in preparing a final draft.

In both college and general writing, correct manuscript form and appearance contribute to the effectiveness of your work. If your instructor, department, or organization has formal guidelines, follow them carefully; otherwise use the guidelines below.

Materials. Submit typed papers on standard 8½- × 11-inch paper. Use good-quality paper, not onionskin. Type with a good ribbon and clean keys. Submit handwritten papers on wide-lined notebook paper, not on sheets torn from spiral notebooks or legal pads. Use blue or black ink for handwritten papers.

Margins and spacings. For typed papers, use a 1½-inch margin at the top and left side, a 1-inch margin at the right and the bottom. Double-space college papers and reports. For handwritten work, leave blank the top and left margins on notebook paper and allow approximately an inch at the right and bottom. Indent each paragraph five spaces in typed papers and approximately one inch in handwritten papers. Double-space footnotes, headings, and long quotations. Center the title on the top line or an inch and a half from the top. Leave an extra space between the title and the first line.

Pagination. Use ordinary arabic numerals (1, 2, etc.) without the word *page* or parentheses in the upper right-hand corner of all pages beyond the first.

General appearance. Endorse or head the paper as your instructor suggests; this usually includes your name, the name of the course, the date, and the name or number of the assignment.

Correct your final draft carefully so that your typed copy is as neat as possible with minimal last-minute corrections. Make such corrections unobtrusively, using a caret (∧) for insertions and a single line to cross out words. Most instructors do not mind a few neatly inked-in corrections on typed papers.

44 sp

Proofread for proper spelling, and work on your spelling weaknesses.

Unfortunately, there is not easy shortcut to effective spelling. Some writers who are otherwise very skillful struggle all their careers with poor spelling. If you are a poor speller and cannot seem to improve much, allow extra time to look up spellings. If you frequently misspell the same words, make a list of them. The suggestions below should help you with some of the more common spelling problems; however, for many words, only memorization or reference lists will help.

ie **or** *ei:* Place *i* before *e*, except after *c* and in words pronounced with other than the long *e* sound:

CORRECT:	field	ceiling	sleigh	height
	grief	conceit	vein	stein
	niece	deceive	weigh	foreign
	relief	conceive	neighbor	heir

EXCEPTIONS:	fiery, seize, species, weird

Final e: Drop a silent final *e* before suffixes beginning with a vowel; keep it before suffixes beginning with a consonant:

CORRECT: writ*ing*   hope*ful*   guid*ance*
             love*ly*   nine*teen*   sincere*ly*

EXCEPTIONS: dye*ing* (clothes), nin*th*, tru*ly*, courage*ous*

Changing y to i: When adding a suffix, change a final *y* to *i* except before a suffix beginning with *i:*

CORRECT: fly, flying, flier
            rely, reliance
            forty, fortieth

Plurals: Most plurals add *-s* to the singular; plurals of nouns ending in *s, ch, sh,* or *x* add *-es.*

CORRECT: girls   tables   typists   spoonfuls
            dishes   taxes   churches   bosses

Singular nouns ending in *y* preceded by a consonant change the *y* to *i* and add *-es.*

CORRECT: cities, tragedies, replies, supplies

Singular nouns ending in *o* preceded by a consonant usually add *-es,* but note these exceptions:

CORRECT: potatoes, tomatoes, heroes, zeroes
            hypos, pros, jumbos
            ghettos or ghettoes, mosquitos or mosquitoes

The Glossary of Usage (**69**) lists some words easily confused because of similar spelling; a few others are

advice, advise   inequity, iniquity
ascent, assent   paradox, parody
censor, censure   passed, past
decent, descent, dissent   prophecy, prophesy
definite, definitive   stationary, stationery
device, devise   to, too
idea, ideal   weather, whether

Here is a list of one hundred commonly misspelled words:

absence	dissatisfied	occurred
accommodate	eighth	omitted
acquaintance	embarrass	parallel
adequately	environment	permissible
aggravate	existence	personnel
alleviate	exaggerate	possess
all right	familiar	preceding
altogether	feasible	predominant
amateur	February	prejudice
analysis	forth	prevalent
apparatus	gauge	privilege
apparent	government	procedure
argument	grammar	proceed
athletic	harass	prominent
becoming	hindrance	psychology
bureaucracy	hurriedly	questionnaire
calendar	hypocrisy	receive
category	imitation	recommend
cemetery	incredibly	repetition
committee	independent	ridiculous
competition	intelligence	rhythm
condemn	irrelevant	separate
conscientious	irresistible	sergeant
conscious	knowledge	schedule
consistent	leisure	succeed
continuous	license	supersede
criticize	loneliness	susceptible
definitely	maneuver	temperament
description	maintenance	thorough
desirable	mischievous	unanimous
desperate	necessary	undoubtedly
develop	noticeable	vacuum
disappoint	occasionally	villain
disastrous		

EXERCISE 44 _____

Underline the correctly spelled words.

1. independant
2. resistence
3. evidentally
4. larnyx
5. indispensable
6. heighth
7. occurrance
8. mispell
9. preceed
10. procede

11. compatible
12. chastise
13. futiley
14. column
15. incidently
16. reciept
17. accidently
18. develope
19. pursute
20. hurriedly

EFFECTIVE SENTENCES

Since sentences are the primary means of expressing your thoughts, you naturally want your sentences to be clear and fluent as well as correct. Chapter 3 focuses on correct grammatical patterns; this chapter describes some ways to achieve emphasis and conciseness and to avoid ambiguity.

45 sub

Use subordination to relate secondary details to main ideas and to improve stringy or choppy sentences.

Two or more ideas can be connected in a sentence by two means: *coordination* or *subordination*. Coordination gives the ideas equal grammatical emphasis; subordination presents one as the main idea and puts the other(s) in a dependent or de-emphasized relationship to the main idea. Therefore, your sentence structure should depend upon the relationship you want to show between your ideas. Notice how the meaning subtly changes in the following sentences:

TWO SENTENCES: Politicians can say extreme things. They must say them so that no one pays close attention.

COORDINATION: Politicians can say extreme things, but they must say them so that no one pays close attention.

SUBORDINATION: Although politicians can say extreme things, they must say them so that no one pays close attention.

SUBORDINATION: Politicians can say extreme things if they say them so that no one pays close attention.

45a   Use subordinate clauses to relate secondary details to the main idea.

Relative pronouns *(who, whom, which, that)* and subordinating conjunctions (such as *because, since, although,* and others in the list below) introduce subordinate clauses and signal specific relationships between them and the main clause. Notice how each subordinate clause below has a different relationship to its main clause:

EFFECTIVE: *Although* Jessica had spent six hours cramming for a philosophy test, she felt unprepared.

EFFECTIVE: Jessica, *who* had spent six hours cramming for a philosophy test, felt unprepared.

EFFECTIVE: *After* she had spent six hours cramming for a philosophy test, Jessica still felt unprepared.

EFFECTIVE: *Because* Jessica spent only six hours cramming for a philosophy test, she felt unprepared.

The following list of common subordinating conjunctions shows the variety of relationships that subordination can indicate:

Cause: since, because, if, so that, in order that

Contrast or concession: although, though, whereas, while, than

Time: when, whenever, as, before, since, after, as long as, once, until, while

Place: where, wherever

Condition: if, unless, whether, provided that, as long as

Manner: as, as though, as if, how

Similarity: as . . . as

Some subordinate clauses can be used in the same way as nouns (as subjects or objects):

> Churchill said *that Dulles was like a bull with his own China shop.* (clause as direct object)

Some subordinate clauses can also function as modifiers—as adjectives or adverbs. An adjective clause modifies (or qualifies) a noun or pronoun and most often begins with a relative pronoun:

> Churchill said that Dulles was like a bull *who always carried his own China shop.* (clause modifies *bull* and thus functions as an adjective)

An adverb clause modifies a verb, adjective, adverb, verbal (such as a gerund or participle), or the rest of the sentence:

> *When Churchill spoke,* people listened. (clause modifies the verb *listened*)

Be sure to place your main idea, the one you want to stress, in the independent clause, and, when possible, put the main clause last. In which of the following sentences does the writer seem more contented with his or her current reading skills?

> Although I read much more quickly now, I remember less.
>
> Although I remember less, I read much more quickly now.

45b Use subordination to improve long, stringy sentences.

One mark of an inexperienced writer is frequent use of rambling, stringy sentences composed of a series of main clauses strung together with *and* or other coordinating conjunctions. If you subordinate one or more clauses, you will usually make your meaning clearer and the sentence more readable:

INEFFECTIVE: Some women are happy just being at home, *and* they argue that a woman's place is largely in the home *and* that mothers who work should feel guilty.

EFFECTIVE: Women who are happy just being at home argue that a woman's place is largely in the home and that mothers who work should feel guilty.

INEFFECTIVE: James Dickey is a Southern writer *and* is my favorite American poet, *and* he is the author of *Deliverance.*

EFFECTIVE: James Dickey, a Southerner who is my favorite American poet, is the author of *Deliverance.*

EFFECTIVE: James Dickey, the Southerner who wrote *Deliverance,* is my favorite American poet.

INEFFECTIVE: He began the descent to the ocean floor *and* felt as though he were in a dream *and* he sensed that, like having jumped from a skyscraper, he was floating rather than crashing.

EFFECTIVE: As he began the descent to the ocean floor, he felt as though he were in a dream in which he sensed that, like having jumped from a skyscraper, he was floating rather than crashing.

45c Use subordination to improve a series of short, choppy sentences.

Numerous short, choppy sentences are another common sign of an inexperienced writer. Such sentences are

sub

awkward to read and fail to show relationships among
their ideas. Notice in these examples how subordination
improves upon the short, choppy sentences:

INEFFECTIVE: Roger wanted very much to play the bass. He
taught himself twenty-two songs. Then he
took lessons.

EFFECTIVE: Roger wanted so much to play the bass that he
taught himself twenty-two songs before he
took lessons.

INEFFECTIVE: Alice expected to enjoy *Slaughterhouse Five*. She
failed to understand it at first. Then she saw
the movie.

EFFECTIVE: Although she expected to enjoy *Slaughterhouse
Five,* Alice failed to understand it until she saw
the movie.

45d Avoid excessive subordination.

Too many subordinate structures in a sentence can
make it awkward, monotonous, or even confusing:

INEFFECTIVE: Their apartment is in unit seventy-nine, which
is the second unit on the right overlooking the
tennis courts which are behind the clubhouse.

IMPROVED: Their apartment is in unit seventy-nine, the
second unit on the right; it overlooks the tennis
courts behind the clubhouse.

INEFFECTIVE: She bought a bottle of Mateus, which is a
popular rosé, which is a wine that is pink
rather than the usual red or white.

IMPROVED: She bought a bottle of Mateus Rosé, a popular
pink wine.

In these examples, notice how you can eliminate non-
essential information (and wordiness) by deleting *which
is, which are,* and so on at the beginning of a clause.

EXERCISE 45 _____

A. Examine the following sentences. Mark E *for those that are effective,* X *for those needing more or less subordination. B. Improve those marked* X.

1. Mrs. Benaiger often assigned a chapter a day, which most students considered to be a load that was too heavy for an introductory course that all freshmen had to take.
2. Many students dropped out of her classes and waited until the next term so they could take the course from someone else and have fewer assignments.
3. Julian was going to drop her class. He decided not to. He ended up loving the class. He said that he learned a great deal.
4. I plan to register for her section even if I have to take the class at an inconvenient hour or even if I have to wait an extra term to fit it into my schedule.
5. I know I will have to study hard, but I will learn a great deal, and that is what I am going to college for.
6. The occult sciences are alive and growing, which does not speak well for our society, for it is a society that yearns for spiritual values.
7. Politicians use fancy words which they think will impress voters, who are generally sharper than the politicians think.
8. The soldiers did not continue. This was not because they were tired. They were without command. It was not because they had nowhere to go. They had no one to lead them.
9. Thieves stole two dozen cases of Scotch. They stole it from a state liquor store in Cleveland. The theft took place yesterday. They left less expensive whiskey behind.
10. Our regular dentist is Dr. Cox, who is on vacation, so we called Dr. Parnell, who shares an office with Dr. Cox.

C. In the following selection, a paragraph by a noted writer has been reduced to a series of short sentences. Combine as many of these as you think appropriate, using subordination whenever possible.

   I was growing up in Newark in the forties. At that time we assumed that the books in the public library belonged to the public. My family did not own many books. Nor did they have much money for a child to buy them. So it was good to know that I had access to any book I wanted. The only reason for this privilege was my municipal citizenship. I could get books from that grandly austere building downtown on Washington Street. Or I could secure them from the branch library. I could walk to it in my own neighborhood. No less satisfying was the idea of communal ownership. I mean property held in common for the common good. I had to care for the books I borrowed. I had to return them unscarred. And I had to return them on time. The reason was that they were not mine. They were everybody's. That idea had as much to do with civilizing me as any I was ever to come upon in the books themselves.

46   co-ord

Use coordination to give equal grammatical emphasis to two or more points.

Compound sentences contain two or more independent clauses, giving equal grammatical emphasis to each. They are often misused and overused by inexperienced writers (see **45**), but they can be used effectively to present several equally important points.

EFFECTIVE: Those who write clearly have readers, but those who write obscurely have critics.

EFFECTIVE: Growing old is not an activity, for the passage of time is a fatality.

EFFECTIVE: Growing old is not an activity; the passage of time is a fatality.

—Simone de Beauvoir

47 comb

Use coordinate modifiers to combine sentences.

In addition to subordination, coordinate modifiers can help you develop mature, expressive sentences. Instead of constructing separate sentences, skillful writers often combine and relate sentence elements so that a single sentence carries more weight.

You can add colorful or clarifying details to a sentence by adding modifiers to the subject or to the predicate or to the sentence as a whole. You can do this by adding modifiers in front of the main clause to form a periodic sentence (see **48c**), or you can pile up modifiers after the main clause rather than using a string of short or choppy sentences.

INEFFECTIVE:	The early Benedictine monks revived agriculture after the collapse of the Roman Empire. They recolonized the land that was deserted. They introduced industrial techniques that had been nearly lost.
EFFECTIVE:	By recolonizing the land that was deserted and by reintroducing industrial techniques that had been nearly lost, the early Benedictine monks revived agriculture after the collapse of the Roman Empire. (periodic)
EFFECTIVE:	The early Benedictine monks revived agriculture after the collapse of the Roman Empire, recolonizing the land that was deserted, reintroducing industrial techniques that had been nearly lost.

The repetition in sentences that all begin alike can be eliminated by creatively combining them into one richer, more complex sentence. Too many modifiers, however, can overload a sentence and make it hard to read; and not every sentence need be developed in this way. But combining can be valuable in generating effective descriptive and narrative sentences, especially.

INEFFECTIVE: The island was dominated by a dormant volcano; its broad slopes were covered with porous rock; this had been weathered to form a poor but arable soil.

EFFECTIVE: The island was dominated by a dormant volcano, its broad slopes covered with porous lava rock, weathered to form a poor but arable soil.

—Jerzy Kozinski

Noun phrases can develop a sentence by vividly restating a noun in the main clause:

The car stopped in front of the *house,* a crumbling, faded colonial mansion whose columns barely supported the sagging roof.

Verbal phrases can provide details of the action, object, or scene mentioned in the main clause. In a narrative sentence, verbal phrases enable a writer to picture simultaneously all the separate actions that make up the action named in the main clause.

Holding his breath until he was about to burst,
gulping down a quick glass of water,
    Jeff frantically tried to kill his hiccups before
    another spasm occurred.

Absolute phrases can also add details to a single sentence, often by developing one aspect of the subject:

The German Shepherd growled menacingly,
    his huge white teeth bared,
    his eyes alert for the slightest false move, and
    the hair on his neck raised as a warning to the intruder.

Note that the use of coordinate modifiers involves parallelism (see **55**).

EXERCISE 47 _____

A. Develop each of the following into one sentence, using coordinate noun, verb, or absolute phrases.

1. The use of space satellite images increases. These pictures alert California growers about the cotton bollworm. They inform farmers about screwworms that destroy cattle and poultry in Mexico. And they help chart the destruction of the Mediterranean fruit fly.
2. I pictured myself sending a 350-yard drive screaming down the fairway. I then imagined myself chipping the ball effortlessly onto the green. And I dreamed of nonchalantly depositing it right into the middle of the cup before tipping my hat to a cheering gallery of onlookers.
3. Gloria sat on the side of the pool. She removed her over-sized sunglasses. She began to read a paperback novel. Then she dangled her feet in the cold water.
4. It was nearly dark when we arrived at the motel. It was a faded, cream-colored Holiday Inn. It was perched on the edge of the busy interstate. Its gaudy, flashing sign lit up the evening.
5. The campus traffic cop stood in front of my car. He loomed up before me. His eyes were hidden under his hat. His silent stance suggested that I was a criminal.

B. Combine the following groups of sentences, using whatever method works best.

INEFFECTIVE: Jerry's room was a mess. The floor was littered with empty beer cans. The bed was piled high with dirty clothes. The desk was stacked with unopened books.

EFFECTIVE: Jerry's room was a mess, its floor littered with empty beer cans, its bed piled high with dirty clothes, its desk stacked with unopened books.

1. The freshmen wrote silently. Some paged nervously through pocket dictionaries. Some glanced anxiously at their watches. Others filled page after page with words.
2. Writing can be a frustrating task. It requires long hours of thought. It forces us to sharpen our wits. It asks us to accept constructive criticism.

3. The tempting aroma of coffee drifted up the stairs. It was a welcome reminder of home to the sleepy students. It was a suggestion of warmth on a cold morning.
4. The young singer leaped onto the stage. His shirt was open. His chest glistened with gold chains. The fans were screaming. The music blared.
5. The tourists are chattering. They are speaking various languages. They wear sunglasses or carry cameras. They eagerly board the bus. Some stand in the aisles.

48   emp

Use word order and sentence length to emphasize important ideas.

Effective writing not only expresses ideas clearly and relates them to each other appropriately but also emphasizes the most important ideas. Choosing the right words (see Chapter 6) will help emphasize your important points; so will putting those words in the right place.

48a   Emphasize an important word by placing it at the beginning or end of the sentence.

The most emphatic position in most essays, paragraphs, or sentences is at the end. The next most emphatic position is the beginning, so you can emphasize key words by starting and ending sentences with them. Since semicolons are much like periods, words immediately before and after semicolons also receive emphasis. Notice how altering the key words in the following examples improves the emphasis.

INEFFECTIVE: The only real evil is ignorance, as Diogenes said. (leaves the reader thinking about Diogenes, not about what Diogenes said)

INEFFECTIVE:	It was Diogenes who said that the only real evil is ignorance. (empty words at the beginning of sentence)
EFFECTIVE:	Diogenes said that the only real evil is ignorance.
EFFECTIVE:	The only real evil, Diogenes said, is ignorance.
INEFFECTIVE:	For us time was brief and money was a problem.
EFFECTIVE:	We had little time; we had little money.

48b   Use an occasional short sentence.

A very short sentence contrasting with longer sentences stops the flow and catches the reader's attention. You can use such a short sentence to emphasize an especially important point. Notice how effective the short sentences are in the following passages:

EFFECTIVE:	With the jingle and flash of innumerable necklaces, the native woman walked proudly, her head held high, her hair festooned with flowers, her bronze arms glittering. She was magnificent.
EFFECTIVE:	If we read of one man robbed, or murdered, or killed by accident, or one house burned, or one vessel wrecked, or one steamboat blown up, or one cow run over on the Western Railroad, or one mad dog killed, or one lot of grasshoppers in the winter, we never need read of another. One is enough.

—Henry David Thoreau

48c   Use an occasional balanced or periodic sentence.

Most English sentences are *loose* or *cumulative* sentences; that is, the main clause comes first, followed by details supporting the main idea. The order is reversed in a *periodic* sentence, in which the main idea follows the subordinate details. Because it saves the most important idea for last and because it is less commonly used, the periodic sentence is more emphatic. Do not overuse it, however; save it for those ideas you especially want to emphasize.

LOOSE: Professional boxers are relatively civilized if one compares them to the Roman gladiators, who fought with swords until an opponent bled to death, or to medieval knights, who jousted with pointed lances, or even to modern bullfighters, who gore exhausted animals.

PERIODIC: Compared to the Roman gladiators, who fought with swords until an opponent bled to death, or to medieval knights, who jousted with pointed lances, or even to modern bullfighters, who gore exhausted animals, *professional boxers are relatively civilized.*

In a balanced sentence, coordinate structures are enough alike that the reader notices the similarity. You can use a balanced sentence to emphasize a comparison or contrast:

BALANCED: Many of us resent shoddiness in cars, food, and services; few of us resent shoddiness in language.

BALANCED: We do not ride on the railroad; it rides upon us.
—Henry David Thoreau

48d   Use a climactic word order.

By arranging a series of ideas in order of importance, you can gradually build emphasis:

CLIMACTIC: Like all great leaders, Lincoln was hated by many; like all strong Presidents, he was embattled by Congress; and, like many heroes, he was popular only after death.

CLIMACTIC: Clint Eastwood is a star, Robert Redford a superstar, Humphrey Bogart a legend.

48e Write primarily in the active voice.

In most active-voice sentences, the subject does something:

> Jim ⟶ hit ⟶ the ball.

In passive-voice sentences, the subject receives the action of the verb:

> The ball ⟵ was hit ⟵ by Jim.

The active voice is usually more direct, natural, and economical:

PASSIVE: Parental discretion is often advised by the networks.
ACTIVE: The networks often advise parental discretion.

PASSIVE: The block committee meeting was held on Tuesday afternoon. The rising crime rate was discussed and a resolution was drawn up to be sent to the mayor. It was also decided that the block picnic should be held on July 20. A proposal was made by two members that a fund be set up for replacing dead trees, but not much enthusiasm for the idea was shown by other members.
ACTIVE: The block committee met on Tuesday afternoon. It discussed the rising crime rate in the neighborhood and drew up a resolution to send to the mayor. It also decided to hold the block picnic on July 20. Two members proposed that the committee set up a fund to replace dead trees, but other members showed little enthusiasm for the idea.

There are appropriate uses for the passive, as in these examples:

PASSIVE: Franklin D. Roosevelt was elected to an unprecedented fourth term.
PASSIVE: Bill White's article will be published next month.

In each case, to rewrite the sentence in the active voice, one has to reconstruct the subject:

ACTIVE: American voters elected Franklin D. Roosevelt to an unprecedented fourth term.

ACTIVE: *Current Anthropology* will publish Bill White's article next month.

If the writer is discussing Roosevelt or the article (or its author), not voters or *Current Anthropology,* the passive voice is more logical. But, in general, write in the active voice. Passive-voice sentences tend to be artificial, wordy, and dull. They are less emphatic, especially when they obscure the doer of the action:

A tax increase was announced yesterday.

Passive-voice sentences can also lead to dangling modifiers (see **52f**):

To be an engineer, a college education is needed.
By doing a few simple tests, the biochemical structure can be isolated.

Finally, the passive is not an effective way to vary your style. Unnecessary shifts from active to passive can be distracting for the reader (see **56b**).

EXERCISE 48 ——————————————————————

Study the following sentences. A. Mark X for those that need rephrasing for emphasis, E for those that are effective. B. Rephrase those marked X.

1. Johnny Unitas was a great quarterback, Bob Griese was good, Fran Tarkington was outstanding.
2. A thirteen-thousand-dollar scholarship was won in the mathematics competition by Cynthia.
3. Mr. Franklin was vice-president of the bank but acted as if he were an ordinary employee; Mr. Chubb was only a teller but acted as if he ran the place.

4. There were more than seventy-five people at our New Year's party.
5. Before she was stopped, Amy had been driving seventy-five miles an hour in a thirty-five zone, run three stoplights, driven the wrong way on a one-way street, hit three lightpoles and a stop sign, and knocked the park bench from under three sleeping winos. She passed out, drunk.
6. They had no important common interests: Bob liked to arrange dried flowers and Irma rebuilt engines.
7. Making the 1980 winter Olympics was a hollow victory for Randy Gardner since he was unable to compete in the finals of the Lake Placid games.
8. In 1980, the U.S. Olympic Committee agreed to boycott the summer games in Moscow after White House pressure following the Russian invasion of Afghanistan.
9. In the chapel can be found a rare William Morris tapestry.
10. To become a journalist, a degree in journalism is not always essential.

49 awk

Proofread to catch awkward repetitions and omitted words.

Awkward sentences are difficult to read. They may or may not be clear, but they always require extra effort and usually interrupt the flow of thought. In this section we discuss two common causes of awkwardness. But many awkward sentences do not fit into neat categories; they often result from the ineffective choice or arrangement of words, as described in this chapter and in Chapter 6. If awkwardness is a problem for you, try reading your sentences aloud: an awkward sentence usually does not *sound* right.

49a Repeat words only for emphasis or transition.

Repeating a prominent word or expression can provide an effective transition between sentences or paragraphs (see **12b**). Occasional repetition of a key word can emphasize an idea. But use repetition sparingly: too much can create awkward sentences:

AWKWARD REPETITION: During July, the museum will *exhibit works* by Cleveland goldsmith John Paul Miller. These *works exhibit* the artist's exquisite *work* with granulation, the technique of adorning jewelry with miniscule spheres of gold.

IMPROVED: During July, the museum will exhibit works by Cleveland goldsmith John Paul Miller. These pieces display the artist's exquisite use of granulation, the technique of adorning jewelry with miniscule spheres of gold.

EFFECTIVE REPETITION: The Bermuda Triangle "mystery" involves the unexplained disappearances of ships and planes in a vast area of the Atlantic Ocean near Bermuda. This mystery is probably best solved by simply realizing that some vessels sank and that others never disappeared.

EFFECTIVE REPETITION: Like Thoreau, he did not wish to avoid life but to confront the essential facts of life; he did not wish to live what was not life. (The repetition emphasizes the special meaning given to *life*.)

One especially confusing type of repetition is the use of the same word in two senses in the same or adjoining sentences. Find a synonym for one instance of the word.

AWKWARD REPETITION: No one knew the principal reason for the principal's dismissal.

IMPROVED: No one knew the major reason for the principal's dismissal.

49 awk

49b Include all necessary words.

Many sentences are awkward because they use unnecessary words, but many others are awkward or confusing because they omit words. Below are some of the more common types of omissions:

AWKWARD OMISSION: I could see almost everyone in the room was talking and laughing excitedly. (*That* has been omitted after *see*. Omitting *that* is often confusing and awkward.)

IMPROVED: I could see that almost everyone in the room was talking and laughing excitedly.

AWKWARD OMISSION: Both twins were beautiful and wearing evening gowns. (*Were* has been omitted before *wearing*. *Beautiful* and *wearing* are not parallel.)

IMPROVED: Both twins were beautiful and were wearing evening gowns.

AWKWARD OMISSION: The senior class expressed its appreciation to Mr. Taylor, the principal; Mrs. Jackson, the senior class advisor; and Mrs. Baker, the college counselor. (*To* omitted before *Mrs. Jackson* and *Mrs. Baker*. Repeating the preposition shows the parallel elements more clearly. See also **55b**.)

IMPROVED: The senior class expressed its appreciation to Mr. Taylor, the principal; to Mrs. Jackson, the senior class advisor; and to Mrs. Baker, the college counselor.

When you use two verbs that require different prepositions, be sure to include both prepositions:

AWKWARD OMISSION: He could neither comply nor agree to the proposal. (*With* has been omitted after *comply*.)

IMPROVED: He could neither comply with nor agree to the proposal.

EXERCISE 49 _____

Read the following sentences. A. Mark X for those that are awkward, E for those that are effective. B. Reword those marked X.

1. My brother's Packard is one of if not the ugliest car on campus.
2. Since the new flu virus is highly contagious and can easily be spread around an office, anyone catching it should stay home for at least one week.
3. He laid the groundwork for his firing when he laid down his tools and went home early.
4. Coach Huff did not know practically the whole team was breaking training rules regularly.
5. Not all biologists feel a wolf kill is humane or necessary.
6. Never having played baseball, Victor could not catch on to catching the ball.
7. His years of volleyball training made him want to hit rather than grab the ball. Such training was hard to overcome.
8. Ed was aware his older brother had passed the bar exam.
9. Jan was told that she should neither apologize nor concur in the majority decision.
10. When a person assumes a public trust, he should consider himself a public property.

50 var

Vary the length and word order of your sentences.

Most writers favor certain types of sentences. In fact, skillful readers can sometimes identify the work of a particular writer by his or her repetition of certain patterns and structures. Inexperienced writers, though, tend to overuse certain sentence types to the point of monotony. To make your writing more interesting, vary your sentences, mix short sentences with longer ones, and vary the word order occasionally. The samples below demonstrate some of the most common monotonous repetitions:

MONOTONOUS: The state's latest legal battle concerns topless bars. Topless dancing was found constitutional. The county commission then passed an ordinance against serving alcohol in topless bars. The owners are looking for loopholes. (Be careful of too many successive short sentences.)

EFFECTIVE: The state's latest legal battle began when topless dancing was declared constitutional. After a law passed by the county commission prohibited the sale of alcohol in topless bars, the bar owners have begun searching for legal loopholes.

MONOTONOUS: American medical schools are overflowing with students. These schools face the threat of cutbacks in federal aid. The country will produce a glut of physicians in the 1990's without such cutbacks, say Washington officials. But the nation's medical schools say that cuts in federal support would push tuition beyond the reach of minority and lower-income students.

EFFECTIVE: American medical schools which are overflowing with students, face the threat of reduced government aid. Although Washington officials say that such cutbacks are needed to prevent a glut of physicians in the 1990's, the medical schools say that cuts in federal support would push tuition beyond the reach of minority and lower-income students.

51 ref

Make each pronoun point clearly to one antecedent.

Since a pronoun refers to a noun (its *antecedent*), a pronoun's meaning is clear only when it points clearly to that noun. Two or more plausible antecedents will confuse your reader:

AMBIGUOUS: Alex told Waldo that he should be earning more money.

CLEAR: Alex told Waldo, "You should be earning more money."
Or: Alex told Waldo, "I should be earning more money."
Or: Alex complained to Waldo about being underpaid.

AMBIGUOUS: As soon as Mrs. Kennedy christened the ship, she was set afloat in the Thames.

CLEAR: As soon as Mrs. Kennedy christened her, the ship was set afloat in the Thames.

In the second pair of examples, sensible readers will know that the ship, not Mrs. Kennedy, was set afloat; but, since they will notice the comical ambiguity, the sentence is still ineffective.

51a Make each pronoun refer to a noun or to an earlier pronoun.

To keep references clear, make each pronoun refer to a noun used as a subject, direct object, or complement, not as a modifier or possessive:

INEFFECTIVE: Morris questioned the newspaper's honesty even though it had helped him.

EFFECTIVE: Even though the newspaper had helped him, Morris questioned its honesty.

INEFFECTIVE: At Sybil's office, she is the Girl Friday.
EFFECTIVE: Sybil is the Girl Friday in her office.

Also be sure that a pronoun can logically refer to its antecedent:

INEFFECTIVE: I had tonsillitis when I was eight, so my doctor removed them.
EFFECTIVE: I had tonsillitis when I was eight, so my doctor removed my tonsils.
or: When I was eight, my doctor removed my tonsils because they were continually inflamed.

51b   Make each pronoun refer to one word or to a specific group of words rather than to an implied idea.

Use *you* only when referring directly to your reader, not when referring to any person in general. Substitute *one* or an appropriate noun:

INEFFECTIVE: Many people believe that college should help you earn a better living.
EFFECTIVE: Many people believe that college should help a person earn a better living.
Or: Many people believe that college should help one earn a better living.

Except in expressions such as "It is cold," use *it* and *they* only to refer to specific nouns:

INEFFECTIVE: On page 381 of our text, it says that Henry Clay was "the great compromiser."
EFFECTIVE: On page 381 of our text, the author says that Henry Clay was "the great compromiser."
Or: On page 381, our text says that Henry Clay was "the great compromiser."

INEFFECTIVE: They do not have many Catholics in Iran.
EFFECTIVE: Iran does not have many Catholics.
Or: There are few Catholics in Iran.

51c Insert nouns to clarify the reference of *this*, *that*, and *which*.

This, that, and *which* are often vague when they refer broadly to an idea expressed or implied in a preceding clause. To avoid confusion, change the pronoun to a noun or add a noun.

VAGUE: The young residents did the actual cutting even though the surgeon received credit and payment for the operation. This is common in many hospitals.

CLEAR: The young residents did the actual cutting even though the surgeon received credit and payment for the operation. This practice is common in many hospitals.

VAGUE: The professor lectured while his teaching assistants worked with individual students, which is quite common.

CLEAR: The professor lectured while his teaching assistants worked with individual students, a common arrangement.

EXERCISE 51 _____

A. Underline all pronouns used inappropriately in the following sentences. B. Rewrite the sentences that contain errors in pronoun use.

1. Even though the dress had obviously been worn, Alstine's gave a prompt refund. This is standard practice in such stores.
2. The Mini Le Mans track uses scale-model cars on a sharply banked track with very tight turns, which gives the impression of great speed.
3. After Max's apartment was robbed for the sixth time, he moved.
4. I enjoy eating at Augustine's because they treat you like royalty.
5. When Ted yells at you, it means that he cares about you.
6. Politicians use fancy words because it impresses voters.

7. I watched Cassandra sneak out early, but no one else noticed this.
8. The nurse was unsympathetic; this is indicative of much apathy in our society.
9. After Sam finally removed the leg from the desk, he was ready to paint it.
10. Dr. Miller gave her the news that she would soon be moving her office.
11. They drink more wine in Europe than we do in America.
12. C.B. radios are useful for tourists because they can help find direction or other assistance.
13. Pursuing happiness is more than a dream; it is a constitutional right.
14. Sergio appreciates female beauty in all its forms, and this is why he has had three attractive wives.
15. Cicero once told a friend that he could have written him a shorter letter if he had had more time.

52 mm dg

Place all modifiers so that they clearly modify the intended word.

The meaning of English sentences depends largely on word order; if you move words and expressions around, you will often change what a sentence means:

The girl eyed the man sitting in the wicker chair.
The girl sitting in the wicker chair eyed the man.

Nancy Palmer recently published the poem she wrote.
Nancy Palmer published the poem she wrote recently.

The rule of thumb is to place modifiers as near as possible to the words they modify.

52a   Place an adjective phrase or clause as near as possible to the noun or pronoun it modifies.

Single adjectives usually come immediately before the noun or pronoun they modify, adjective phrases and clauses immediately after. When other words come between an adjective and the word it modifies, the sentence may sound awkward, and its meaning may be obscured:

MISPLACED: The customer returned the blender to the store with the broken rotor.

IMPROVED: The customer returned the blender with the broken rotor to the store.

Often you have to do more than move the modifier; you have to rethink and revise the whole sentence:

MISPLACED: Marvin bought a new router attachment for his power drill that he found on sale last week.

IMPROVED: Last week Marvin bought on sale a new router attachment for his power drill.

MISPLACED: My uncle bought an old Chevrolet for seventy-five dollars, which he calls his "fishing car."

IMPROVED: My uncle paid seventy-five dollars for an old Chevrolet that he calls his "fishing car."

52b   Place a limiting adverb, such as *only* or *just*, immediately before the word it modifies.

In speech, most of us are casual about where we place such adverbs as *only, almost, hardly, just,* and *scarcely.* But writing should be more precise:

MISPLACED: Elliott refurbished his antique cars almost until they were like new.

IMPROVED: Elliott refurbished his antique cars until they were almost like new.

MISPLACED: A kilo of salt only weighs 2.2 pounds.
IMPROVED: A kilo of salt weighs only 2.2 pounds.

Notice how moving the modifier changes the meaning of the following sentence:

She had just read *Jane Eyre* for her literature class.
She had read just *Jane Eyre* for her literature class.

52c   Make certain that each adverb phrase or clause modifies the word or words you intend it to modify.

An adverb phrase or clause can appear at the beginning of a sentence, inside a sentence, or at the end:

After the census, New York lost two congressional seats.
New York, after the census, lost two congressional seats.
New York lost two congressional seats after the census.

Be careful, though, that the adverb modifies only what you intend it to modify:

MISPLACED: The victim was found shot twice by his huge circular bed. (Did the bed shoot him?)
IMPROVED: The victim was found next to his huge circular bed, shot twice.

MISPLACED: The President promised that he would soon clarify his stand on television last night.
IMPROVED: The President promised on television last night that he would soon clarify his stand.

MISPLACED: The ex-convict vowed to kill Rockford at least twice.
IMPROVED: The ex-convict vowed at least twice to kill Rockford.

52d   Move ambiguous (squinting) modifiers.

If you find that you have placed a modifier so that it refers ambiguously to more than one word, move it to avoid the ambiguity:

AMBIGUOUS:	Conrad enjoyed working for a short time.
CLEAR:	For a short time, Conrad enjoyed working.
	Or: Conrad enjoyed short periods of work.

| AMBIGUOUS: | Mary assured the supervisor with a straight face that she was not cheating. |
| CLEAR: | With a straight face, Mary assured the supervisor that she was not cheating. |

AMBIGUOUS:	Since termites travel in swarms usually they are hard to exterminate.
CLEAR:	Since termites usually travel in swarms, they hard to exterminate.
	Or: Since termites travel in swarms, they are usually hard to exterminate.

52e Split infinitives only when the alternative is awkward.

Conventional usage requires that you do not insert an adverb between *to*—called the sign of the infinitive—and its verb form *(to quickly run)*. In some instances, splitting the infinitive seems natural; many writers would prefer the following sentence to an alternative: "To suddenly stop offering trading stamps might upset our customers." In college writing, however, it is usually best to avoid splitting infinitives:

| SPLIT: | The chairman proposed to, if no one had any objections, defer discussion of the budget. |
| REVISED: | The chairman proposed to defer discussion of the budget, if no one had any objections. |

| SPLIT: | The aim of the new agency is to swiftly reduce unemployment. |
| REVISED: | The aim of the new agency is to reduce unemployment swiftly. |

52f Make certain that introductory verbal phrases relate clearly to the subject of the sentence.

Modifiers are said to *dangle* when they do not logically modify a word or expression in the sentence. Most often, a *dangling modifier* does not correctly refer to the subject of the sentence:

DANGLING: Listening to Rita Coolidge singing "Mud Island," my stereo died.

In this sentence, the reader will mistakenly assume that the subject of the sentence *(stereo)* is also the understood subject of the verbal *(listening)*. The result is absurd: did the stereo listen? The writer should have written:

IMPROVED: *As I was* listening to Rita Coolidge singing "Mud Island," my stereo died.

The improved sentence illustrates one way of correcting a dangling modifier: supply the necessary words to make the phrase into a complete dependent clause. It is especially natural to supply missing words when the dangling modifier is an *elliptical phrase* (a predicate with the subject and part of the verb implied but not expressed):

DANGLING: While watching the performance, their jewels were stolen.
CORRECTED: While *they were* watching the performance, their jewels were stolen.

At other times, the best way to correct a dangling modifier may be to revise the main sentence, as in the following examples:

DANGLING: *Driving recklessly,* Allen's Corvette crashed into a light pole. (dangling participial phrase)
CORRECTED: Driving recklessly, Allen crashed his Corvette into a light pole.

DANGLING: *Besides finishing the report on water tables,* my afternoon will be taken up with telephone calls. (dangling phrase with gerund)
CORRECTED: Besides finishing the report on water tables, I will spend the afternoon making telephone calls.

DANGLING: *To succeed,* a great deal of determination and luck are needed. (dangling infinitive)
CORRECTED: To succeed, one needs a great deal of determination and luck.

These examples illustrate two common causes of dangling modifiers. In the first two sentences, the word that the phrase is intended to modify is not the subject of the sentence but a possessive modifying the subject *(Allen's my)*. In the last sentence, the main clause is in the passive voice. Note that the revisions are not only logical but also more direct.

Note: Some verbal phrases (often known as *absolute constructions*) refer not to a single word but to the whole idea of a sentence; hence, they do not dangle.

ACCEPTABLE: *Generally speaking,* most books contain errors.
ACCEPTABLE: *Considering the cost of gasoline,* the bus fare looks quite reasonable.

52g   Be certain that concluding clauses and phrases modify the word intended.

ILLOGICAL: Jack Nicholson won an Oscar for *One Flew over the Cuckoo's Nest,* his greatest role. (Was the movie his role?)
CORRECTED: Jack Nicholson won an Oscar for his greatest role, McMurphy in *One Flew over the Cuckoo's Nest.*

Avoid adding a verbal phrase to the end of a sentence as a substitute for a parallel verb:

AWKWARD: Lee studied business in college, majoring in accounting.
IMPROVED: Lee studied business in college and majored in accounting.

EXERCISE 52 _____

Read the following sentences. A. Mark E for those with modifiers used correctly, X for those with misplaced or dangling modifiers. B. Revise the sentences marked X.

1. To illustrate the theory, a look at a recent experiment is in order.
2. Even though dressed as a boy, Rosalind's love is not disguised in *As You Like It*.
3. Featuring mostly four-part harmonies, the popularity of the Oak Ridge Boys has recently soared.
4. For the first time, sexual battery in the state legislature was discussed.
5. Slowly and gracefully, you watch the skier ascend in the chair lift.
6. Though aware of government corruption, I wonder if most people dislike politicians.
7. Our missing poodle was found hiding under some bushes with the help of the entire neighborhood.
8. Finding the door ajar, she darted out and disappeared into the dark.
9. When tying a figure-eight knot, be sure to firmly grasp both ends.
10. The man Jack had criticized bitterly protested.

53 pred

Make subject and predicate relate to each other logically.

As a main verb, *to be* links a subject with a complement: The *piano* is an old *Steinway;* The *news* is *good*. A common error called *faulty predication* occurs when the subject and complement cannot be logically joined:

FAULTY: His job was a reporter for the *Sentinel Star.*
CORRECT: He worked as a reporter for the *Sentinel Star.*
    (he = reporter)

FAULTY: Burglars and muggers are common crimes today.
CORRECT: Burglary and mugging are common crimes today.
    (burglary and mugging = crimes)

In general, avoid following a form of *to be* with adverb clauses beginning with *where, when,* and *because:*

FAULTY: Someone said that diplomacy is when one lies gracefully for his country.

CORRECT: Someone said that diplomacy is lying gracefully for one's country.

FAULTY: The reason Hubert was fired was because he was rude to many customers.

CORRECT: The reason Hubert was fired was that he was rude to many customers.
Or: Hubert was fired because he was rude to many customers.

Faulty predication can occur with verbs other than *to be* whenever the subject and predicate do not fit together logically:

FAULTY: Abused spouses must be dealt with severely.

CORRECT: Spouse abuse must be dealt with severely.

EXERCISE 53 _____

A. Mark E *for those sentences in which subject and complement are compatible,* X *for those with faulty predication. B. Then reword the sentences marked* X.

1. An inverted sentence is where the verb comes before the subject.
2. Jerry's flat tire was an irritating experience.
3. The reason I was promoted was that my father was the boss.
4. My new position is much better paid than my old one.
5. Roofers and bricklayers are two of the hardest construction jobs, but they pay no better than easier work.
6. If nothing else, a movie is one way to spend an evening.
7. College is when many young people grow up.
8. Jeff believes that medicine is the best means of becoming rich.
9. Northwest Africa is called "the West" in Arabic because it has long been the western outpost of Islam.
10. Dale's only problem is when the assigned reading involves long nineteenth-century novels.

54 comp

Compare only things that are logically comparable.

A common fault is to compare a characteristic of one thing with another thing instead of with its corresponding characteristic:

FAULTY: Bernini's handling of marble is warmer than any other sculptor. (comparing *handling* to *sculptor*)

CORRECT: Bernini's handling of marble is warmer than *that of* any other sculptor.

FAULTY: A teacher's income is generally lower than a doctor. (*income* compared to *doctor*)

CORRECT: A teacher's income is generally lower than a doctor's.
Or: A teacher's income is generally lower than that of a doctor.

Many comparisons are faulty because the word *other* has been omitted:

FAULTY: New York is larger than any American city.

CORRECT: New York is larger than any other American city.

Many faulty comparisons are ambiguous:

FAULTY: Lately I've been calling Mary much more often than George. (Who calls whom?)

CORRECT: Lately I've been calling Mary much more often than George has.
Or: Lately I've been calling Mary much more often than I have called George.

FAULTY: Pensacola is farther from Chicago than Miami.

CORRECT: Pensacola is farther from Chicago than it is from Miami.

Many comparisons are incomplete because words such as *as* are omitted:

FAULTY: Jefferson is as good if not better than other community colleges.

CORRECT: Jefferson is as good as, if not better than, other community colleges.
Or: Jefferson is as good as other community colleges, if not better.

EXERCISE 54 _____

A. Mark E *for those sentences with effective comparisons,* X *for those with ineffective comparisons. B. Reword those marked* X.

1. When I was a teenager, I vowed to trust my father more than any man.
2. St. Paul's Cathedral is as great if not more so than any other Wren church.
3. I saw Cassandra more often than Audrey.
4. The poetic style of Vaughan is much like Traherne.
5. Dan Fouts's passing is better than any other quarterback.
6. In the 1980 Shakespeare season, *Hamlet* at Stratford was superior to any production there.
7. Nureyev's movements in *Giselle* were like a cat.
8. Tom could never tell Bob Seeger's raspy baritone from Rod Stewart.
9. The temperature is higher in Dallas this year than it has been for over thirty years.
10. The cathedral in York contains more medieval stained glass than any church in England.

55 //

Use parallel structures effectively.

When you express two or more ideas that are equal in emphasis, use parallel grammatical structures: nouns with nouns, infinitives with infinitives, adverb clauses with adverb clauses. The parallel structures clearly and emphatically indicate parallel ideas:

EFFECTIVE: The hero is destroyed by his own strength, devoured by his own hunger, and impoverished by his own wealth. (verb phrases)

EFFECTIVE: It may be better, Eliot said, to do evil than to do nothing. (infinitive phrases)

EFFECTIVE: Because of his acute sense of hearing, because of his playful imagination, and most of all because of his amazing intelligence, the dolphin is a rare creature of the sea. (introductory phrases)

55a In parallel structures, use only equal grammatical constructions.

A common error among inexperienced writers is faulty parallelism—treating unlike grammatical structures as if they were parallel. This practice upsets the balance that the reader expects in a coordinate structure. Below are some of the more common types of faulty parallelism:

FAULTY: Denise has two great passions: to act and becoming a gourmet.

CORRECT: Denise has two great passions: to act and to become a gourmet.
Or: . . . acting and becoming a gourmet.

FAULTY: Myron is intelligent, charming, and knows how to dress.

CORRECT: Myron is intelligent, charming, and well dressed.

55b Repeat necessary words to make all parallels clear to the reader.

Awkward, confusing sentences often result if you do not repeat needed prepositions, signs of infinitives *(to)*, auxiliary verbs, or other words needed to make a parallel clear:

FAULTY: Knotts Berry Farm is famous for its "jailbirds" who call visitors by name and preserves and jellies of every kind imaginable.

CORRECT: Knotts Berry Farm is famous for its "jailbirds" who call visitors by name and *for* preserves and jellies of every kind imaginable.

FAULTY: Mr. Simmons, the counselor, told Carmelita that she should be more realistic and failing one course would not ruin her record.

CORRECT: Mr. Simmons, the counselor, told Carmelita that she should be more realistic and *that* failing one course would not ruin her record.

55c   Always use parallel structures with correlative conjunctions such as *both . . . and* or *neither . . . nor.*

The *correlative conjunctions* connect two closely related ideas; use the same grammatical form for both ideas. The most common correlatives are *both . . . and, either . . . or, not only . . . but also, neither . . . nor, whether . . . or.*

FAULTY: Gene Burns is well respected both for his mellow, authoritative voice and as a shrewd analyst of local politics.

CORRECT: Gene Burns is well respected both for his mellow, authoritative voice and for his shrewd analysis of local politics.

FAULTY: He is admired not only by those who share his liberal views but also conservatives respect his integrity.

CORRECT: He is admired not only by those who share his liberal views but also by conservatives who respect his integrity.

A. Mark with E *those sentences that are effective, with* X *those with parallelism. B. Reword those marked* X.

1. I cannot decide whether to play my guitar or to read some science fiction.
2. Reading is more relaxing than to play handball.
3. Three stars were drafted from the baseball team: one was a pitcher, one played shortstop, and one as a designated hitter.
4. Glover, the shortstop, will either go directly to the major leagues or play only one year in the high minors.
5. The English courses are interesting, enjoyable, and to the students' advantage.
6. Many women do not mind having their chairs pulled out for them, their doors opened, or a man picking up the tab.
7. During my freshman year, I received much helpful advice and many new friends.
8. I believe that everyone should study and be opposed to the proposed ordinance.
9. The real test of excellence in a leader is not simply to represent the voters in a narrow sense, but he should move ahead of them, ignoring their more transient and petty interests. And, in a sense, he must misrepresent them.
10. Vibrant brunette seeks a tall, articulate man who must be a nonsmoker, Jewish, have a good mind and body, be capable of commitment, a New Yorker, a sense of humor as well as enjoying hiking, backgammon, Greek poetry, and classical guitar.

56   shift

Be consistent in your use of verbs and pronouns.

To present your information smoothly and clearly, be consistent in the tense, voice, and mood of verbs and in the person and number of nouns and pronouns. Unnecessary shifts—from past to present or from singular to plural, for instance—make awkward reading and can confuse meaning. Some shifts are necessary—to indicate passing time, for instance—but it is best to make such shifts only when you feel they are necessary.

56a Avoid unnecessary shifts in tense, voice, and mood.

A change in **tense** usually signals to your reader a change in time, so be sure not to give a false signal by switching tenses unnecessarily. A shift such as the following is often just the result of carelessness:

SHIFT IN TENSE: As he *turned* the corner, he *became* aware that someone *is* following him.

CORRECTED: As he *turned* the corner, he *became* aware that someone *was* following him.

Be careful not to shift time when you are using one of the perfect tenses:

SHIFT IN TENSE: We had paid our dues and are ready to begin attending meetings. (past perfect with present)

CORRECTED: We have paid our dues and are ready to begin attending meetings. (present perfect with present)
Or: We had paid our dues and were ready to begin attending meetings. (past perfect with past)

See **22** for a discussion of verb tenses. Active and passive **voice** can be mixed in one sentence (she *ran* twice and *was defeated* twice), but an unnecessary shift in voice can spoil the focus of a sentence:

56 shift

SHIFT IN VOICE:	Electrolysis is used by Dr. DeKleva and he also performs minor surgery.
IMPROVED:	Dr. DeKleva uses electrolysis and performs minor surgery.
SHIFT IN VOICE:	The report showed that white-collar criminals almost never serve hard time while long sentences are served by petty burglars.
IMPROVED:	The report showed that white-collar criminals almost never serve hard time while petty burglars serve long sentences.

Active voice is usually more direct and natural than passive voice (see **48e**).

A change in mood should reflect a change in the way the writer views the action or situation being described: "If I *were* willing to lie, I *would tell* you I enjoyed the story; but I *am* not willing to lie." Unmotivated shifts are distracting:

SHIFT IN MOOD:	If I were the President, I would take action, not act as if I was still in Congress.
CORRECTED:	If I were the President, I would take action, not act as if I were still in Congress.

See **24**.

56b Be consistent in the number and person of your nouns and pronouns.

Shift number (singular or plural) only to show a valid change: I wanted to go to Europe, but *we* could not afford the trip. (See also **19**.)

FAULTY:	The class of 1972 was academically outstanding, but they were unusual.
IMPROVED:	The class of 1972 was academically outstanding, but it was unusual.

FAULTY: The staff was given a brief explanation of the
                new medical policy as part of our hospitalization
                plan.

IMPROVED: The staff was given a brief explanation of the
                new medical policy as part of its hospitalization
                plan.

Similarly, keep the person of your pronouns consistent.
Be especially careful to avoid slipping into the universal
you (second person) when you are writing in the third
person *(she, he, it)*:

FAULTY: Deer hunters in the Ocala National Forest must
                wear bright clothing so you will not get shot.

IMPROVED: Deer hunters in the Ocala National Forest must
                wear bright clothing so they will not get shot.

FAULTY: Other hunters will shoot at you if they see
                movement in the brush.

IMPROVED: Often other hunters will shoot carelessly if they
                see movement in the brush.

EXERCISE 56 _____

A. Mark E *for those sentences without awkward shifts,* X *for those
with awkward shifts. B. Reword those marked* X.

1. After physics had been mastered, Jeff had little trouble
   with engineering.
2. Our summer in Europe should be a bargain, but you have
   to plan on unexpected expenses.
3. Raymond Chandler's classic mystery *The Big Sleep* was
   remade into a disappointing 1978 film, which is set
   in England.
4. A person should always be careful about what you sign
   your name to.
5. Each teacher uses a different approach, but they all get
   their presentation across.
6. The emerald ring was purchased for two hundred dollars,
   but she sold it for four hundred.

7. My new pair of Gloria Vanderbilt jeans is very stylish, but they were overpriced.
8. The metamorphosis of a tent caterpillar is not complete until they become flying moths.
9. Most of the convention speeches were effective on television but were lost on the delegates in the hall.
10. The acoustics in Orchestra Hall were such that you can hear from any seat in the house.

WORDS

Getting the right word in the right place to say exactly what you intend can be one of your greatest challenges as a writer. To meet that challenge, you need to know what words mean and how to use them. As you become more sensitive to words—to their ability to clarify or obscure, and to their suitability for your purposes and audiences—you will use them with increasing confidence.

A good dictionary will help you decide whether the word you think is the right one actually expresses what you intend. It will also warn you if a word is considered slang or obsolete or in some other way inappropriate for college writing. The following sections will help you to use your dictionary more efficiently and will offer other advice about choosing words wisely.

57 lev

Write at a level appropriate to your subject and audience.

The English language includes many dialects—different ways of speaking or writing in particular geographical areas or among particular groups of people. The predominant dialect used by educated writers and speakers of American English is called Standard English. It is the variety of English expected in college papers, business reports, and books like this one. Most dictionaries mark the words not usually used in Standard English as *nonstandard, substandard,* or *dialect. Nowheres,* for example, is labelled *dial* in *Webster's New Collegiate Dictionary.* (Note: some words may be Standard in one sense but not in another. *Learn* is nonstandard when used to mean "teach.") The abbreviations for these labels vary; your dictionary will have a section at the front or back explaining its labels and abbreviations.

Standard English is written and spoken in many styles, which we can arbitrarily divide into three "levels": Formal, Informal, and General. Each level is appropriate in some situations but not in others.

Formal English is found in technical reports, scholarly books and articles, and many types of professional or academic writing. It uses an extensive, elevated vocabulary and sentences more complex than those found in other levels of writing. It avoids contractions and colloquial expressions and therefore sounds different from the way people speak:

> Money and the habitual resort to its use are conceived to
> be simply the ways and means by which consumable goods
> are acquired, and therefore simply a convenient method by
> which to procure the pleasurable sensations of
> consumption; these latter being in hedonistic theory the
> sole and overt end of all economic endeavor. Money
> values have therefore no other significance than that of
> purchasing power over consumable goods, and money is
> simply an expedient of computation.
>
> —Thorstein Veblen

Informal English, on the other hand, has a more conversational tone. Writers of Informal English regularly use contractions, colloquial expressions (*a couple of* instead of *two*, *really* instead of *very*), and slang. They usually write in loose sentences with more *and*'s and fewer subordinate clauses than are used in other levels of writing. Informal English is gaining popularity in journalism but is generally not considered appropriate for college papers.

> Muhammad Ali believes he is the most famous man in the world, and he may be onto something. . . . His picture hangs in African mud huts, where they don't always even know what he does for a living; Arab kings lay villas on him like Kleenex; he is the toast of England and the fastest route to an argument in America and altogether the noisiest piece of work since Telstar made possible the global shriek.
>
> —Wilfred Sheed

General English follows a middle course between Formal and Informal. Most of its sentences are less complex than those of Formal English but tighter than those of Informal English. In the right circumstances, General English might use relatively formal words like *haughty* and *attire* or informal words like *stuck-up* and *threads*, but most of the time it uses words like *proud* and *clothes*. General English is usually the best choice for college or business writing.

> Beginnings are apt to be shadowy, and so it is with the beginnings of that great mother of life, the sea. Many people have debated how and when the earth got its ocean, and it is not surprising that their explanations do not always agree. For the plain and inescapable truth is that no one was there to see, and in the absence of eyewitness accounts there is bound to be a certain amount of disagreement.
>
> —Rachel Carson

EXERCISE 57 _____

A. Label each of the following paragraphs F for Formal, I for Informal, and G for General English. B. Be prepared to discuss the circumstances in which each paragraph would be appropriate.

1. America's neglect of foreign language study has produced misunderstandings and setbacks at a time of increased international communication. Sometimes ignorance of languages other than English produces minor or amusing embarrassments, as when "Body by Fisher" was translated "Corpse by Fisher" in some countries. But the U.S. is more seriously embarrassed by being alone in the world in its ignorance of foreign languages. A 1980 Presidential Commission revealed that nine out of ten Americans know only English, ninety percent of U.S. colleges require no foreign language study, and fewer than twenty-five percent of high school students learn languages. Because other industrial nations have competent language education programs, they are more successful in the increasing arena of international business. In America, the neglect of foreign language study has produced a generation whose inability to communicate has serious political and economic as well as cultural consequences.

2. It is a question whether Knowledge can in any proper sense be predicated of the brute creation; without pretending to metaphysical exactness of phraseology, which would be unsuitable to an occasion like this, I say, it seems to me improper to call that passive sensation, or perception of things, which brutes seem to possess, by the name of Knowledge. When I speak of Knowledge, I mean something intellectual, something which grasps what it perceives through the senses; something which takes a view of things; which sees more than the senses convey; which reasons upon what it sees, and while it sees; which invests it with an idea. It expresses itself, not in a mere enunciation, but by an enthymeme: it is of the nature of science from the first, and in this consists its dignity.

3. Colleges have been turning out unskilled workers for decades. Until five years ago, most of these unskilled

workers took their degrees in sociology, philosophy, English, or history and moved directly into the middle class. Some filled executive positions in government and business, but many went into education, which is the only thing they knew a great deal about. Once there, they taught another generation the skills necessary to take tests and write papers.

4. Tim had everything you might imagine a guy would need to become the number one collegiate quarterback in the country. He was tall and fast and had a super smile, and he had style: he could charm the press and get plenty of publicity for himself without ever being really pushy. It's hard to believe, but he gave it all up to enter a monastery.

5. As an intensification and extension of the visual function, the phonetic alphabet diminishes the role of the other senses of sound and touch and taste in any literate culture. The fact that this does not happen in cultures such as the Chinese, which use nonphonetic scripts, enables them to retain a rich store of inclusive perception in depth of experience that tends to become eroded in civilized cultures of the phonetic alphabet. For the ideogram is an inclusive *gestalt*, not an analytic dissociation of senses and functions like phonetic writing.

58 d

Keep your level of usage consistent.

Appropriate diction requires a consistent style. Mixing formal and informal language can produce distracting and absurd results:

It seemed inconceivable that the thieves could hope to penetrate the supposedly impregnable chamber; their rip-off was simply unreal.

Here the slangy conclusion clashes with the standard, if somewhat formal, level of the rest of the sentence. Just

as you would not wear bluejeans with a dinner jacket,
you do not want to call attention to yourself by mixing
styles of writing inappropriately.

INAPPROPRIATE: The unique excellence of the tube is also its
tragic flaw.

APPROPRIATE: The unique excellence of television is also
its tragic flaw.

INAPPROPRIATE: As Orwell observed, the English language
is unquestionably hard up.

APPROPRIATE: As Orwell observed, the English language
is unquestionably in difficulty.

EXERCISE 58 _____

*Study the levels of usage in the following sentences. A. Mark
with X those that mix levels of usage, with C those that are consistent. B. Revise those marked X.*

 1. Shakespeare's characters, though they speak memorable
    poetry, are often tough to relate to.
 2. The nation gives meaning to the flag, but the flag does
    not give meaning to those who wave it.
 3. Some people are convinced that, having said nothing,
    they have said a great deal.
 4. Professor Baxter is articulate, but somehow I suspect that
    he isn't quite all together.
 5. Sylvia enjoys history, but ancient Rome doesn't turn
    her on that much.
 6. The administration is working to improve the registration
    process, which has been a hassle for the students.
 7. One good way to keep the proverbial wolf from the door
    is with a sheepskin.
 8. Show me a thoroughly satisfied person, and I will show
    you a failure.
 9. The candidate's largely flaky performance in a television
    press conference helped to defeat him.
10. My research assistant telephoned to inquire what was
    going down in the laboratory.

59 idiom

Use the idiom of written English.

An idiom is a customary expression peculiar to a language. Native speakers of English naturally say "with the naked eye," for example, not "with a bare eye," though it is impossible to explain why. You may have difficulty with some of the idiomatic uses of some prepositions: When do you say *differ from,* when *differ with*? Do you say *to the contrary* or *on the contrary*? If your ear cannot guide you, your college dictionary usually can. Here are some troublesome phrases:

Unidiomatic	*Idiomatic*
absolve of	absolve from
accept to	accept by
accuse with	accuse of
accustom with	accustom to
adhere in (*or* by)	adhere to
adjacent of	adjacent to
agree in	agree to (a proposal)
	agree on (a course of action)
angry at (a person)	angry with (a person)
apologize about	apologize for
bored of	bored with (*or* by)
comply to	comply with
concur about	concur with (a person)
	concur in (a decision or action)
conform in	conform to (*or* with)
derived of	derived from
different than	different from
in accordance to	in accordance with
in search for	in search of
intend on doing	intend to do
interfere about	interfere with (= prevent)
	interfere in (= meddle)

Unidiomatic	*Idiomatic*
oblivious about	oblivious of (*or* to)
plan on doing	plan to do
preferable than	preferable to
similar with	similar to
superior than	superior to

EXERCISE 59 _____

A. Use your dictionary to determine which of the following sentences are idiomatic. B. Correct those that are not.

1. Porter tried to *dissuade* his friends *about* smoking.
2. Is Social Security *beneficial to* helping the elderly pay their bills?
3. Minnie has always had a *distaste for* baroque music.
4. Ken is caught in a vicious circle *in which* he cannot escape.
5. Far *superior than* his recent works, Roth's new novel is both enjoyable and lucid.
6. Surprisingly, Nick said that he was not *interested to have* a Porsche.
7. Sara was too *angry at* him to *apologize about* her own rudeness.
8. Ellen *graduated* high school at fourteen and college at seventeen.
9. They could not *acquiesce to* the jury's decision.
10. The course helped Ralph develop a positive *attitude of* reading poetry.

60 vague

Use specific and concrete words.

Consider the following sentences:

> We protected all of the plants in the yard.
> We mulched the shrubs, mounded around the rose bushes, and covered the eucalyptus tree.

The second sentence is more specific; it identifies the kinds of plants and the ways of protecting them. It is longer, but the extra words give the reader a clearer picture.

Specific terms give more information than general ones. *Surgeon*, for example, implies *doctor*, but *doctor* does not identify a person as a surgeon. If you find yourself writing *people* when you mean *U.S. citizens* or *college students* or *black voters*, you are not asking yourself this important question: Am I identifying what I am referring to as specifically as I should? The following list shows how little effort it takes to become more specific:

general	*specific*	*more specific*
building	house	bungalow
contest	footrace	Boston Marathon
go	run	sprint
go	walk	shuffle
religion	Christianity	Roman Catholicism
officer	Cabinet officer	Secretary of State

The best choice is usually the most specific expression that says what you mean. In the following examples, notice how the specific sentences clarify the general ones:

GENERAL: The patient's wound was treated.
SPECIFIC: The nurse bandaged the patient's minor wound.
SPECIFIC: The intern stitched the patient's four-inch laceration.

GENERAL: He studied.
SPECIFIC: He read three chapters in his geology text.
SPECIFIC: He memorized his French vocabulary list.

Abstract terms often combine with general terms in dull writing. An abstract term names something intangible, like an idea or a quality: *democracy, finance, linguistics.* A concrete term, on the other hand, points to something physically real: *desk, checkbook, motorcycle.* We could not communicate complex ideas without using abstract terms, but dull writing tends to be unnecessarily abstract. Sentences filled with *aspects, cases, factors, circumstances,* and *instances* will deaden your writing. Many writers mistakenly convert verbs *(explain, prefer)* into abstract nouns *(explanation, preference)* and use those nouns with vague verbs like *be, have,* or *make:*

> He offered no explanation for his preference for
> European drama.

We can improve the sentence by changing the abstract nouns back to verbs:

> He did not explain why he preferred European drama.

Notice how the following abstract sentence, taken from a newspaper report, is improved by avoiding the abstract nouns *decline* and *use:*

ABSTRACT: The U.S. Department of Agriculture statistics show a decline in the annual per capita use of eggs during the period from 1964 to 1974.

MORE CONCRETE: According to U.S. Department of Agriculture statistics, the average American ate fewer eggs in 1974 than in 1964.

Often you may not be able to make your writing more concrete simply by changing a few words. If your sentences are filled with abstract and general terms, you may find that you need to get into your subject more deeply, to find specific examples. Vague language often indicates vague or incomplete thinking.

VAGUE: Bobby Deerfield has a routine life until love enters his empty world.

SPECIFIC: Bobby Deerfield—a man who is emotionally half dead, whose human relationships are as mechanical as the formula 1 car he drives or the commercials he grinds out for extra money—starts coming to life again because of his love for Lillian.

EXERCISE 60 _____

A. Mark the sentences that use specific terms with S, *the vaguely
worded ones with* X.

1. Kwanza, established in 1966, has become a black cultural
   holiday celebrated in many parts of the United States.
2. This holiday already includes many nice aspects
   and customs.
3. The space program continues to make a significant
   contribution to our society.
4. Since Sputnik first beeped its way around the world in
   1957, the U.S. has more than caught up with the
   Russians in space.
5. The atmosphere surrounding the novel's hero is one
   of foreboding.
6. In many cases consumers are easily misled by advertising.
7. The manipulation of children's minds by toy commercials
   on television is an established part of advertising.
8. A depressed feeling often enters my mind when I read
   certain poems.
9. Many people tend to think that a college degree is a major
   factor in achieving success.
10. The government official visited the company's new facilities.

*B. Expand the following dull sentences by adding specific, concrete
words.*

1. The president must be many things to many people.
2. After considerable struggle, we caught some fish.
3. California is not only our largest state but also one of the
   most varied.
4. Alfred Hitchcock's movies contain a great deal of suspense.
5. Dietetic variations of many foods are now available.

61 ww

Find the exact word to express your meaning.

A well-chosen word, Eric Sevareid once said, is worth a thousand pictures. If you are to select the word that expresses precisely what you intend to say, you must understand its denotation, what it literally means. If you write *notorious* when you mean *famous,* or *erotic* when you mean *erratic,* you may confuse your readers and cause them to doubt your competence as a writer. The Glossary of Usage (**69**) lists a number of easily confused words.

IMPRECISE:	Chemical research includes effort, time, and efficiency. (Effort, time, and efficiency do not constitute chemical research.)
PRECISE:	Chemical research *requires* effort, time, and efficiency.
IMPRECISE:	The President's analyzation of the current economic situation differs from that of his advisors.
PRECISE:	The President's *analysis* of the current economic situation differs from that of his advisors.

EXERCISE 61 _____

A. Use your dictionary to determine the difference between these paired words:

1. apprehend—comprehend
2. simple—simplistic
3. notable—notorious
4. illusion—allusion
5. disinterested—uninterested

6. fortunate—fortuitous
7. feasible—possible
8. forceful—forcible
9. exceedingly—excessively
10. censor—censure

B. Is the italicized word in each of the following sentences correct? If not, supply the correct word.

1. An Olympic athlete's determination has to be *infallible.*
2. In his speech, the senator gave *tacit* approval to the conference.
3. At the *onset* of the class, the instructor gave a surprise quiz.

4. The stories are similar in one *respect:* they involve social outcasts.
5. I am always glad to see Kevin, whose appearance at my party was *gratuitous.*
6. John did not wish to be *implicated* in his wife's problems.
7. Stan had to build and *maintenance* the new aircraft.
8. The author likes to give free *reign* to his imagination.
9. The *underlining* reason for the novel's melancholy tone is the author's unhappy youth.
10. With further education and reading, I hope to become more *opinionated.*

62 **ww**

Make sure the connotations of your words are appropriate.

You will choose the right words only if you know their connotations, their secondary or implied meanings. The dictionary, for example, defines *politician* as one who actively engages in politics. But if you call a fellow student "a real politician," you call up not the literal meaning of *politician*, its denotation, but its connotations: your fellow student is a smooth operator. Consider the differences in tone in each of these sentences:

The faculty senate *discussed* the proposed grading system.
The faculty senate *debated* the proposed grading system.
The faculty senate *argued about* the proposed grading system.
The faculty senate *quarreled over* the proposed grading system.

After three hours of *questioning,* the *detained protesters* were *released.*
After three hours of *grilling,* the *political prisoners* were *liberated.*

Many words have powerful political, sexist, or other social overtones. Because they may evoke personal, emotional responses in those who hear or read them, you must be conscious of their connotations.

A. Are the connotations of the following words favorable or unfavorable?

adolescent, cheap, radical, motherly, liberal, pragmatic, imperialism, disadvantaged, Pentagon, sisterhood, romantic, primitive, educator? *Explain.*

B. How do the connotations of these paired words differ?

1. invincible—unbeatable
2. smart—elegant
3. distinguished—distinctive
4. tough—durable
5. design—shape

6. brilliance—ingenuity
7. childish—childlike
8. startled—shocked
9. unusual—exotic
10. spinster—bachelor

63 fig

Use figures of speech to create vivid images.

Everyday speech is filled with *metaphors* (implied comparisons such as "my room is a nightmare") and *similes* (explicit comparisons such as "a voice like honey"). Similes and metaphors are the most common *figures of speech*—words used in an imaginative rather than a literal sense. Carefully selected figures can be a powerful and vivid way to make points clear by creating pictures for the reader, as when film critic John Simon compares Charles Bronson's acting to "a desperately tight pair of pants that the least animation might split down the middle." Compare the following:

DULL: Churchill used the English language effectively during wartime.

VIVID: "Churchill mobilized the English language and took it to war."

—John F. Kennedy

DULL: Writers use trite expressions when their minds are inactive.

VIVID: Writers use trite expressions when their minds have been switched to automatic pilot.

DULL: Her face was large, child-like, and blank.

VIVID: "Her face was as broad and innocent as a cabbage."

—Flannery O'Connor

If, however, you cannot create a fresh metaphor that fits your subject, rely on an accurate literal statement. A dull, overused metaphor (see **65**) will only demonstrate that you are not original; a wildly inappropriate or strained metaphor will spoil what you have to say.

STRAINED: George's face, as cold as winter water, acted as a moat against the prying eyes of the world.

STRAINED: Blowing gently in the warm wind, Judy's hair, like sweet syrup, brushed my shoulder.

STRAINED: The thick fog, penetrating the lower reaches of the mountain air, made the valley below pregnant with mystery.

EXERCISE 63 _____

A. Complete each of the following with an original metaphor or simile.

1. After Stuart was fired, the office was as quiet as ____ .
2. Food in our cafeteria is as appetizing as _____
3. She began to sob, the tears _____ .
4. The old woman's hair was so thin that _____ .
5. He walks like _____; his posture is clearly improving.
6. Sam ran across the campus as fast as _____ _____ .
7. Jan's fifty-dollar-an-ounce perfume smelled _____ .

8. The frightened newcomer was shaking like _____ .
9. When my kid brother Marvin gets dirty, he _____ .
10. The old, charred books _____ in my hands
    like pieces of _____ .

B. *What figures of speech are used in the following examples?*

1. Prejudice has been defined as the chains forged by
   ignorance to keep people apart.
2. "Blotnik's old mind hobbled slowly, as if on crutches."
                                        —Phillip Roth
3. Her eyes looked "like two small pieces of coal pressed into
   a lump of dough."
                                        —William Faulkner
4. Mark Twain said that a man wrapped up in himself makes
   a very small package.
5. Writers often try to flaunt their sophistication by flinging
   meaningless words upon a stage of lined paper, but they
   tend to empty the auditorium before they complete
   the first paragraph.

64   fig

Make your figures of speech consistent with each other and with your subject.

Metaphorical language is so common that writers may
be unaware of the comparisons their words evoke. For
example, when you speak of "grasping" or "catching"
rather than "understanding" what a writer is saying,
you are making a simple comparison between the
mind and hands. If you speak of being "flooded with
memories," you are using another metaphor: the mind
is the land; the memories the floodwaters. But if you
were to say, "When I grasped what he was saying, it
flooded me with memories," you would have a **mixed
metaphor,** two images that conflict with one another.

Mixed metaphors are a sure sign that you are not thinking about the pictures your words create:

MIXED: Fishing in troubled waters at the American Legion convention, Senator Whipsnade went out on a limb on the abortion issue.

MIXED: If the President keeps the ship of state on an even keel, America will be pulled out of the moral quagmire of recent years.

The images here are both trite and absurd: a senator fishing from a tree limb, a president sailing out of a bog—and pulling the country behind him. You can avoid mixing metaphors if you examine figures of speech in your early drafts. Revise trite figures of speech whether they conflict with other images or not (see **65**) and make sure that your images call up pictures that fit your subject.

EXERCISE 64 _____

Explain why the figures of speech in the following sentences are effective or ineffective.

1. After his defeat, Senator Hall said, "This slap in the face is simply the last straw."
2. The sun penetrates the sea in dancing swords of light.
3. Heat stood in the room like an enemy.
4. Emily's mind is a steel trap which captures ideas like flies.
5. Time, like a hovering eagle, keeps nibbling away at my youth.
6. *Patriotism* is a word all dressed up in red, white, and blue.
7. In the splendor of the Grand Tetons, the majestic mountains play tag with the clouds.
8. The bottom line on inflation boils down to some tough decisions which Congress may find hard to swallow.
9. Evelyn didn't have a leg to stand on after the judge warned her that she was skating on thin ice.
10. The captain of the ship belongs on the bridge, not nipping at the heels of his political foes.

65 trite

Avoid trite expressions and unwarranted euphemisms.

In conversation, we all use stale expressions without thinking about what they mean. But writers have time to think and so should try to make the most of their words.

Clichés. Many of the figures of speech that come most readily to mind were once fresh images. But through overuse, they have lost their effectiveness. We too easily substitute these trite expressions, or clichés, for original thought. No reader will be impressed by such hackneyed images as *light as a feather, busy as a bee,* or *dead as a doornail.* Here is a brief list of clichés that have lost their value as figures of speech:

acid test	grind to a halt
beat around the bush	in a nutshell
by leaps and bounds	nipped in the bud
crystal clear	no stone unturned
explore every avenue	playing with fire
frosting on the cake	silver lining

Fillers. Also common are useless phrases such as *in a very real sense, so to speak, as it were, needless to say, it goes without saying,* and *as a matter of fact.* These phrases add words but no meaning. Here are some others to avoid:

all in all	last but not least
better late than never	part and parcel
each and every	point with pride
easier said than done	rain or shine
few and far between	short and sweet
first and foremost	safe and sound
golden opportunity	without rhyme or reason

Using an original metaphor, Richard Altick sums up the point: A writer should provide "traction for the readers' minds rather than allow them to slide and skid on a slippery surface paved with well-worn phrases."

Euphemisms. A euphemism refers indirectly to something unpleasant or embarrassing. For example, many people use *pass away* or *expire* to mean *die*. A euphemism is sometimes the best way to avoid hurting someone's feelings; but many euphemisms are trite, many are wordy, and many conceal truths that should be plain.

TRITE AND WORDY:	under the influence (drunk)
	stretch the truth (lie)
	woman of the streets (prostitute)
MISLEADING:	civil disturbance (riot)
	protective reaction strikes (bombing)
	inoperative statement (false, retracted statement)

EXERCISE 65 _____

A. To see how easily clichés come to mind, complete the trite expressions in the following "speech":

"First and _____ as you travel down the _____ to success, you will face many challenges _____ and beyond the call of _____. If you persevere, you will pass life's greatest tests with _____ colors; and you can then point with _____ to your achievement. For you will then be truly in a class _____ _____. In the _____ analysis, when all is _____ and _____, it goes without _____ that each and _____ _____ of you can succeed only if you _____ the line and keep your _____ to the wheel as well as your _____ to the grindstone. Last but not _____, I must remind you that all of this is _____ said than _____."

B. *Find a euphemism for each of the following:*

1. fat
2. corpse
3. bossy
4. old
5. wino

6. cheap
7. steal
8. teacher
9. spy
10. ugly

C. *Find equivalents for the following clichés and euphemisms:*

1. raining cats and dogs
2. phony as a three-dollar bill
3. when hell freezes over
4. quiet as a mouse
5. Her bark is worse than her bite.

6. clear as a bell
7. severe nutritional deficiency
8. semi-private room
9. encore telecast
10. electronic surveillance

66 flowery

Avoid pretentious and unfamiliar words.

Although you should try to build a rich vocabulary, try to use it precisely, not just show it off. "Pomposity," "flowery diction," "overwriting," and "fine writing" are just some of the terms used to describe the common mistake of using big words where more familiar words would be more appropriate to the audience and subject. Use a long, formal word only when it expresses your meaning exactly, and avoid falsely poetic, foreign, and artificially formal terms:

PRETENTIOUS: The several members of the fraternal organization caroused in a buoyant spirit of nocturnal wassailing.

IMPROVED: Some of the fraternity members had a wild drinking party.

PRETENTIOUS: Perspicacious persons who take pen in hand, albeit bewitched by the glitter of polysyllabic utterance, do so with the intent to eschew obfuscation.

IMPROVED: Despite the attraction of fancy words, clear writers avoid obscure language.

EXERCISE 66 _____

Translate the following pretentious sentences into more direct English.

1. The coach shook up the players in a salutary fashion prior to the initiation of play.
2. Replete with breathless enthusiasm for the expectation of verdant woods and purling streams, I launched myself on the road to a plethora of diversionary pastoral pleasures.
3. The patient was *in extremis,* threatening to pass away at any moment.
4. By the sheer perspiration of his brow, Ted succeeded in building an empire of fast-food restaurants.
5. Percipient weather prognosticators indicate that significant amounts of precipitation are anticipated in these United States.
6. The militant minions of our left-leaning opposition must be vanquished if we are to secure the preservation of our party.
7. The unauthorized ignition of tobacco-containing substances constitutes felonious behavior.
8. My contemptuous manifestations of derision toward my colleague's piscatorial pursuits evoked irate retorts about my character.
9. He then effected a total metamorphosis in demeanor and politely threatened to initiate legal action.
10. Thus I retorted, "I need a lawsuit the way I need an additional orifice in my cranium."

67 jargon

When writing for the general reader, avoid jargon and highly technical language.

Nearly every specialized field develops its own specialized language: psychologists speak of *syndromes* and *psychoses,* computer operators discuss *core capacity* and *interface,* art critics refer to *texture* and *value contrast.* Among specialists, a specialized vocabulary can convey exact meanings. Among nonspecialists, however, the same vocabulary is only jargon, usually pretentious and confusing. If you want to use a technical term, ask yourself two questions: Do I really need the term? Will my readers understand it? If you do need the term and your readers might not understand it, be sure to define it.

Jargon also refers to the many unnecessarily technical expressions that grow up in most fields. Some of these expressions are euphemisms (see **65**), some just inflated language. Here are a few samples of educational jargon:

> learning facilitator (= teacher)
> exceptional student (= slow or fast learner)
> underachiever (= slow student)
> economically deprived (= poor)
> learning resources center (= library)
> experiential approach (= learning by doing)

Big words such as the following are often misused to give a technical flavor to nontechnical writing:

ameliorate (improve)	exhibit (show)
endeavor (try)	factor (item, point, cause)
inaugurate (begin)	*per se* (in itself)
individual (person)	peruse (read)
initiate (begin)	presently (now)
maximum (most)	utilize (use)
optimum (best)	viable (workable)

Here is Keats' famous line "Beauty is truth, truth beauty" as translated into modern jargon:

> The condition characterized by being aesthetically pleasing to the eye of the beholder is identical to that condition characterized by an unyielding regard for veracity and, of course, there is the fact that the reverse of the foregoing is also true.*

Such language, Randall Jarrell said, sounds as if it were written on a typewriter *by* a typewriter.

EXERCISE 67 _____

Rewrite the following sentences, eliminating jargon.

1. Before she quit her job, Carol exhibited all the symptoms of acute paranoia and felt that everyone was criticizing her.
2. Subsequent to the theater's fire, the schedule of performances was of necessity reconstructed in its entirety.
3. A vast majority of the specimens presently under examination exhibit deteriorative tendencies suggestive of a virus as the causal factor.
4. The university afforded an extraordinarily stimulating intellectual environment, participation in which was one of the most important factors in determining my whole intellectual and professional career in academia.
5. Meaningful interpersonal relationships will hopefully develop subsequent to implementation of the innovative dormitory visitation policy.
6. Optimizing my potentialities as an announcer of athletic contests via audiovisual media is my chief career objective.
7. Personnel who utilize the appropriate methodology are able to bring to a conclusion all of their attempted endeavors.
8. A college education is not a finalization, not a terminal activity; rather it can be perceived as the inception of a lifelong maximal utilization of the mind.

* Kenneth W. Houp and Thomas E. Pearsall, *Reporting Technical Information,* 3rd ed.

9. All of those persons in a state of current employment within our organization must be in attendance when I tender my resignation.
10. Kindly extinguish all superfluous illumination upon exiting the premises.

68 **wdy rep**

Avoid needless repetition, wordiness, and redundancy.

As you revise, look for ways to eliminate anything that does not add to your meaning. Writers often pad sentences with intensives, clichés (see **65**), and jargon (see **67**):

WORDY: *At this point in time,* those who are *in the process of* writing often overload their sentences with ready-made phrases; this is *indicative of the fact that* wordiness is *indeed* rampant *due to the fact that, quite frankly,* writers fail *to give consideration to* conciseness.

IMPROVED: Because writers do not try to be concise, they often overload their sentences with ready-made phrases.

WORDY: It is our supposition that the safety device in question possesses the capability of being used by the airlines.

IMPROVED: We suppose that airlines can use this safety device.

Avoid long verb phrases *(give consideration to* or *come to a conclusion);* instead use simple, concrete verbs *(consider, conclude).* Avoid unneeded intensives *(indeed, really, quite frankly),* windy openers *(it is, there are),* and stock phrases such as these:

due to the fact that (= because)
in all probability (= probably)
in excess of (= more than)
in many instances (= often)
in a similar fashion (= similarly)
in the neighborhood of (= about)
on a daily basis (= daily)
in the event that (= if)
on the part of (= by *or* among)
a large number of (= many)
a small number of (= few)
during the time that (= while)
small-sized (= small)

EXERCISE 68A _____

Reduce each phrase to one word:

outside of	in the near future
plan ahead	advance forward
can possibly	future plans
recur again	possible likelihood
question as to whether	visible to the eye
rectangular in shape	disappear from view
quite exact	red in color
cease and desist	absolutely essential
past history	sufficient enough
contain within	most unique
as of now	complete monopoly
seldom ever	blend together with
for a period of	rules and regulations

Replace each of these phrases with a single verb:

conduct an investigation	have a necessity for
undertake the removal of	take a measurement
result in damage to	place a call to

68a Eliminate meaningless intensives.

We tend to fill our speech with words such as *very,*
certainly, quite, really, and *simply.* But in writing, we should

eliminate most of these words because they are vague, insincere, or unnecessary. Clear thoughts do not usually need modifiers such as *very (clear), quite (clear),* or *really (clear).* So too it is best to avoid imprecise, extravagant modifiers like *fabulous, fantastic, terribly, awfully.*

68b Eliminate obvious repetition and redundancy.

Other forms of wordiness include obvious repetition, redundancy (expressing the same idea in different ways, as in *cease and desist, basic essentials,* or *the reason is because),* and unnecessary negatives *(not unnecessary).* See the Glossary of Usage (**69**) for some common redundant and round about expressions and **49b** for repetition in sentences.

OBVIOUS REPETITION:	When any two stories are compared, one must consider many aspects. Some of these aspects are readily discernible. These aspects can, in fact, be similarities or differences.
IMPROVED:	When comparing two stories, one must consider both similarities and differences.
REDUNDANT:	Throughout the entire story, Young Goodman Brown is tempted by the devil.
IMPROVED:	Throughout the story, Young Goodman Brown is tempted by the devil.
NEEDLESS NEGATIVES:	It is not surprising that Wyatt's autobiography is not unexciting to read.
IMPROVED:	As expected, Wyatt's autobiography is exciting.

EXERCISE 68B _____

A. Improve the following sentences by eliminating unnecessary words. Reword the sentences, if necessary.

1. It is the unemployment situation which needs attention at the present time.
2. One reason why Tom was so successful was because Tom was smart.
3. Though close to the point of death, my uncle remembered back to his youth in the city of Brooklyn.
4. Can we not cooperate together, even though it is true that we are few in number and that the final outcome is not encouraging?
5. The letter was written by someone whose name must of necessity remain absolutely anonymous.
6. It is worth noting the fact that the feast of Corpus Christi was established as such by the Catholic Church in 1264.
7. The dean is currently in the process of evaluating the frank, candid responses to the faculty questionnaire.
8. There is truth to the contention that the causes of the Civil War were in a very real sense economic.
9. This particular device is hexagonal in shape.
10. Sports are certainly an important, vital part of today's contemporary lifestyle.

B. Explain the redundancy in the following and reduce it:

1. present incumbent
2. personal friendship
3. free gift
4. advance planning
5. past experience

69

Glossary of Usage

This glossary discusses words that are commonly confused and usages that appear frequently, especially in
speech, but are disapproved by many dictionaries and

books on style. Look over the entries, noting any usages with which you are unfamiliar; and refer to this glossary or to a good college dictionary whenever you are unsure of the way you are using a particular word. For a discussion of the varieties of writing referred to in this glossary, see **57**.

a, an   Use *a* before a consonant sound, *an* before a vowel sound: *a* university, *a* horror; *an* uncle, *an* hour.

absolutely   Often meaningless intensifier (*absolutely* the finest cook); redundant with words such as *complete* and *perfect*.

accept, except   See *except, accept*.

adapted, adopted   *Adapted* means "changed"; *adopted* means "accepted." After the mayor **adopted** the housing rule, it was **adapted** to suit local needs.

administrate   Use *administer*.

adverse, averse   *Adverse* means "opposite" or "unfavorable": *adverse* criticism, *adverse* winds. *Averse* means "reluctant" or "disliking": He is *averse* to manual labor.

affect, effect   *Affect* is usually a verb; *effect* is usually a noun. As a verb, *effect* means "bring about":

His injury did not **affect** his performance.
The protest had little **effect**.
The new chairman **effected** several changes.

afflict, inflict   *Afflict* typically takes *with* and an animate object: He was *afflicted with* measles. *Inflict* takes an inanimate object: The judge *inflicted* the maximum penalty.

again, back   Unnecessary after words meaning *again* or *back*, such as *refer*, *revert*, and *resume*.

In reaching its decision, the court **referred** [not *referred back*] to a 1948 Supreme Court ruling.

ahold   Use *get hold*: Dan tried to *get hold* [not *ahold*] of himself.

ain't Most writers avoid this colloquial contraction.

all ready, already *All ready* means "fully prepared" or that everyone or everything is ready: The letters were *all ready* to be signed. *Already* is an adverb meaning "at or before this time": The book has *already* sold a million copies.

all right *Alright* is not a standard spelling.

all the farther Use *as far as:* This is *as far as* we can go.

allude A verb meaning "mention indirectly": He often *alludes* to Shakespeare. Do not confuse it with *refer*, "to mention directly." Also do not confuse the noun *allusion* with *illusion*, a false perception or impression.

a lot Two words; do not spell as one.

alternate(ly), alternative(ly) As an adjective, *alternate* means "by turns, first one and then the other": *alternately* hot and cold weather. *Alternative* means "another choice," such as an *alternative* course of action.

altogether, all together *Altogether* is an adverb meaning "completely": *all together* is an adjective phrase meaning "in a group":

> The hikers were **all together** at the campsite.
> They were **altogether** unprepared for the storm.

alumnus, alumna, alumni A male graduate is an *alumnus*, a female graduate an *alumna; alumni* is the plural for both sexes (although *alumnae* is sometimes still used for female graduates).

among, between Use *among* with more than two, *between* with two. But you may also use *between* with more than two items to show individual relationships: The differences *between* inexpensive French, Spanish, and California wines are less obvious than the differences *between* inexpensive and expensive wines from any one country.

amoral, immoral　The first means irrelevant to morality whereas *immoral* means contrary to moral standards.

amount, number　Use *number* for things that can be counted, *amount* for quantities of things that cannot be counted:

> A large **number** of books have been stolen.
> The old furnace wasted a large **amount** of fuel.

analyzation　Use *analysis*.

and etc.　See *etc.*

anticipate　Use *expect* when you mean "look forward": The patient *expected* [not *anticipated*] an encouraging prognosis.

anyone, any one　*Anyone* means "any person"; *any one* refers to a single person or thing from a group:

> **Anyone** can learn to spell better.
> Choose **any one** point of view and stick with it.

anyway, any way　Use *anyway* to mean "in any case" or "nevertheless," *any way* to mean "any course" or "any direction." To mean "in any manner," use either one.

> We played well but lost **anyway.**
> The traffic will be heavy **any way** you go at that hour.
> Do it **any way** [or **anyway**] you choose.

Anyways is nonstandard.

appraise, apprise　*Appraise* means to set a value, as on real estate; *apprise* means to notify, tell, or inform: The attorney was *apprised* [not *appraised*] of the case.

apprehend, comprehend　*Apprehend* means to catch the meaning of something, whereas *comprehend* means to understand it fully.

as　Often ambiguous when used to mean *since, when,* or *because:* She forgot her lines *because* [not *as*] she was nervous. *As* is often unnecessary: He was voted [as] the most likely to succeed. Do not use *as* to mean "whether" or "that": I can't say *that* [not *as*] I understand. See also *like as*.

as regards   See *concerning*.

awhile, a while   *Awhile* is an adverb; *a while* is a noun: wait *awhile*; wait for *a while*.

bad, badly   Use *bad* as an adjective, *badly* as an adverb:

> I wanted a drink so **badly** that I was ready to do almost anything.
> It was **bad**. I feel **bad**. He looks **bad**.

basically   Like *essentially* and *ultimately*, *basically* is overused and often adds little emphasis: [*Basically,*] the problem is serious.

being   Often a weak connective in sentences: He writes well, being the son of a novelist. Instead of *being that* or *being as*, use *because* or *since*: He writes well *because* [not *being that*] he is the son of a novelist.

beside, besides   *Beside* means "at the side of"; *besides* means "in addition to"; either may be used to mean "except":

> The map lay **beside** the lamp.
> **Besides** her regular job, she plays bass in a blues band.
> No one **beside** [or **besides**] you had a key.

better   Avoid as a synonym for *more*: *More* [not *Better*] than half of the workers were present.

between   See *among, between*.

both   Redundant with words such as *agree* or *together*: We [both] agreed to stop bickering.

but   Avoid redundant combinations such as *but however* or *but nevertheless*. Use *that* rather than *but that* or *but what* in sentences such as "I do not doubt *that* [not *but that*] he will succeed.

can, may In strict usage, *can* expresses ability; *may* expresses permission:

> **May** I go fishing?
> Yes, if you **can** find your rod.

cannot Spell as one word unless you wish to place especially heavy emphasis on the *not*.

can't hardly, can't scarcely Avoid these double negatives; use *can hardly* or *can scarcely*.

case, line Both are often deadwood:

> In [the case of] English, single adjectives usually
>   precede nouns.
> I would like to buy [something in the line of] a mystery.

center around *Center on* is more exact, but either phrase is usually roundabout and imprecise:

> The story **concerns** [not *centers around*] a jewel thief.

cf. The abbreviation of the Latin *confer* ("compare"). Except in notes, *compare* is preferable.

close to Not a substitute for *nearly* or *almost:* Nearly [not *close to*] fifty guests are coming.

complement, compliment *Complement* means "to complete"; *compliment* means "to praise."

comprise, compose *Comprise* means "to consist of" or "to include"; *compose* means "constitute" or "make up the parts of":

> Thirteen chapters **compose** [or **constitute**] the book.
> The book **comprises** thirteen chapters.

considerable, considerably Avoid using the adjective *considerable* as an adverb:

> The injury to the first-string center hurt the team
>   **considerably** [not *considerable*].

consist in, consist of *Consist* means "to reside in" or "in here": Virtue *consists* in doing good. *Consist of* means "to be composed of": The book *consists* of seven chapters.

continual, continuous *Continual* means "frequently repeated" and is not the same as *continuous,* "uninterrupted":

Robbery is a **continual** problem in our neighborhood.
Chicago suffered forty-three days of **continuous** sub-
freezing weather.

could of An error for *could have.* See *of.*

council, counsel, consul A council is a governing body; counsel is advice or the act of giving advice; a consul is a government official in a foreign country:

The town **council** met last night.
Mr. Adamson **counseled** me to choose a career other
than medicine.
The **consul** was expelled from the country.

couple *Couple* takes a plural verb when it refers to people, as does *pair:* The couple *are* [not *is*] in Bermuda.

credible, credulous, creditable All have to do with belief, but they are not interchangeable. *Credible* means "believable"; *credulous* means "naive"; *creditable* means "deserving praise."

data Plural for the rarely used singular *datum.* *Data* is best used as a plural.

different *Different from* is standard usage: Frye's approach to the poem is *different from* [not *than*] Ellman's approach. Watch for needless use of *different:* I read three [different] novels last winter. Use *various* to indicate diversity unless you wish to stress unlikeness. *Differ from* indicates dissimilarity (Boys *differ from* girls); *differ with* indicates disagreement (She *differed with* his view of the film).

disinterested, uninterested *Disinterested* means "impartial"; *uninterested* means "not interested."

done Nonstandard as a substitute for *did:* They *did* [not *done*] the work already.

due to the fact that Use *because.*

each and every   Use one word or the other.

economic, economical   *Economic* usually concerns economics *(economic policy)*, whereas *economical* always means "thrifty."

effect   See *affect, effect.*

e.g.   The abbreviation for the Latin *exempli gratia* ("for example"). Use *for example*.

elicit, illicit   *Elicit* is a verb meaning "draw forth": The article *elicited* an angry response. *Illicit* is an adjective meaning "unlawful": The police cracked down on *illicit* gambling.

emigrate, immigrate   *Emigrate* means to move out of a country; **immigrate** means to move in. An American who emigrates to England is immigrating from the English standpoint.

eminent, imminent   *Eminent* means "prominent" or "famous"; *imminent* means "upcoming, about to happen":

   An **eminent** economist predicted **imminent** disaster.

enthuse   A colloquial substitute for "be enthusiastic" or "show enthusiasm."

equally as   Just *as* is sufficient: The film was [*equally*] *as* good as the book.

etc.   An abbreviation of the Latin *et cetera* ("and other things"). It is often a lazy or evasive substitute for specifics: Work was delayed by rain, etc. Do not use *and etc.*, in which *and* is redundant.

everyone, every one   See *anyone, any one.*

except, accept   *Except,* meaning "other than," is not a substitute for *but.* Also, do not confuse *except* with *accept,* "to receive" or "to agree."

   The British might have scored a decisive victory, **but** [not
       except] they did not pursue the retreating American army.
   Everyone **except** Aunt Agatha **accepted** the invitation.

expect   Informal when used to mean "suppose" or "think" as in "I expect it will rain." *Suppose, assume, think,* and *believe* are preferable.

factor   A factor helps to produce a given result, so *contributing factor* is redundant. *Factor* is often misused to mean "item" or "point": There are several *points* [not *factors*] in favor of the new proposal.

farther, further   *Farther* usually refers to physical distance, *further* to additional time or degree:
>   We managed to drive **farther** than we expected during the first three days.
>   The economists decided to wait for **further** developments before making a decision.

feature   As a verb, *feature* should not be used to mean "contain" (The magazine *contained* [not *featured*] many recipes) but to mean "give prominence to" (The magazine *featured* an article by Truman Capote).

few, little; fewer, less   *Few* and *fewer* refer to things that can be counted; *little* and *less* to things that cannot be counted: *few* apartments, *little* space; *fewer* calories, *less* food.

finalize   Jargon for *complete*.

flaunt, flout   *Flaunt* means "to display ostentatiously"; *flout* means "to treat with scorn":
>   He made himself unpopular by **flaunting** his large vocabulary.
>   The rebels **flouted** all the campus rules.

flounder, founder   *Flounder* is to struggle awkwardly; *founder* is to sink or collapse:
>   Henrietta **floundered** through high school but came to life in college.
>   Despite heroic efforts by the crew, the ship **foundered.**

former, first; latter, last   Use *former* and *latter* when you refer to one of two items; with three or more items, use *first* and *last.*

good, well   *Good* is an adjective: The air smells *good*. *Well* is usually an adverb: The choir sings *well*. *Well* is also used as an adjective referring to health: I have stayed *well* since I started the new diet.

hardly   See *can't hardly*.

hopefully   Widely used but also widely condemned as a substitute for "I hope" or "it is hoped."

i.e.   The abbreviation for the Latin *id est* ("that is"). Use *that is*.

if and when   Like *when and if*, a wordy and trite phrase. Use one word or the other.

imminent   See *eminent, imminent*.

immunity, impunity   *Immunity*, an exemption, as from a disease, can be confused with *impunity* (freedom from punishment): Journalists are free to express their views with *impunity*.

imply, infer   *Imply* means "to suggest"; *infer* means "to conclude":
> The press secretary **implied** that the President would fire the attorney general.
> From the press secretary's remarks, I **inferred** that the President would fire the attorney general.

inflict, afflict   See *afflict, inflict*.

in regards to   The standard forms are *in regard to* or *as regards*. But *concerning* is usually preferable to either phrase.

inside of   Use just *inside* or *within*.

irregardless   Nonstandard for *regardless*.

its, it's   *Its* is the possessive (belonging to *it*): The company issued *its* report. Compare *his, hers*. *It's* is the contraction for *it is* or *it has*. There is no such word as *its'*.

kind of a   Drop the *a*: That kind of [a] story always amuses young readers.

latter See *former, first; latter, last.* Do not confuse *latter* with *later.*

lay, lie See *lie, lay.*

learn, teach Students learn; instructors teach:

My grandfather **taught** me how to cast a fly.
I **learned** to cast a fly before I was six years old.

leave, let *Leave* means "to depart or go away from"; *let* means "to permit." Do not use *leave* for *let.*

less See *few, little; fewer, less.*

let's us Since *let's* is the contraction for *let us,* do not add a second *us.*

level Often used in wordy phrases: *level an attack* [= *attack*]; *at the literal level* [= *literally*]. "He *levelled* with me" is colloquial.

lie, lay *Lie* means "to rest" or "to recline"; *lay* means "to put or place (something) down." The past of *lie* is *lay;* the past of *lay* is *laid:* She *laid* the book on the table and *lay* down to rest.

like, as In making comparisons, use *like* as a preposition, *as, as if,* or *as though* as a conjunction introducing a dependent clause:

Like Hamlet, he is indecisive.
The lab researcher will examine the slides **as** she always has—slowly and carefully.
After the race, all of the runners looked **as though** they might faint.

Some writers mistakenly go out of their way to avoid using *like:* The hotel looks *similar to* [preferably *like*] the one in Johnstown.

line See *case, line.*

loose, loosen, lose A *loose* screw (adjective); *loosen* a tie (verb); *lose* a bet (verb).

may, can See *can, may.*

may, might When expressing a hypothesis (if you could hear me sing . . .) or a past condition (if you had seen me on the stage . . .), use *might,* not *may:* . . . you *might* [not *may*] have made me a star.

media The plural of *medium.* Compare *criterion, criteria; phenomenon, phenomena.*

moral, morale *Moral* can be an adjective meaning "ethical" (a *moral* action) or a noun referring to the ethical meaning of a story or action (the *moral* of the play). *Morale* is a noun meaning "mental and emotional condition": The *morale* of Richard's army was extremely low.

most Informal as a substitute for *almost,* as in "he comes here *most* every evening."

myself *Myself* can be used as a direct object referring to the subject of the sentence (I hurt *myself*) or as an intensive (I will do the job *myself*). Do not use it as a substitute for *I:* Two of us finished the puzzle: John and *I* [not *myself*].

nohow, nowheres Nonstandard forms. Use *in no way, not at all, nowhere.*

not too, not that Colloquial substitutes for *not very,* as in "I'm *not that* concerned with politics."

number, amount See *amount, number.*

of Do not use *of* for *have* in verb phrases: *could have, would have, might have, must have:* I should *have* (not *of*] attended the meeting.

off of Use just *off:* He would not get *off* [*of*] the subject.

oftentimes Use just *often.*

on account of Use this phrase as a preposition (*on account of* the rain), not as a conjunction (*on account of* it rained). *Because* or *because of* is preferable: *because of* the rain; *because* it rained.

orientate *Orient* is simpler and preferred by many careful writers.

ought Do not use with auxiliaries such as *had* and *did:* Eve wondered if she *ought* [not *hadn't ought*] to leave.

outside of Use just *outside*.

overall Often needless jargon: the [overall] effect.

party Except in law, *party* is a poor substitute for *person:* Would the *person* [not *party*] who requested a change in seating please come to the counter?

percent, percentage Use *percent* with numbers *(ten percent), percentage* without numbers: A high *percentage* [not *percent*] of those responding rated inflation as the chief problem. Do not use *percentage* loosely for *part:* A large *part* [not *percentage*] of the work was done before we arrived.

plenty Informal as an adverb meaning "very": She must be *very* [not *plenty*] rich.

plus *Plus* is technically a preposition meaning "with the addition of," not a conjunction:

> After the game, Bill was tired **and** [not *plus*] his leg hurt.
> The principal **plus** the interest comes to $368.55.

practical, practicable Something *practical* works well in practice; something *practicable* can be put into practice but has not yet shown that it works:

> Conversion to solar energy is **practicable** in many parts of the country, but few systems have so far proved **practical**.

precede, proceed See *proceed, precede*.

predominant, predominate *Predominant* is the adjective (the *predominant* opinion); *predominate* is the verb: For twenty years, conservative opinion *predominated* in the court.

presently   Use *now*.

previous to, prior to   Use *before*.

principal, principle   *Principal* can be an adjective or a noun: the *principal* cause; the *principal* of our school; the *principal* plus the interest charged by the bank. *Principle* is always a noun meaning "basic rule of truth": Although customs vary, the *principles* of good behavior are very much the same in both countries.

proceed, precede   *Proceed* means "to go forward," "to continue"; *precede* means "to go before." *Proceed* is not a good choice if the meaning is simply "go."

quite, rather   See *rather, quite*.

quotation, quote   *Quote* is the verb, *quotation* the noun: an apt *quotation* [not *quote*].

raise, rise   *Raise* takes a direct object *(raise something)*; *rise* does not:

They **raise** the flag every day.
Farmers **rise** early.

rather, quite   Both can weaken the force of a strong modifier: a [quite] huge fireplace. *Rather* often adds no meaning and produces ambiguity: does *rather clear* mean "very clear" or "a little clear"?

real, really   *Real* is the adjective, *really* the adverb: a *real* distinction; *really* late. But *really* is often just an empty word: They [really] worked hard.

reason is because   Redundant. "The reason is *that* [not *because*] he is shy.

refer back   See *again, back*.

relevant   If you call something *relevant* or *irrelevant*, be sure to say *to what* it is relevant or irrelevant.

respectfully, respectively *Respectfully* means "with respect"; *respectively* means "singly in the order given":

They treated the ambassador **respectfully.**
Her three children weighed **respectively** eight, nine, and ten pounds at birth.

rise, raise See *raise, rise.*

sensual, sensuous *Sensual* usually refers to sexual gratification, *sensuous* to the senses generally.

set, sit *Set* takes a direct object (*set* something down); *sit* does not (*sit* down). See p. 85.

shall, will The distinction between these words has largely broken down. See p. 78.

should of An error for *should have.* See *of.*

some In writing, avoid the colloquial use of *some* for *somewhat:* I feel *somewhat* [not *some*] better today.

somewheres Nonstandard for *somewhere.*

stationary, stationery *Stationary* means "fixed in course or position"; *stationery* refers to writing materials.

supposed to, used to Be careful not to drop the *-d* from the end of *supposed* or *used* before *to.*

sure, surely *Sure* as an adverb is colloquial; in writing, use *surely:* We *surely* [not *sure*] enjoyed the concert.

teach, learn See *learn, teach.*

than, then These words are commonly confused:

The balloon rose faster **than** they expected.
Then it drifted out over the lake.

their, there, they're Watch for misspellings: *Their* books are here (possessive adjective); *There* are my glasses (adverb); *They're* coming tonight (contraction of *they are*).

theirselves Nonstandard for *themselves.*

thusly   Error for *thus*.

till, until   Both are acceptable; *til* and *'til* are not.

to, too, two   Spelling errors with these words are common but unnecessary. *To* is a preposition (*to* the fair) or the sign of an infinitive (*to* run). *Too* means either "also" or "excessively." *Two* is a number.

> John, **too,** found the path **to** the top **too** steep.
> It takes **two to** argue.

try and   *Try to* is preferred by many stylists, though *try and* is common.

-type   This suffix should usually be omitted in phrases like *a temperamental-type person*.

unique   *Unique* means "single" or "without equal" and therefore does not need qualification: not *very unique* or *quite unique* but just *unique*.

used to   See *supposed to, used to*.

utilize   Often bureaucratic jargon for *use*, especially with reference to people.

wait on   Use *wait on* to mean "serve" but not as a substitute for *wait for*:

> The army stopped to **wait for** [not *on*] reinforcements.
> She feigned illness and persuaded everyone to **wait on** her.

ways   Use *way* for distance: a long *way* [not *ways*] to go.

where   Avoid using *where* as a substitute for *that:* I read in the paper *that . . .* [not *where . . .*].

whose, who's   Be careful not to confuse the possessive *whose* (*Whose* notes are these?) with *who's*, the contraction for *who is*.

-wise   Avoid this suffix, a common type of jargon: *gardenwise, profitwise*.

your, you're   *Your* is the possessive (*your* copy), *you're* the contraction for *you are*.

7

THE RESEARCH PAPER

The research paper (also called the library paper or term paper) is a documented essay: it contains numbered endnotes or footnotes identifying the books and articles the writer has consulted.

70

Select an interesting, manageable subject.

Research papers too often become long recitations of facts and opinions copied out of library books. The best way to avoid producing anything so unoriginal and to eliminate needless drudgery is to choose a topic you already know something about and want to know more about. Then your research will not only satisfy your curiosity but will also allow you to write with authority about a subject that means something to you. By examining facts, sifting evidence, and comparing opinions, you will be able to arrive at your own conclusions and keep your own contribution at the center of your paper.

If you are free to choose your own subject, do not try to read eveything you can find on sports, nature, art, or whatever general field most interests you. You must focus on one small corner of that field: not sports but the problem of violence in hockey; not nature but the causes of weed pollution in certain lakes; not art but the influence of Cézanne on cubist painting. An arguable topic—one that has at least two sides—or one involving a problem will let you approach the question in an interesting way. Your instructor may propose a general subject, such as "television advertising," and challenge you to develop your own topic. Out of that you might develop these:

> Types of deception used in television commercials
> Sexual stereotyping in television commercials
> Government regulation of television advertising
> How advertisers influence programming

You can save yourself time if you avoid certain predictable kinds of unsuitable topics:

1. Topics too complex or controversial to be handled in anything less than a book: "atheism in the United States"
2. Topics so limited that you can find only a few brief sources: "developing Ektachrome"
3. Topics so new that little has yet been published on them
4. Topics so cut-and-dried that you can do little more than summarize your sources: "the life of Benjamin Franklin"
5. Topics about which you can learn little that is not already known to most people: "cigarettes are harmful"
6. Topics about which you have such strong feelings that you might not be able to evaluate what you read objectively.

EXERCISE 70 _____

*A. Decide which of the following topics would be suitable for
a documented paper of eight to ten pages. Mark these with
E. Mark with X those that would be unsuitable.*

1. Why do we laugh at the Marx Brothers?
2. Abortion is immoral.
3. Pollution of our resources is one of the chief problems facing America today.
4. Fairy tales are not harmful to children.
5. Five arguments against capital punishment.
6. Baseball has a long and colorful history.
7. Transcendental Meditation: The solution for our anxious age.
8. Democracy works better than communism.
9. Women make better drivers than men.
10. Commercial aviation disasters are often the result of pilot error.
11. Church and state must remain separate.
12. Franklin D. Roosevelt could have prevented war with Japan.
13. Jazz as a distinctive American art form.
14. Shakespeare's boyhood in Stratford-upon-Avon.
15. Television in the courtroom.
16. Who really killed John F. Kennedy?
17. The rise of Adolf Hitler.
18. There IS intelligent life on other planets!
19. Job opportunities for respiratory therapists.
20. Spin-offs from the space program in our daily lives.

B. Focus the following topics more sharply.

1. The metric system
2. Television news
3. Science fiction
4. Criminal justice
5. Suicide
6. Country music
7. Alcoholism
8. Photography
9. Energy sources
10. Noise pollution

71

Prepare a working bibliography.

Before you settle on a topic, be sure that you can find enough material to develop a paper on that topic. Begin to build a working bibliography, a list of the books, articles, reviews, reports, and other materials you will investigate. For each source you locate, write the author's name, the title, and other necessary information (along with the library call number) on a 3″ x 5″ card. Use the bibliographical form explained in **77**. If you have complete and correct information, you will save time later when you type the notes and bibliography.

Bibliography Card: Book

Mandell, Richard D.
The <u>Nazi</u> <u>Olympics</u>
New York: Macmillan, 1971

GV
722
1936
.M3

Bibliography Card: Periodical

Brasher, Chris
"The Last Olympics?"
The Illustrated London News,
July 1980, pp. 32-33
AP4
.I449

Since it often lists other sources, an encyclopedia article often provides a good working bibliography. Or you can start with the subject index of your library's card catalog. In addition to the card catalog, periodical indexes, and reference books listed below, the reference librarian may suggest government documents, looseleaf services, pamphlets, and other specially classified material.

The card catalog. This index to the library's collection is composed of author, title, and subject cards arranged alphabetically. Use the subject cards, which cite the heading under which books are catalogued, to locate material in the library's circulating collection.

Library of Congress Catalog Card

```
                  1  OLYMPIC GAMES
  2
      GV
      612     3  Gilbert, Doug, 1938-
      .6         4  The miracle machine / Doug Gilbert. — New York : Coward,
     .G54          McCann & Geoghegan, c1979.
                5  314 p., ₁10₁ leaves of plates : ill. ; 24 cm.
                6  Includes index.
                   ISBN 0-698-10952-X : $10.95


                7  1. Sports—Germany, East.  2. Sports and state—Germany, East.  3. Physi-
                   cal education and training—Germany, East.  4. Olympic Games, Montréal,
                   Québec, 1976.   I. Title.
                8  GV612.6.G54  1980      9  796.4'8'09431     10  79-13603
                                                                      MARC

              Library of Congress              79
```

1. Subject heading. This is typed at the top of the card in capitals. Author cards have no heading. Title cards have the title typed in this position.
2. Call number used by library.
3. Author's name
4. Title, place of publication, publisher, and date of publication
5. Number of pages, note on illustrations, size
6. Note on contents, here showing that book contains an index
7. Subject headings suggested by Library of Congress
8. Library of Congress call number
9. Dewey Decimal System call number
10. Library of Congress order number of this card

Guide to Books in Print (1957–   ), *Essay and General Literature Index* (1934–   ), *Book Review Digest* (1905–   ), and *The Library of Congress Catalog of Books: Subjects* (1950–   ) can provide you with titles of works that are not in your library's collection or that you overlooked in the card catalog.

Periodical Indexes. Since some of the most current information is available in magazine and journal articles, the various indexes to periodical literature are essential in almost every library research project. Just as the card catalog is the key to books, so the periodical guides are the keys to articles. Do not limit yourself to the best-known and most general of these indexes, the *Readers' Guide to Periodical Literature*.

General indexes:

> *Humanities Index* (1974–   ); formerly the *Social Sciences and Humanities Index* (1965–73) and the *International Index* (1907–65).
> *New York Times Index* (1913–   ).
> *Poole's Index to Periodical Literature* (1802–1906).
> *Readers' Guide to Periodical Literature* (1900–   ).
> *Social Sciences Index* (1974–   ); formerly the *Social Sciences and Humanities Index* (1965–73) and the *International Index* (1907–65).

Specialized indexes:

> *Applied Science and Technology Index* (1958–   ).
> *Art Index* (1929–   ).
> *Biography Index* (1946–   ).
> *Biological and Agricultural Index* (1964–   ).
> *Business Periodicals Index* (1958–   ).
> *Education Index* (1929–   ).
> *Index to Legal Periodicals* (1908–   ).
> *MLA International Bibliography* [literature, language] (1921–   ).
> *Music Index* (1949–   ).
> *Public Affairs Information Service Bulletin* (1915–   ).
> See also the various abstracts: *Abstracts of English Studies,* 1958– ; *Biological Abstracts,* 1927– ; *Chemical Abstracts,* 1907– ; *Psychological Abstracts,* 1927–, etc.

Reference books. Also cited in the card catalog are the library's encyclopedias, dictionaries, atlases, and many other basic reference tools. An excellent descriptive guide to these sources is Eugene P. Sheehy's *Guide to Reference Books* (9th ed., 1976). Here are a few:

General dictionaries:

> *The Oxford English Dictionary.* 13 vols.
>   1933 + supplements.
> *The Random House Dictionary of the English Language.* 1967.
> *Webster's Third New International Dictionary.* 1972.

General encyclopedias:

> *Chambers's Encyclopedia.* 15 vols. 1973.
> *Encyclopedia Americana.* 30 vols. 1978.
> *The New Encyclopaedia Britannica.* 30 vols. 1979.

Special encyclopedias:

> *Encyclopedia of Education.* 10 vols. 1971.
> *Encyclopedia of Philosophy.* 8 vols. 1967.
> *Encyclopedia of World Art.* 15 vols. 1959-68.
> *International Encyclopedia of the Social Sciences.* 17 vols. 1968.
> Langer, William L. *An Encyclopedia of World History.*
>   5th ed. 1972.
> *McGraw-Hill Encyclopedia of Science and Technology.* 15 vols.
>   4th ed. 1977.
> *The New Catholic Encyclopedia.* 15 vols. 1967.
> *Van Nostrand's Scientific Encyclopedia.* 5th ed. 1976.

Other:

> *Britannica Book of the Year* (1938–   ).
> *Current Biography* (1940–   ).
> *Dictionary of American Biography.* 10 vols. 1974.
> *Dictionary of National Biography* (British). 22 vols. 1882-1953.
> *Facts on File* (1940–   ).
> Spiller, Robert E., et al. *Literary History of the United States.*
>   4th ed., rev. 1974.
> *Statistical Abstract of the United States* (1878–   ).

The Times Atlas of the World. 1980.
Ward, A. W., and A. R. Waller, eds. *Cambridge History of English Literature.* 15 vols. 1907–33.
World Almanac and Book of Facts (1868–).

EXERCISE 71 _____

Compile a bibliography of at least ten sources (both books and articles) on a topic that interests you. Use at least four of the following reference works. After each entry, cite the title of the work that referred you to that book or article.

1. Card catalog—subject index
2. *Readers' Guide to Periodical Literature*
3. *Essay and General Literature Index*
4. *Social Sciences Index, Humanities Index,* or *Applied Science and Technology Index*
5. Either *Public Affairs Information Service* or *The New York Times Index*
6. One of the general or specialized encyclopedias listed above (under "Reference Books")

72

Evaluate your sources of information.

Analyzing the material you find is always important. Not everything in print is reliable, and some sources carry more weight than others. A short article in a popular magazine will probably not be as authoritative as a book or journal article, but even a book may represent just one person's thinking about a subject. Always be careful to distinguish between facts and opinions. As you examine any source ask yourself these questions:

1. Is the writer a recognized authority on the subject, one whose work is cited by other writers?

2. Does the work seem to be biased? Does the author give sufficient attention to other points of view?
3. Is the work recent enough to provide up-to-date information?

Primary and secondary sources. Primary sources are the actual texts of reports, novels, and documents as well as interviews, recordings, and other original material. Secondary sources are the critical and historical accounts based on primary materials. For a paper on the space shuttle, for example, your primary sources might include reports from NASA as well as interviews with or letters from space officials. For a paper on educational television for children, reports of experiments in childhood learning as well as the programs themselves would be your primary sources. Clearly, observing the programs would be essential to understanding the topic; you would not wish to get most of your information second-hand. Nor could you fully understand and evaluate what critics say about country music unless you had first attended concerts or listened to recordings (your primary source). Whatever your topic, locate and use as many primary sources as possible.

Secondary sources may help you find additional primary sources, and they can point out ways of interpreting those sources. By examining a number of secondary sources, you can determine which ones offer the most convincing interpretation of the facts. Since you will probably not have time to read all the available secondary sources in their entirety, check their indexes and tables of contents and skim chapters you think might help you. Also check each secondary source for a bibliography that might direct you to other sources.

EXERCISE 72 _____

What cautions would you have to take in using the following sources for papers on the subjects cited? Would any of the sources be appropriate?

1. *Gun control:* a 1981 pamphlet by the National Rifle Association
2. *Auto safety:* Ralph Nader's 1965 book, *Unsafe at Any Speed*
3. *I.Q. Tests:* a 1947 article in the *Harvard Educational Review*
4. *Coal as an Energy Source:* a 1980 article in *Reader's Digest*
5. *Themes in Country Music:* a 1974 article in *Harper's Magazine*
6. *Sex education in schools:* a 1981 article in *McCall's* magazine
7. *United Nations and the third world:* a 1981 UNESCO report
8. *Future of the Olympics:* 1980 pamphlet by the U.S. Olympic Committee
9. *Portrayal of Blacks on TV:* 1981 *New York Times* article
10. *Spin-offs from the space program in our daily lives:* a 1963 NASA report

73

Prepare a preliminary thesis statement and working outline.

As early as possible in your research, formulate a tentative statement of the main point you expect to make in your paper (see **4**). You will need to change this preliminary thesis statement if further research gives you a new perspective, but writing down the thesis early will help you concentrate your note-taking on material that supports, contradicts, or in some other way bears directly on your main point.

Next, consider the subpoints you will need to support your thesis, and arrange these into a rough outline (see **5**). For example, if you are working on the future of the Olympic movement, your preliminary thesis and rough (working) outline might look like this:

Thesis: The Olympic Games are fated to die unless reforms are made.

   I. Ancient ideals need to be restored.
  II. Political rivalries should be abolished.
 III. Commercial trends should be curbed.

As you develop the topic further, you will find ways to develop each of the subtopics: what was the original Greek idea, and how do the modern Games differ? How have politics and greed entered into the Games? How can specific solutions be found? You may also find new subtopics or discover that you have to change some of the ones you have. You might also find that you need to sharpen your thesis statement. For example, you could specify how changes in the Olympics would solve the recent problems:

> The Olympics can return to the ideals of peace, fellowship, and sportsmanship by avoiding political nationalism and commercial exploitation.

Think of your working outline as a flexible guide in your search for pertinent information. If you code your note cards to the sections of your rough outline, you will be able to see if you are finding enough information for each section and if you are turning up useful information that calls for changes in your outline.

EXERCISE 73 _____

Suggest a thesis statement and a working outline of at least three main parts for three of the following topics.

1. Altering college admissions standards for disadvantaged applicants
2. The Lamaze method of childbirth
3. Training for mentally retarded children
4. I.Q. tests as a measure of one's potential
5. The effect of television on the popularity of football

6. The problem of illegal aliens
7. How secure is Social Security?
8. Hollywood's treatment of the American Indian
9. Governmental help for the railroads
10. The effect of evangelism on presidential politics

74

Take thorough, accurate notes on your sources.

Your aim in taking notes is to record accurately and concisely the important facts from your sources. A 4" × 6" note card will provide room for substantial notes as well as for a subject heading and a key to the corresponding bibliography card. Use one card for each idea you record so that you can later sort the cards as you refine your organization. Each card should contain the following information:

1. *Subject.* In a few words at the top of the card, identify the information the card contains.
2. *Source.* List the author's name or an abbreviated title. Or you might number your bibliography cards and use the appropriate number to identify each note card.
3. *Page number.* If a quotation runs from one page to the next, use a slash line to indicate the page break. You may later want to use just part of the quotation.

The note itself may be a quotation, a paraphrase (rewording) of the original material, or a summary.

Quotation. Although most note-taking should not be word-for-word copying, quote your source directly whenever you think you might want to give your

Note Card

> Brasher, p. 32   effect of TV
>
> Television has had a major effect on the modern Olympics. TV turns the games into big commercial ventures, adding pressure for athletes. Drug abuse began in 1960 Rome Games, when live TV coverage in Europe began. "By 1968 satellites were able to beam live television into every country in the world and the audience was incalculable. What a prize for a manufacturer if he could get his product on to the feet of a man whom the world was going to see win an Olympic gold medal."

reader the exact wording of your source. When quoting, follow these guidelines:

1. On your note card, place quotation marks around all direct quotations to remind yourself that the wording is not yours. This distinction is essential.
2. Copy your source exactly, including punctuation marks. If an error appears in the original, put [*sic*], meaning "this is the way I found it," in your notes.
3. Use an ellipsis mark of three spaced periods (. . .) to indicate omitted material within a direct quotation; avoid ellipses before quotations of only parts of sentences (see **36a** and the sample note card above).
4. Use square brackets for your own insertions in a quotation: "Last year [1981] Americans spent more than $3 billion on pet foods alone."

Paraphrase (rewording). Direct quotation is not the only way to record the material you will use. You can reword passages from your sources, being careful to capture the ideas of an author without copying his or her sentence structure or word choice. You do not have to change every word in your source; simply write in your own style, and note the exact location of the ideas you are rephrasing. When your source contains phrases that you think deserve direct quotation, you can combine paraphrase and quotation, as shown in the sample note card on p. 230, but be sure to distinguish carefully between your words and those of your source.

Note: Plagiarism, borrowing others' ideas and words without giving proper credit, is a serious offense. When you put your name on any piece of writing, the reader assumes that you are responsible for the information, ideas, wording, and organization and that you will acknowledge the source of any fact or idea that is not your own. Unintentional plagiarism can result from sloppy note-taking, from not distinguishing between your own thoughts and words and those of your sources. Enclose all directly quoted material in quotation marks. You must acknowledge all ideas taken from your sources—not just direct quotations.

Summary. Instead of copying or carefully paraphrasing background information or other material that you will not need to present in detail, write a brief summary. Record the important facts; skip unimportant details. Early in your note-taking, you may want to take summary notes on sources you expect to investigate more carefully later. If you make photocopies of important sources, summary notes can help you arrange ideas without rereading everything in your photocopies.

Note Card: Quotation (original material)

> cultural heredity
>
> "Human beings owe their biological supremacy
> to the possession of a form of inheritance quite
> unlike that of other animals : exogenetic or
> exosomatic heredity. In this form of heredity,
> information is transmitted from one gener-
> ation to the next through non-genetic channels--
> by word of mouth, by example, and by other
> forms of indoctrination; in general, by the
> entire apparatus of culture."
> P.B. Medawar, "Unnatural Science, <u>The</u> <u>New</u> <u>York</u>
> <u>Review</u>, 3 Feb. 1977, p. 14.

Note Card A (unacceptable)

> cultural heredity
>
> The biological supremacy of human beings
> is due to their unique form of inheritance
> called exogenetic or exosomatic (p.14). Such
> heredity is transmitted from one generation
> to the next through non-genetic, cultural channels,
> such as example and word of mouth.
> P.B. Medawar, "Unnatural Science" <u>The</u> <u>New</u>
> <u>York</u> <u>Review</u>, 3 Feb. 1977, p. 14.

This note is unacceptable because the first sentence is copied closely without acknowledgment; the second sentence closely follows the original wording. It will be difficult to determine later if these notes are quoted or paraphrased.

Note Card B (unacceptable)

cultural heredity

Human beings have a biological supremacy due to a type of inheritance unlike that of other animals: exogenetic or exosomatic heredity. This means that one generation transmits heredity information to another generation through cultural, non-genetic channels.

P.B. Medawar, "Unnatural Science" The New York Review, 3 Feb. 1977, p. 14.

This note is unacceptable because it will be unclear later whether the first sentence is quoted directly or not and whether the second is a paraphrase or summary from material on a different page.

Note Card C (acceptable)

> cultural heredity
>
> according to P.B. Medawar in _The New York Review_, man is superior to other animals because he possesses "exogenetic or exosomatic heredity" (p. 14). This means that one generation transmits heredity to another generation through such non-genetic means as word of mouth, example, and other instruction; in short, says Medawar, through culture. (p. 14)

This note is acceptable because no plagiarism will result from such a note; the source is clearly introduced and acknowledged while the expert's key terms are assimilated into the student's own writing.

Note Card: Paraphrase with Quotation

> Lucas, p. 21
>
> Olympic rebirth
>
> When it was revived in 1896, the Olympic movement was intended to express Baron Pierre de Coubertin's grandiose, romantic dream of recapturing "a Greek intensity, a medieval chivalric idealism, and a modern sense of pride and passion."

Note Card: Summary

Lucas, p. 21   Olympic rebirth

The modern Olympic movement began
in 1896 with Coubertin's dream of re-
capturing certain Greek, medieval, and
modern ideals.

As you read and take notes, consider possible subtopics which will complete the ideas in your rough
outline (see **73**). These subtopics will help guide your
reading and note-taking, and your reading will provide
ideas for more subtopics. You will then be organizing
the paper as you prepare to write it. If you are investi-
gating ways to restore the tarnished image of the
Olympic Games, you might develop these subtopics:

> Flags and national anthems
> Drugs and steroids
> A permanent site
> Presentation costs
> Security costs
> National scorekeeping

The order of the subtopics, as well as the subtopics
themselves, will doubtless change as you find material
and as your ideas develop.

EXERCISE 74 _____

Read the following selections (documentation below), then read the students' paraphrased versions. Revise the student paragraphs, adding whatever is needed to avoid plagiarism.

ORIGINAL: An increasing number of public colleges and universities are adopting enrollment restrictions to defend their thinly stretched budgets against the pressure of record numbers of students.

In some cases the pressure for limiting enrollment comes from faculty members who feel they are being asked to teach bigger classes but are not being given bigger salaries.

Colleges and universities have been encouraged to limit their growth rather than expand their capacity not only because of a current shortage of financial support but also because of population projections that indicate a downturn in enrollments within a few years.

The immediate cause of the push to cut back admissions is this fall's generally unexpected upsurge in enrollment at many public institutions. A shortage of attractive job prospects apparently has encouraged more people to go to college and stay there longer.[1]

STUDENT: There has been some debate on campus recently over whether the state universities should put a cap on enrollment. But the problem is not just regional. Nationwide, an increasing number of public colleges and universities are adopting enrollment restrictions. Several reasons have been put forth: faculty rebellion at teaching more students with no increase in pay; a current shortage of financial support; fear of overexpanding in the face of an expected drop in population; and this fall's generally unexpected upsurge in enrollment.

ORIGINAL: The secularization of sport, which began as soon as athletics were pressed into the cause of patriotism and character building, became complete only when sport became an object of mass consumption. The first stage in this process was the establishment of big-time athletics in

[1] Jack Magarrell, "They're Putting Lids on Enrollments," *The Chronicle of Higher Education,* 3 November 1975, p. 1.

the university and their spread from the Ivy League to the large public and private schools, thence downward into the high schools. The bureaucratization of the business career, which placed unprecedented emphasis on competition and the will to win, stimulated the growth of sports in another way. It made the acquisition of educational credentials essential to a business or professional career and thus created in large numbers a new kind of student, utterly indifferent to higher learning but forced to undergo it for purely economic reasons. Large-scale athletic programs helped colleges to attract such students, in competitive bidding for enrollments, and to entertain them once they enrolled.[2]

STUDENT: Sports have become a major industry due in large part to what has happened to athletics in universities. First, athletics were seen as serving the causes of patriotism and character building. Big-time sports, which helped colleges attract students, in competitive bidding for enrollments, and to entertain them once they enrolled spread from the Ivy League to colleges elsewhere and then to the high schools. At the same time the business world, with its emphasis on competition, advanced the state of big-time sports by making the acquisition of educational credentials essential to a business or professional career. As a result, many students began to attend college for economic reasons rather than to pursue learning; and sports were essential in keeping them on the campuses.

[2] Christopher Lasch, *The Culture of Narcissism* (New York: Norton, 1978), pp. 119-20.

75

Organize, write, and revise the rough draft.

If you revise your rough outline as you collect information, you should be nearly ready to write your rough draft by the time you finish taking notes. But first review and refine the organization. Start with your thesis statement: does it clearly express what you now see as the central, unifying idea of the paper? (See **4**.) If, for example, your initial thesis were "The Olympic Games are fated to die unless reforms are made," your research may lead you to a more limited, precisely focused thesis:

> The 1984 Olympics will only succeed if athletes, not nations, compete in a spirit of fellowship and sportsmanship.

A sentence outline (see **6**) can be especially useful at this point. Write a sentence stating each of the main ideas supporting your thesis. Then complete the outline with sentences that represent the subdivisions of your main points. You will be able to see how well the parts of your paper fit together, and you may be able to use many of the sentences as topic sentences for your main subsections. In its final form, the outline could serve as a guide for the reader to the contents of the paper. See the sample outline on pages 259 and 261.

Handling source material. Identify your sources so that readers can make their own judgment about their content and reliability. Make sure that material from your sources supports the points you wish to make and that your own voice is not drowned out by excessive quotations. If all the quoted and paraphrased passages were to be removed from the paper, it should still make sense. These guidelines will help you achieve that goal:

1. Write a topic sentence in your own words for each of your main paragraphs. Even if you later incorporate a quotation into a topic sentence or drop the topic sentence altogether, writing it in your own words will help you make sure that the paragraph expresses your thought. (See **9.**)
2. Use direct quotations only to emphasize significant points or to show your reader how your source expressed a key idea.
3. Avoid long paragraphs of quotations.
4. Make short quotations part of your own sentences: Frances FitzGerald says that history textbooks have changed so much that "many an adult would find them unrecognizable."[1]
5. Introduce quoted and paraphrased material so that your reader will know whose work you are citing: As B. F. Skinner said, "The goal of science is the destruction of mystery."[2]
6. After each paraphrase or quotation, place in parentheses an abbreviated reference to the source and the page number. You can add full footnotes in your final draft.

Revising the rough draft.   You will probably need to revise your paper several times to make it read smoothly and say exactly what you want it to say. Check especially to see that your paragraphs are unified and sufficiently developed (see **10** and **11**) and that you have supplied transitions to guide your reader through the paper (see **12**).

Before typing your final draft, make sure that it is free of errors (spelling, mechanics, grammar, punctuation) and that its sentences are logical and its diction clear. Compare the final draft with your outline to make sure that they are consistent. (If not, decide which needs to be changed.) Be sure to transcribe the notes correctly from your bibliography cards according to the format in **76.** Type from your bibliography cards a bibliography of those materials you have cited in the paper. Eliminate sources you have not used, but include each source which appears in your annotation. Arrange the cards in alphabetical order by author (or title if there is no author), and type one continuous list according to the format outlined in **77**.

76

Use endnotes to document source material.

Annotation can take the form of endnotes or footnotes. Most college papers, except formal theses and dissertations, list the annotation as endnotes on a separate page following the body of the paper. This form of noting is simpler to handle and has become more widely accepted than footnotes, but it is best to check with your instructor about which form to follow.

Annotation has two important functions: to give credit to the sources you have consulted and to enable your readers to look up the original material. Documenting by using numbered notes also protects you against possible plagiarism (see **74**); it distinguishes your thoughts and words from those you have taken from other sources. The form for endnotes and footnotes (or other systems of documenting sources) is usually set by the publishers of the leading journals in each field: those for chemistry by the American Chemical Society, those for biology by the American Institute of Biological Sciences, and so on. In the humanities, the most common authority is the *MLA Handbook for Writers of Research Papers, Theses, and Dissertations* (New York: Modern Language Association, 1977). That style is followed in most respects here and in many guidebooks, including James D. Lester's *Writing Research Papers: A Complete Guide,* 3rd ed. (Glenview, Ill.: Scott, Foresman, 1980). Lester also includes brief instructions for documenting science papers. Because styles differ, check with your instructor before choosing any one style; once you have chosen a style, follow it exactly.

What must you document? Since you have read extensively to prepare your research paper, you may think at first that nearly every sentence in the paper will have to be noted. But your readers should not be overwhelmed by quotes and endnotes; readers are interested in what *you* have to say, in how you have used your reading. Short dictionary definitions and facts that are common knowledge do not require notes, and widely known quotations can be acknowledged in the text: "Those who are ignorant of history," Santayana said, "are condemned to repeat it." *Do* use notes for the following:

1. All directly quoted material:

According to A. J. Liebling, "Newspapers write about other newspapers with circumspection."[1]

[1] The Press (New York: Ballantine Books, 1964), p. 35.

2. All paraphrased and summarized material:

The prestige of a college education, John W. Gardner says, has led many people to assume (falsely) that there is no other type of learning after high school.[2]

[2] Excellence (1961; rpt. New York: Harper, Perennial Library, 1971), p. 103.

3. Facts and data which are not common knowledge:

Dylan Thomas was twenty years old when he left Wales in
1934 for London.[3]

   [3] Paul Ferris, <u>Dylan Thomas</u> (New York: Dial Press,
1977), p. 23.

Sometimes, when several items are taken from the
same source, one note will suffice. If, for example, three
or four sentences in a paragraph give statistics derived
from a single book, use one note at the end of the paragraph to signify that all the data cited in the paragraph
comes from that book. In such a situation, you need not
have a note for each fact. So too in quoting extensively
from a primary source, you can use a note for just the
first reference, as in this example:

   [1] William Shakespeare, <u>King Lear</u>, in <u>The Complete
Works of Shakespeare</u>, ed. David Bevington, 3rd ed.
(Glenview, Ill.: Scott, Foresman, 1980), p. 1211 (V.ii.10).
All subsequent references are to this edition.

In later references to the play, give the act, scene, and
line number in parentheses just after the quotation:

King Lear's dying words are, "Look there, look there!"
(V.iii.316).

You can follow the same procedure when you analyze a
poem or any other primary source.

Endnote Form. Since endnotes are used in most research papers, as in the sample student paper (see

p. 291), we have used the endnote form on the following pages. Follow these guidelines in typing your notes:

1. Number the notes consecutively throughout the paper.
2. Place the note numbers in the text immediately after the quoted or paraphrased material. Use Arabic numerals raised slightly above the line.
3. Place note numbers *after* all punctuation marks (except the dash).
4. Place endnotes in numerical order on a separate page titled *Notes*. Indent the first line 5 spaces, begin with the number raised slightly above the line, and leave a single space between the number and the first word of the note. (Footnotes go at the bottom of the page on which the citation occurs.)
5. Double-space the lines of an endnote (but single-space the lines of a footnote); and double-space between the notes.
6. Cite authors' names in normal order, first names first. If no author or editor is named in your source, begin the note with the title.
7. Note that the form for notes is different from that of bibliography entries (see **77**); use commas, not periods, between author and title.
8. Use italics (underlining) for titles of books and periodicals; use quotation marks for articles, poems, essays, and parts of books.
9. End each note with a period.
10. For later references to the same source, use the abbreviated form shown below. For a second reference to the same page in the source just cited, it is simpler and clearer to repeat the author's last name ("Smith, p. 21.") rather than use *Ibid.* (meaning "the same").
11. Cite the publisher's city without the state unless the state is needed for clarity: Glenview, Ill.: Scott, Foresman, 1982. Use only the first city printed on

the title page and the most recent copyright date.

12. After the complete title of a book, cite the edition used, if it is not the first (for example, 9th ed.), as well as the number of volumes (3 vols.) if there are more than one.

13. In notes (but not in your text) use standard abbreviations:

anon.	anonymous
ch., chs.	chapter(s)
ed., eds.	edition(s), editor(s), or edited by
et al	and others
n.d.	no date (of publication)
no., nos.	number(s) of issues
n.p.	no place (of publication) or no publisher
p., pp.	page(s)
rev.	revised
rpt.	reprinted

trans.	translated by
vol., vols.	volume(s)

Sample Notes: Books

First full reference:

    [1] Peter Conrad, <u>Imagining America</u> (New York: Oxford Univ. Press, 1980), p. 72.

Later reference to the same book:

    [2] Conrad, p. 79.

If two or more works by the same author have been cited, use this form:

    [3] Conrad, <u>Imagining America</u>, p. 85.

If author's name is cited in paper:

    [4] <u>The Life of Byron</u> (Boston: Little, Brown, 1976), pp. 164-66.

Two or three authors:

[5] Walter J. Ong and Wayne Altree, <u>Why Talk</u>? (San Francisco: Chandler and Sharp, 1973), p. 25.

More than three authors:

[6] Albert C. Baugh et al., <u>A Literary History of England</u>, 2nd ed. (New York: Appleton, 1967), p. 797.

Translated and edited books:

[7] Homer, <u>The Iliad</u>, trans. E. V. Rieu (Baltimore: Penguin, 1963), p. 30.

[8] Gerald J. Schiffhorst, ed., <u>The Triumph of Patience</u> (Gainesville, Fla.: Univ. Presses of Florida, 1978), p. 44.

Chapter or part of a book:

[9] Marshall McLuhan, "Hybrid Energy," in his <u>Understanding Media</u> (New York: McGraw-Hill, 1964), p. 48.

Essay in a collection of essays:

[10] John Gregory Dunne, "A Riot on TV," <u>The New Republic</u>, (11 Sept. 1965), rpt. in <u>Mass Media and the Popular Arts</u>, ed. Frederick Rissover and David C. Birch (New York: McGraw-Hill, 1971), p. 148.

For such anthologies, cite the original source and date as well as the collection in which you found the essay reprinted.

More than one volume:

[11] Lucian, "Of Pantomime," The Works of Lucian,

trans. H. W. and F. G. Fowler (Oxford: Clarendon Press,

1905), II, 245. Hereafter cited as Works.

Note that the abbreviation for *page* drops when a volume is cited. When volumes are published in separate years, place the volume number *before* the publication data.

Revised and reprinted editions:

[12] James D. Lester, Writing Research Papers: A

Complete Guide, 3rd ed. (Glenview, Ill.: Scott, Foresman,

1980), p. 50.

[13] F. Scott Fitzgerald, The Great Gatsby (1925; rpt.

New York: Scribner's, 1953), p. 50.

Encyclopedias:

[14] "Lipoprotein," The New Columbia Encyclopedia,

1975 ed.

Volume and page number may be omitted in an alphabetically arranged work.

Sample Notes: Periodicals

Journal:

[15] Donald Monk, "Hemingway's Territorial Imperative,"

Yearbook of English Studies, 8 (1978), 125.

Follow this form when the pages are numbered consecutively throughout the volume; follow the same format for weekly, monthly, or quarterly journals paged consecutively, but cite the week, month, or year.

Later references:

[16] Monk, 128.

Magazine:

[17] "Battle Over Bilingualism," Time, 8 Sept. 1980, p. 64.

Use this form for magazines paged anew in each issue; omit volume number; use p. (page) or pp. (pages).

Later references:

[18] "Battle Over Bilingualism," p. 65.

For a monthly magazine, cite month and year.

[19] Mariana Popp, "Africa--American Style," Ebony, Jan. 1978, pp. 86 and 92.

This citation shows that the quotation extends to a second page separated from the beginning of the article.

Book review:

[20] E. Z. Friedenberg, "Splitting Up," rev. of The Question of Separatism: Quebec and the Struggle Over Sovereignty, by Jane Jacobs, The New York Review of Books, 20 Nov. 1980, p. 35.

Newspaper:

[21] Haynes Johnson, "Let's Have Genuine Debates,"
Miami Herald, 3 Sept. 1980, Sec. A, p. 7, col. 3.

[22] "In Search of Identity," Editorial, _New York
Times_, 27 May 1973, Sec. E, p. 14, col. 1.

Sample Notes: Other Sources

Pamphlet:

[23] U.S. Civil Service Commission, _The Human Equation:
Working in Personnel for the Federal Government_ (Washington, D.C.: GPO, May 1970), p. 43.

Unpublished thesis or dissertation:

[24] Bonnie K. Scott, "James Joyce in His Irish Milieu,"
Diss. Univ. of North Carolina (Chapel Hill) 1974, p. 72.

Interview or letter:

[25] Personal interview with Dr. Susan L. Willis,
Associate Professor, Auburn Univ., Montgomery, Ala.,
2 Feb. 1981.

Film:

[26] Milos Forman, dir., _One Flew Over the Cuckoo's
Nest_, with Jack Nicholson, Fantasy Films, 1975.

Television or radio program:

[27] "Blood Money," _60 Minutes_, CBS-TV, 16 March 1980.

Recording:

²⁸ Elton John, "This Song Has No Title," <u>Goodbye

Yellow Brick Road</u>, MCA 2-10003, 1974.

EXERCISE 76 _____

A. From the following raw materials, construct endnotes as they should appear in a research paper.

1. An article by McCarthy (William) in *PMLA*, vol. 92 for January 1977, entitled, "The Continuity of Milton's Sonnets." The quotation begins on p. 96 and continues on the next page.
2. Quoting from p. 487 of Douglas N. Morgan's *Love: Plato, the Bible and Freud,* published by Prentice-Hall of Englewood Cliffs (New Jersey) in 1964.
3. A reference to an April 1968 article in *Esquire* magazine by Claude Brown, "The Language of Soul," but reprinted on p. 236 in a 1977 anthology, *Exploring Language,* edited by Gary Goshgarian (Boston: Little, Brown).
4. "The Last Laugh," an article in *The New York Review* (8/4/77), pp. 29–33, by George Plimpton, including an opinion on p. 32 that you would like to use.
5. A second reference to Plimpton on the same page as no. 4.
6. A second reference to Claude Brown (no. 3) on the same page as the earlier note.
7. The use of material on pp. 184–85 of *Economic Failure, Alienation, and Extremism* by Michael Aiken, Lewis A. Ferman, and Harold L. Sheppard, published by the University of Michigan Press (Ann Arbor) in 1968.
8. A second reference to the book cited in no. 7., p. 189.
9. The use of p. 114 of an article in *Science* entitled "Science and the New Humanism," by Hudson Hoagland, appearing in vol. 143 for 1964.
10. Douglass B. Feaver's article in the *Washington Post,* "Solutions to Transportation Problems Gain Little Speed," 31 Aug. 1980, p. 2, col. 1, sec. E.

B. Examine these endnotes as they might appear at the end of a paper. If their format is correct, mark C; if incorrect, mark X and make the needed corrections.

¹ Alan Wheelis, "Will and Psychoanalysis," *Journal of the American Psychoanalytic Association*, 4 (1956), p. 256.

² Wheelis, p. 266.

³ Albert Camus, *The Stranger*, translated by Stuart Gilbert (New York: Vintage Books, 1946), p. 97.

⁴ Susan Sontag, "Baby," *Playboy*, Feb. 1974, p. 74.

⁵ Wheelis, 256.

⁶ Hilda M. Hulme, *Explorations in Shakespeare's Language* (New York: Longman, 1977).

⁷ Kurt Vonnegut, Jr. "The Hyannis Port Story," *Innovative Fiction: Stories for the Seventies*, ed. Jerome Klinkowitz and John Somer (New York: Dell, 1972), p. 3.

⁸ H. V. Hodson, *The Nuclear Deterrent*, "The Illustrated London News," Aug. 1980, p. 31.

⁹ Gail Cunningham, *The New Woman in the American Novel* (New York: Barnes and Noble, 1978), p. 12.

¹⁰ Hodson, "The Nuclear Deterrent," p. 31.

77

Use these guidelines in constructing a bibliography.

A bibliography is an alphabetical list of the books, articles, and other sources you have cited in your paper. Although some instructors may require you to list all the works you consulted in preparing your research paper, the most common practice is to list only those sources you have used and cited. Copy from your bibliography cards the complete information for each such source, and type the list on the last page of your paper (see the sample on p. 295).

The form for bibliography differs slightly from that for annotation.

1. Since the list is alphabetical, place authors' last names first. (If no author or editor is given, alphabetize by title.)
2. If you cite two or more works by the same author, use a twelve-space line of dashes followed by a period instead of repeating the author's name:

Ong, Walter J. The Barbarian Within. New York: Macmil-

    lan, 1962.

------------. The Presence of the Word. New Haven: Yale

    Univ. Press, 1967.

3. Separate the items within the entry with periods, not commas.
4. Although your endnotes or footnotes contain the *specific* page cited, in your bibliography you must include the *full* page reference for all periodical articles and chapters of books (for example: *Esquire*, Feb. 1981, pp. 60–62, 64–65, 133–34).

Sample Bibliography: Books

Single author:

Conrad, Peter. Imagining America. New York: Oxford Univ.

    Press, 1980.

Two or three authors:

Marchetti, Victor, and John D. Marks. The CIA and the

    Cult of Intelligence. New York: Knopf, 1974.

More than three authors:

Baugh, Albert C., et al. A Literary History of England.

    2nd ed. New York: Appleton, 1967.

Translated and edited books:

Homer. The Iliad. Trans. E. V. Rieu. Baltimore: Pen-

    guin, 1963.

Schiffhorst, Gerald J., ed. The Triumph of Patience:

    Medieval and Renaissance Studies. Gainesville: Univ.

    Presses of Florida, 1978.

Essay in a collection of essays:

Dunne, John Gregory. "A Riot on TV." The New Republic,

    11 Sept. 1965. Rpt. in Mass Media and the Popular

    Arts. Ed. Frederick Rissover and David C. Birch.

    New York: McGraw-Hill, 1971, pp. 148-49.

Your footnote or endnote should cite the specific piece which you used in the collection.

Encyclopedias:

O'Brien, Donald M. "Fire Fighting and Prevention."

    Encyclopedia Americana, 1973 ed.

Reprinted, revised, and subsequent editions:

Fitzgerald, F. Scott. The Great Gatsby. 1925; rpt. New

    York: Scribner's, 1953.

Lester, James D. <u>Writing Research Papers: A Complete</u>

    <u>Guide</u>. 3rd ed. Glenview, Ill.: Scott, Foresman,

    1980.

More than one volume:

Parrington, Vernon L. <u>Main Currents in American Thought</u>.

    3 vols. New York: Harcourt, 1927-32.

Sample Bibliography: Periodicals

Journal:

Fisher, Philip. "The Future's Past." <u>New Literary</u>

    <u>History</u>, 6 (1975), 587-606.

As in footnotes, drop "p." for "page" when the volume is listed; note that the complete pages are given for all articles.

Magazine:

"Battle Over Bilingualism." <u>Time</u>, 8 Sept. 1980, pp. 64-65.

Will, George F. "The Myth of Alger Hiss." <u>Newsweek</u>,

    20 March 1978, p. 96.

Book review:

Anderson, Jervis. "Life with Father, Duke Ellington."

    Rev. of <u>Duke Ellington in Person</u>, by Mercer Ellington.

    <u>New York Times Book Review</u>, 28 May 1978, p. 8.

Newspaper:

```
"In Search of Identity."  Editorial.  New York Times,

     27 May 1973, Sec. E, p. 14, col. 1.
```

Sample Bibliography: Other Sources

Pamphlet:

```
U.S. Civil Service Commission.  The Human Equation:

     Working in Personnel for the Federal Government.

     Washington, D.C.: GPO, May 1970.
```

This government publication is handled like a book, with the agency which produced it listed as author. When no date is given for a publication, use "n.d." (no date).

Unpublished thesis or dissertation:

```
Scott, Bonnie K.  "James Joyce in His Irish Milieu."  Diss.

     Univ. of North Carolina (Chapel Hill) 1974.
```

Interview or letter:

```
Willis, Dr. Susan L.  Personal interview.  2 Feb. 1981.
```

Film:

```
Forman, Milos, dir.  One Flew Over the Cuckoo's Nest.

     With Jack Nicholson.  Fantasy Films, 1975.
```

Recording or television/radio program:

"Blood Money." <u>60 Minutes</u>. New York: CBS-TV, 16 March

1980.

John, Elton. "This Song Has No Title." In <u>Goodbye Yellow</u>

<u>Brick Road</u>. MCA Records, MCA 2-10003, 1974.

EXERCISE 77 _____

Arrange the following sources into a bibliography as it would appear at the end of a research paper. Compare your version with that at the end of the sample paper, p. 295.

"Plot to Kill the Olympics." *Newsweek* (3 Sept. 1972), pp. 58–59.
"Terror at the Olympics." *Newsweek* (18 Sept. 1972), pp. 24–34.
C. Robert Paul and Jack Orr, *The Olympic Games: The Thrills and Drama from Ancient Greece to the Present Day.* New York: Lion Press, Inc., 1968.
The President's Commission on Olympic Sports. *The Final Report of the President's Commission on Olympic Sports.* Washington, D.C.: GPO, 1977, 2 volumes.
VanderZwaag, Harold J. "Amateurism and the Olympic Games," in Peter J. Graham and Horst Ueberhorst, ed., *The Modern Olympics* (Cornwall, N.Y.: Leisure Press, n.d.)
Chris Brasher. "The Last Olympics?" *The Illustrated London News,* July, 1980, pp. 32–33.
Doug Gilbert, *The Miracle Machine* (New York: Coward, McCann, and Geohegan, 1980).
"Game Playing in Montreal: Controversy Over Taiwanese Participation." *Time,* 26 July 1976, pp. 32 and 39.
Mandell, Richard D. *The Nazi Olympics.* New York: Macmillan, 1971.
"Olympics Send Russians Off on a Profit-Making Spree." *U.S. News and World Report,* 5 December 1977, p. 55.

Politics, Commercialism, and the Olympics

By

Chris Higgins

Composition 1

Dr. Schiffhorst

November 25, 1980

The thesis sentence is typed at the top of the outline.

A sentence outline, such as the one shown here, supplies topic sentences for many of the paragraphs in the paper and provides a skeleton of ideas to guide the student in writing. In its final form, it gives the reader a brief guide to the paper's contents.

258

OUTLINE

Thesis: The Olympics can and should work to re-establish idealism, abolish political rivalries and commercial exploitation, and allow a true Olympiad to be reborn.

I. What was the "original Greek ideal"?

   A. The athletes of the ancient Games lived up to the Greek ideal of a sound mind in a sound body.

   B. The modern Olympiad, based on similarly high standards, envisioned an ideal world forum for peace through sport.

II. These ideals of sportsmanship and peace have been undermined by commercialism and political nationalism.

   A. Television has heightened commercial and nationalistic pressures.

   B. Presentation and other costs have contributed to the commercialization of the Olympic Games.

      1. The host city must provide expensive facilities.

    2. Security costs have become a necessity because of international terrorism.

    3. Spectator expense is another area in which commercial exploitation flourishes.

    4. Commercialism has affected the athletes themselves.

  C. Political nationalism is perhaps dealing the mortal blow to the original Olympic ideals.

    1. Protests and boycotts based on racism or ideology have typified the modern Games.

    2. Nationalism has created the super-athlete, made superior by stimulants and steroids.

III. Solutions can and should be found for the problems facing the Olympics, or the Games will die.

This page is not numbered. The title is repeated as a heading. Quadruple space between the title and the first line of the text.

The introductory paragraph catches the reader's attention and then focuses that attention on the thesis statement, which appears at the end of the introduction.

The second paragraph contains information found in various sources. The encyclopedia article (note 1 on the following page) is cited as one convenient source of many of these background facts.

Politics, Commercialism, and the Olympics

Are the Olympics fated to die? Will 1984 mark the
end of the modern Olympic movement? Unfortunately, the
answer may be "yes" because the powerful forces of commercialism and political nationalism have corrupted the
original Olympic ideal. But the Olympic movement can and
should work to re-establish that idealism, abolish political rivalries and commercial exploitation, and allow a
true Olympiad to be reborn.

What we call the "original Olympic ideal" is a mixture of fact and legend. Tradition tells us that the
ancient Games, held every four years in honor of Zeus,
began in Olympia, Greece, in 776 B.C. and became the
greatest festival in the Greek world. Although nationalistic rivalries between city-states often ran high, the
emphasis was on the competition of athletes, who prepared
morally as well as physically in accordance with the Greek
idea of education: A victory was seen as a victory of
beauty, meaning bodily grace and perfection as well as the
possession of a reasoning mind and a pure conscience. And

Page numbers for all pages except the first are placed at the top of the page, flush with the one-inch right-hand margin. Quadruple space from the number to the first line of the text.

attaining beauty was the pursuit of anyone wishing to
acquire virtue. Victorious athletes were crowned with
wild olive branches, symbolic of peace and vitality.[1]
Before professionalism and corruption helped end the Games
in the fourth century A.D., they were marked by a high
degree of disciplined sportsmanship. Athletes were required to train under close supervision for ten months and
to take an oath that they had faithfully trained before
participating in the Games. Wars were suspended during
these popular summer games, and a model of amateur athletic
competition that rewarded individual excellence in an
atmosphere of peace and honest sportsmanship was established.

The Olympic movement as we know it, however, began
in 1896 with the grandiose plan of Baron Pierre de Coubertin. In reviving the Games, he proposed a version of the
ancient Olympiad for the whole world based on the belief
that sport would mean improved international communication.
The resulting modern Olympiad was modeled on the best elements in the original Greek system and was intended to

The source for the information about the modern Olympiad is Lucas, whom the student quotes directly to catch the author's original wording. Note how the student incorporates the direct quotation (see notecard) into her own sentence.

Lucas, p. 9   ideals

"The Olympics must be preserved. No other social institution in the world has, as its sole reason for existence, the brotherhood of man, the physical health of mankind, and the joy of international athletic competition."

Brackets are used for inserting clarifying information in note 3. The final paragraph here states the student's own views and requires no annotation.

emulate the high standards of the Greeks. Coubertin's ideal of universal communication has always been controversial, yet its basic idea remains sound. As John Lucas has said, "no other social institution in the world has, as its sole reason for existence, the brotherhood of man, the physical health of mankind, and the joy of international athletic competition."[2] Coubertin's vision, based on the Greek scholar-athlete ideal, was intended to achieve a world forum for athletic excellence and peace. Such a dream should reduce, not inflame, national rivalries. As Coubertin stated in 1896, "the most important thing [in the Olympic Games] is not to win but to take part, just as the most important thing in life is not the triumph but the struggle. The essential thing is not to have conquered but to have fought well."[3]

Not surprisingly, the goal of a trouble-free world championship has rarely been achieved, though the Olympics remain a dream for young people around the world. Ironically, television, which has carried the achievements of top athletes into millions of homes, creating a vast audi-

Since Brasher has been properly identified in the text and in note 4, the sentence following the note requires no annotation. Compare the student's paraphrase here with the direct quotation on her notecard:

Brasher, p. 32   Drugs

"I do not believe it is any coincidence that the first Olympics competitor to die of drugs was a Danish cyclist during the 1960 Games in Rome. If the 1968 Games were the first to be televised live, the 1960 Games were the first to be televised live throughout Europe."

ence for a new age of heroes, has played a major role in heightening international rivalries. The United States hockey team's defeat of a supposedly superior Soviet team at the Lake Placid Winter Games in 1980 was one of the significant stories of that year, thanks in part to wide TV coverage. And, since 1968, when the Mexico City Games were the first to be televised worldwide, the power of television as a commercial tool has dangerously affected the amateur nature of the Olympics, turning them into high-pressure events for athletes, their nations, and sponsors. Former Olympic champion Chris Brasher aptly observes in The Illustrated London News how external forces can build and control sporting events that are big in themselves to command worldwide television coverage. "By 1968 satellites were able to beam live television into every country in the world and the audience was incalculable. What a prize for a manufacturer if he could get his product on to the feet of a man whom the world was going to see win an Olympic gold medal."[4] Brasher goes on to point out that the problem of drugs first surfaced

Here is a portion of the rough draft of this paper with corrections. Notice how the student has improved the writing by eliminating repetition and wordiness, using subordination, connecting sentences, and adding details for development.

More recently, pressures on the host city, spectators, & athletes have

Today, commercial exploitation has reached olympic

proportions. Presentation costs alone are represent a major [part expense

of the total commercialization of] the Olympic Games in of staging for the world TV audience.

These sentation costs are a financial burden borne by the host city. nation

which hosts the Games (and the host nation changes every

four years). These costs involving primarily facilities and

security, The host nation must provide The sponsoring

city with necessary facilities. must provide such Olympic facilities. These facilities include as

stadiums, gymnasiums, among other things. swimming pools, and housing. In order to T

illustrate the cost of these structures, U.S. News and

World Report partially itemized the costs for Moscow,

[which was] the host for the 1980 summer Games: "300 million dollars for new

and modernized facilities, 30,000 Moscow hotel rooms . . .

and an Olympic village eighteen apartment blocks long,

sixteen stories high." (5) (US News, p. 55)

270

in 1960, when the Rome Games were the first to be televised live throughout Europe.

More recently, commercial pressures on the host city,
the spectators, and the athletes have reached olympic proportions. Presentation costs alone are a major expense
in staging the Olympic Games for the world television
audience and for the tens of thousands of spectators and
participants. These costs, involving primarily facilities
and security, are a financial burden borne by the host
city. The sponsoring city must provide such Olympic
facilities as stadiums, gymnasiums, swimming pools, and
housing. To illustrate the cost of these structures,
U.S. News and World Report partially itemized the expenditures for Moscow, host for the 1980 Summer Games: "300
million dollars for new and modernized facilities, 30,000
Moscow hotel rooms . . . and an Olympic village eighteen
apartment blocks long, sixteen stories high."[5]

Bureaucratic and legal problems, along with national
pride, contribute to the exorbitant presentation costs,
many of which are unnecessary. For example, Jean Drapeau,

Note 6 provides annotation for the three sentences preceding it, all of which present facts summarized from a Time article.

The student's own opinion is clear between notes 6 and 7.

mayor of Montreal, proposed a 310 million dollar budget
for the 1976 Olympics. Of that budget, reported *Time*
magazine, 70 million dollars were set aside for a stadium
to be built with a roof which could be raised or lowered.
By the time expensive extras were included, the stadium
costs alone totaled 564 million dollars--exceeding the
total proposed budget by 254 million dollars.[6] Such
blatant extravagance is outrageous. Student leaders in
Mexico City (site of the 1968 Games) protested their government's Olympic budget; one student said, "It seems
ridiculous to see a government spend $80 million on an
imperialistic spectacle while millions of its citizens
live at sub-human levels."[7]

Security costs constitute the other half of presentation expenditures in the Olympic Games. The Olympic
dream of peaceful competition was shattered during the
1972 Munich Games when, as *Newsweek* reported, a Palestin-
ian terrorist group called Black September attacked the
Israeli dormitories in the Olympic village in a horrifying
massacre that shocked the world. The attack lasted nine-

teen hours and left seventeen people dead.[8] The security
of the participating athletes therefore became a major
concern of the 1976 Games in Montreal. The Canadian government spent over 100 million dollars and enlisted 9,000
armed forces to protect the Olympic village from attack.[9]
Security costs have become a necessary item in Olympic
budgets because some nations have ignored the Olympic
ideal of peaceful competition.

Spectator expenses have also mushroomed. These costs,
which help the host city meet its expenses, include
tickets, souvenirs, coins, lotteries, stamps, meals, and
lodging. Spectators purchasing a ticket to view Olympic
events spend an average of twenty-five dollars. Exploitation occurs when a fan pays a scalper an exorbitant price
(from one to two hundred dollars) to see an outstanding
performer. As many news accounts have revealed, scalping
is evident also in other spectator expenses, notably meals
and lodging, which may double in price during the event.

Finally, commercialism has affected the athletes.
This exploitation is most evident in money given to the

Note the effective transition in the first full paragraph as the student leads the reader from the commercial to the political aspects of the topic.

athletes by equipment manufacturers to use their sporting goods. According to Olympic rules, a competitor must be an amateur and must not allow his or her "person, name, picture, or sports performance to be used for advertising. . . ."[10] But many athletes devote so much time to perfecting their skills that they have no time left to earn a living; for them, accepting under-the-table money seems justifiable.

Although commercialism has had a hand in strangling the modern Olympic ideal, political nationalism, also magnified by worldwide TV, is perhaps dealing the mortal blow to the Games. The Olympics in the twentieth century have been plagued by petty political disputes, boycotts, and terrorism. Wars and political animosities were suspended during the ancient Games, but this civilized ideal has not been a mark of the modern Olympiad, which has spawned ultranationalism, a very different thing from pride in one's country.

The 1936 Olympics, held in Berlin, were the first games threatened by international boycott because of Nazi

A quotation that exceeds four typed lines is indented ten spaces, and no quotation marks are used. The student uses long quotations sparingly and introduces them to establish the reader's interest.

Because the facts following note 11 are repeated in numerous sources and are well-known, the student does not provide annotation.

racial views and fascist policies. As Richard Mandell
says in The Nazi Olympics,

> Expressions of disgust and tentative move-
> ments for the formation of a boycott . . . were
> voiced in Sweden, the Netherlands, and Czecho-
> slovakia. . . . Spain, like the Soviet Union,
> had no team in Berlin in 1936. . . . The Ameri-
> cans actually produced a serious and frightening
> (for the Nazis at least) protest movement.[11]

While Leni Riefenstahl's classic documentary Olympische
Spiele glorified "Aryan beauty and strength," the true
hero in Berlin was Jesse Owens, the American black athlete
who won four gold medals. Since 1936, boycotts have been
used repeatedly (especially since 1968) by nations and
political groups wishing to express differences over race,
religion, or ideology. In Mexico City's 1968 games, Black
Power militants made a demonstration to call attention to
racial strife in America, and African athletes in 1976
protested South Africa's racial policies. In 1972, the

It is clear from note 12 that a book by Gilbert has been used as the source of the facts about drugs.

10

International Olympic Committee voted to oust white suprem-
acist Rhodesia, giving in to the demands of black African
and some United States athletes. The Munich Games of 1972
are also remembered for the Black September massacre mentioned earlier. In the 1976 Montreal Olympics, Taiwan
was expelled because the I.O.C. for the first time allowed
a host country--Canada, which recognized mainland China--
to refuse entry to a qualified team for political reasons.
The 1980 Games in Moscow were boycotted by a number of countries, led by the United States, because of opposition to
the Soviet Union's invasion of Afghanistan. Who has been
hurt by such protests? The Olympic athletes and the movement itself, not the nations expelled or opposed.

In addition, nationalism has created the super-
athlete, made superior by stimulants and anabolic steroids.
In The Miracle Machine, Doug Gilbert reports that drugs,
including amphetamines, heroin, caffeine, and nitroglyc-
erine, were once used by athletes to give them an extra
edge over their competitors.[12] Fortunately, tests have
been developed to detect the presence of stimulants in

the system. Any stimulant found in the blood of an Olympic athlete immediately disqualifies that athlete from competition.

Unfortunately, the drive to eliminate the use of anabolic steroids has not been successful. One reason for this lack of success, according to Brasher, is that it took more than a decade for scientists to produce a proper screening test. Brasher goes on to identify another problem:

> . . . an athlete can use anabolic steroids during his winter and spring training and then stop taking them for three weeks before the Games. His muscles have benefitted throughout many months of training so that his performance during the Games is enhanced. Observers like myself believe--but we have no proof--that the majority of medal winners in the "heavy" events (shot, discus, javelin, weight-lifting) in the last three Olympic Games have taken steroids during their training build-up.[13]

12

What is wrong with using a muscle-building agent to increase strength? First, competition should be based on the natural skills of the athlete; therefore, using a drug to enhance those skills violates that basic competitive rule. There is also an obvious, practical reason for athletes not to use anabolic steroids: They have alarming side effects. Possessed by a desire to win, a desire to beat the rest of the world symbolically, those who display intense nationalism have spawned a generation of Frankenstein-like athletes around the world.

Perhaps the most blatant example of nationalism contributing to the pressures to win Olympic gold has been seen in East Germany. This small country of seventeen million people has seized on those Olympic sports that receive the most TV coverage--swimming, gymnastics, track and field--to establish its national identity. As a result of intense training from early childhood, East German athletes are able to defeat competitors from much larger countries in a propaganda effort transmitted around the world by TV satellites. National prestige, not the excel-

By stating "Brasher and others are right," the student does two things: she indicates that this suggestion has been advanced by several writers, and she indicates her agreement with them.

The student's own views are clear as she offers solutions to the problem posed by the thesis and prepares for the conclusion.

lence of individual athletes, has been the motivating force.

The futile game of one-upmanship played by all the nations participating in the Olympic Games is killing the international event. Commercial exploitation and political nationalism, like cancerous tumors, must be removed from the Olympics. How can this be accomplished? First, to rid the Olympics of commercialism, the International Olympic Committee should find a permanent home for the Games (perhaps Olympia, Greece, the site of the ancient Games). Brasher and others are right in suggesting that a permanent home, in a neutral country, would ease the financial burden placed on host nations. All participating nations could contribute to a general fund for maintaining the facilities and for security. The athletes should be supported financially by their nations to reduce the temptation to take bribes from sporting goods manufacturers. Second, to eliminate nationalism from the Olympics, competitors must agree to suspend political hostilities during the Games and allow athletes to com-

The conclusion sums up the paper's key ideas and restates the thesis in different terms.

pete free of the pressure to win medals for their nations'
glory. And the I.O.C. should resist pressures from countries seeking to use the Olympics as a political or propaganda weapon. Finally, to downplay politics and allow
athletes to have the spotlight, Olympic officials should
ban national uniforms, flags, and anthems as well as
national scorekeeping.

If the International Olympic Committee and the various national Olympic committees implement these reforms,
the Games will survive in a revitalized form, providing
young people of all nations, creeds, and colors with in-
valuable opportunities to meet and compete in the spirit
envisioned by Coubertin. The athletes themselves, not
their nations, will be the winners. The Olympic ideals
of discipline, excellence, and sportsmanship can and
should be re-established; if they are not, the Olympics
will die. Perhaps the meaning of the original Greek
prize--peace and vitality--can be restored for the
benefit of the Olympics and the world.

Center the word "Notes" two inches from the top. The page is not numbered (but any further pages of notes would be numbered). Use four spaces before beginning the first note.

in note 1, no page is required for alphabetically-arranged books.

in note 4, omit the volume number for weekly and monthly periodicals that are paged anew with each issue.

in note 9, a second reference to a source already cited requires only an abbreviated reference, usually author and page; here, a shortened version of the title is given since there is no author.

Notes

[1] "Olympic Games," The New Columbia Encyclopedia, 1975 ed.

[2] John Lucas, The Modern Olympic Games (South Brunswick, N.J.: A. S. Barnes, 1980), p. 9.

[3] President's Commission on Olympic Sports, The Final Report of the President's Commission on Olympic Sports (Washington, D.C.: GPO, 1977), I, 1.

[4] Chris Brasher, "The Last Olympics?" The Illustrated London News, July 1980, p. 32.

[5] "Olympics Send Russians off on a Profit-Making Spree," U.S. News and World Report, 5 Dec. 1977, p. 55.

[6] "Game Playing in Montreal: Controversy over Taiwanese Participation," Time, 26 July 1976, p. 39.

[7] "Plot to Kill the Olympics," Newsweek, 2 Sept. 1968, p. 58.

[8] "Terror at the Olympics," Newsweek, 18 Sept. 1972, p. 24.

[9] "Terror at the Olympics," p. 24.

in note 10, use "n.d." if no publication or copyright date is cited for the book (use "n.p." if no city is listed for the publisher).

in note 13, simply repeat author's last name and supply the page number for a source already identified.

[10] Harold J. VanderZwaag, "Amateurism and the Olympic Games," in The Modern Olympics, ed. Peter J. Graham and Horst Ueberhorst (Cornwall, N.Y.: Leisure Press, n.d.), p. 93.

[11] Richard D. Mandell, The Nazi Olympics (New York: Macmillan, 1971), pp. 68-69.

[12] Doug Gilbert, The Miracle Machine (New York: Coward, McCann and Geohegan, 1980), p. 203.

[13] Brasher, p. 33.

Center the word "Bibliography" two inches from the top of the page, skip four lines before beginning the first source, and leave the page unnumbered. Here the student lists in alphabetical order all the works used to prepare, and cited in, the paper. (Some writers list other works which they have read and used, even if these works are not cited in the notes.)

Supply the complete pages for periodical articles. The Time article occupies two non-consecutive pages.

A state is supplied after the publisher's city (South Brunswick, N.J.) only to provide clarity.

The President's Commission is used as the "author" of the report.

Bibliography

Brasher, Chris. "The Last Olympics?" The Illustrated
    London News, July 1980, pp. 32-33.

"Game Playing in Montreal: Controversy Over Taiwanese
    Participation." Time, 26 July 1976, pp. 32, 39.

Gilbert, Doug. The Miracle Machine. New York: Coward
    McCann and Geohegan, 1980.

Lucas, John. The Modern Olympic Games. South Brunswick,
    N.J.: A. S. Barnes, 1980.

Mandell, Richard D. The Nazi Olympics. New York:
    Macmillan, 1971.

"Olympic Games." The New Columbia Encyclopedia. 1975 ed.

"Olympics Send Russians Off on a Profit-Making Spree."
    U.S. News and World Report, 5 Dec. 1977, p. 55.

"Plot to Kill the Olympics." Newsweek, 2 Sept. 1972,
    pp. 58-59.

President's Commission on Olympic Sports. The Final
    Report of the President's Commission on Olympic
    Sports. 2 vols. Washington, D.C.: GPO, 1977.

The final item indicates use of a chapter in an edited volume.

"Terror at the Olympics." Newsweek, 18 Sept. 1972,

    pp. 24-34.

VanderZwaag, Harold J. "Amateurism and the Olympic Games."

    In The Modern Olympics. Ed. Peter J. Graham and

    Horst Ueberhorst. Cornwall, N.Y.: Leisure Press, n.d.,

    pp. 92-99.

SPECIAL APPLICATIONS

The techniques of clear, effective writing are essentially the same in all situations, whether in the composition classroom, in another classroom, or on the job. But some types of writing have special requirements in addition to those already discussed in this book. This chapter is designed to help you with some of the special types of writing you will be likely to face in college or in business.

78

Use conventionally accepted style and form for business letters.

No other type of writing today is as stylized as the business letter. Although conventional practices concerning letter form and tone vary somewhat, you must follow some standards if you want your reader to accept and respect your letters. The suggestions below present the most commonly accepted conventions.

78a Arrange the parts of your letter according to standard form.

The eight parts listed below are required in all business letters. Arrange them as shown in the sample. Single-space within each part, but double-space between parts and between paragraphs. Use at least one-inch margins at the sides and one and one-half inches at top and bottom. Balance a short letter to fill as much of the page as possible.

Letterhead or return address. If no printed letterhead is available, type your return address so that it ends at the right-hand margin. Start one and one-half inches from the top.

Dateline. Center the correct date two lines below the letterhead. If you type your return address, type the date immediately below the last line of the address.

Inside address. Four to eight spaces below the dateline, put the name, title, and mailing address of the person to whom you are writing. The inside address may require three, four, or five lines, each starting at the left margin.

Salutation. Write the salutation flush with the left margin two spaces below the inside address. If the letter is addressed to an individual, use *Dear Ms. X, Dear Mrs. X,* or *Dear Miss X* for female addressees, *Dear Mr. X* for males—or, when appropriate, use a title such as *Dr.* or *Professor.* If the letter is addressed to a job title without a specific person's name (such as Director of Personnel), use *Dear Sir* or *Dear Madam.* Some writers prefer *Dear Sir or Madam.* If the letter is addressed to a group, such as a company or department, use *Gentlemen* or *Ladies.* Put a colon (:) at the end of the salutation.

Body.   Begin the body two lines below the salutation. Either indent the first line of each paragraph five spaces or start it at the left margin. Double-space between paragraphs.

Complimentary close.   Put the complimentary close two lines below the end of the body, starting five spaces to the right of the center. Use only standard closings such as *Sincerely yours* or *Yours truly.* Capitalize the first word and put a comma after the last.

Signature.   Type your name four spaces directly below the complimentary close. Women may type *Mrs., Miss,* or *Ms.* in parentheses before their names to indicate their preference.

Written signature.   Sign your name in the space between the complimentary close and the typed signature.

In addition to these eight required elements, certain others are sometimes needed:

Identification line.   When typing someone else's letter, list that person's initials followed by your own in the following manner: DEF: 1f. Start it at the left margin two lines below the typed signature.

Enclosure notation.   If you enclose anything with the letter, place an enclosure notation two spaces below the identification line or typed signature. Use one of the following forms:

Enc.   or   Encs. 2.

Carbon-copy notation.   If anyone other than you and the addressee is to receive a copy of the letter, include a carbon-copy notation. Put it on the left margin two spaces below the previous notation. Use the following form:

```
cc: Mr. Anthony Canteras.
```

Second-page heading. If a letter requires more than one page, use plain paper instead of letterhead for the second and subsequent pages. Leave a one-inch margin at the top, type a second-page heading as shown below, skip three spaces, then continue the letter. A second page must have at least two lines of body.

```
Mr. Ralph Bushee                2              February 2, 1981
```

Envelopes. Placement of the address is important so that the address can be read by the post office's optical scanners. The last line should be no more than three inches and no less than one-half inch from the bottom of the envelope. Leave at least one inch from the end of the longest line to the right-hand edge.

78b Use the all-purpose letter pattern.

Nearly any letter you will have to compose can be developed using a three-phase pattern. Begin by getting to the point within the first two sentences, stating the basic purpose of your letter much as you would the thesis of an English composition. Then develop your point by adding specific details and examples as needed. Be concise, and use short paragraphs so that your reader can refer quickly to each specific point you make. Finally, write a brief one- or two-sentence paragraph to close the letter smoothly. Note how the sample letter on the next page follows this pattern.

Adapt your tone to your reader and the situation, and be cordial but businesslike. Avoid the jargon often associated with business letters: *in reference to, pursuant to, yours of the 12th received,* and so on. You can communicate more clearly and effectively without such phrases (see **67**).

RETURN ADDRESS	2415 Overdene Avenue Rockford, Illinois 62320
DATELINE	March 10, 1981

INSIDE ADDRESS	Mr. James Robinson, Director Personnel Department Chicago Public Schools 228 N. La Salle Street Chicago, Illinois 60610
SALUTATION	Dear Mr. Robinson:

BODY

    I would like to be considered for a position teaching English in a Chicago high school.

    As the enclosed résumé shows, I am well qualified to teach remedial English, especially among students to whom English is a second language. I am well aware of the difficulties of such a position, but, with my preparation and determination, I am confident I can succeed.

    I would be happy to come into the city at your convenience to discuss any available position. You may reach me at my campus phone (815) 299-8820. Thank you for your consideration.

COMPLIMENTARY CLOSE   Sincerely yours,

WRITTEN SIGNATURE   *Steven M. Gallarza*

SIGNATURE   Steven M. Gallarza

        Enclosure

79

Prepare a clear, concise résumé to emphasize your strengths.

Few things you ever write will be as important to you as the résumé you submit to prospective employers. The facts do not speak for themselves; a well-prepared résumé will enhance your qualifications.

79a Include the appropriate information in your résumé.

When preparing a résumé, select facts about your background that will present you as positively as possible. Do not lie or concoct fictitious credentials, but select those that present the best impression.

Personal data. By law, you do not have to furnish personal data to prospective employers, but many people include it on their résumés. If you include personal information, choose from among the following: date of birth, height and weight, sex, marital status, number of children, religious preference, health, military status.

Educational background. Begin with the college you are currently attending and work backwards to the high school from which you graduated. Give dates of attendance or degrees, names of degrees or majors and minors, memberships in organizations and honor societies, and gradepoint average if it is impressive.

Work experience. Begin with your present or most recent job and work back to your high-school graduation date; you may include significant part-time work from your high-school days. Give your past employers' names and addresses, dates of employment, and job descriptions.

Professional skills. If you have experience or training in the field you are applying in, develop a special section summarizing your skills. The exact skills will vary with your field, but the following suggestions should help: equipment, procedures, or special techniques used; supervisory positions held; unusual promotions or awards; certifications or registrations.

Related skills or activities. If you have acquired through elective courses, hobbies, or other means any skills that might be useful in the desired position, you may include them. You may also mention community activities. Include anything that might give you a slight edge over other candidates. Do not bother listing interests or hobbies merely to give the reader a notion of what you are like.

Position desired. Many applicants name the actual position being sought; others list a broader "objective." Use either if you wish, but your accompanying letter of application should state the position you are seeking; stating that position in your résumé may prevent your being considered for other openings.

References. Including references is usually unnecessary, but feel free to do so, especially to fill out an otherwise very short résumé. If you do include references, give the names, titles, and business addresses of three or four people who know you well and who can be trusted to speak favorably about you. Try to get variety, selecting people who know you in various ways.

Résumé of Steven M. Gallarza
2415 Overdene Avenue, Rockford, Illinois   62320
Telephone: 815-921-3752

Position Desired

English teacher in urban high school, preferably remedial
    classes.

Educational Background

Sept. 1979-present Northern Illinois University, DeKalb, IL.
    Expect to receive B.A. in English June, 1981. Minors in
    Spanish and special education. Active in many student
    groups. NIU G.P.A. 3.4 of 4.0.

June 1977-June 1979 Rock Valley College, Rockford, IL. AA
    degree, majoring in English. G.P.A. 3.8 of 4.0.

April 1977 Received GED diploma, State of Illinois.

Sept. 1970-June 1973 Auburn High School, Rockford, IL. Left
    to join U.S. Navy.

Work Experience

August 1979-present ITT, DeKalb, IL. Second shift assembly.
    Supervisor Michael Stoddard.

February 1977-July 1979 Sundstrand, Inc., Rockford, IL. Main-
    tenance work. Supervisor Bud Steinberg.

July 1973-January 1977 U.S. Navy E-5. Honorable Discharge.

Related Skills and Activities

Special tutor for Upward Bound program NIU. Volunteer reading
    teacher for Adult Literacy League. Three years' work
    with Spanish-speaking migrant labor families.

References available upon request
March, 1981

79b   Carefully prepare your résumé in an effective form.

The following checklist will help you to prepare an effective résumé:

1. Use correct grammar, but you may use phrases and clauses instead of complete sentences.
2. Use common abbreviations to save space.
3. Single-space within sections; double-space between sections.
4. State everything as positively as possible.
5. Make the final copy clean and neat, even if you must have a professional typist prepare it.
6. Put your name, address, and telephone number at the top.

80

Know how to approach an essay examination.

Essay examinations test both your knowledge of material and your ability to organize and present it. They enable your instructor to determine how well you can put facts into perspective and draw conclusions from them. Some questions ask you to provide facts; most ask you to state an opinion based on your study of the facts. Although it is no substitute for studying the material, learning how to approach an essay question properly will improve the quality of your answers.

80a   Read an essay question carefully to see what it requires you to do.

If you do not read a question carefully, you may end up writing about the general subject rather than answering the specific question. Look especially for key words that will help you determine how to approach and organize an answer:

analyze: break the topic into its parts and show how each part relates to the whole. In analyzing literature, for example, you might focus on how the author uses character, setting, and symbolism to convey a theme.

comment, criticize: state your opinion of the issue or statement in the question.

compare: explain both the similarities and differences.

contrast: explain the differences.

define: give the meaning of a term or concept (and show how it is different from related terms and concepts).

describe: explain what the subject is or looks like: what happened?

discuss: examine the topic in detail.

evaluate: judge the worth or quality of something, such as by making positive and negative points about it.

explain: make something clear or state the reason(s) for something.

illustrate: provide examples to explain a general statement.

interpret: explain the meaning of facts.

list, outline, review, summarize: give the main points of a concept or story, often in a numbered series.

prove: give reasons why a statement is true or false.

Before you begin to formulate an answer, make certain that you understand exactly what the question asks you to do. Do not squander valuable time summarizing a story or theory unless the question asks you to do so.

80b   Develop an essay answer much as you would a short theme.

Before you begin to write, decide on your basic answer, plan your overall organization, and begin deciding what specific details to use. You will usually not have time to develop a full outline, but you can take a few minutes to jot down notes. Consider also the length of time you will have. Plan an answer which you can complete in the time allotted.

Develop a good beginning that lets the reader (your instructor) know that you understand what is asked of you and that you do have an answer. Try in one or two sentences to state the essential answer, much as in a thesis statement in a theme (see **13**). Often you can turn the question into your opening statement:

QUESTION: Compare the motif of reality and illusion in *Hamlet, Macbeth,* and *Othello.*

THESIS: The motif of reality and illusion is interwoven with the theme in each of the three plays, but in varying degrees of complexity.

After opening with this thesis, you could go on to identify the theme of each play and to show how the motif of illusion relates to the theme in each. You should illustrate your points with references to particular scenes, but you should not spend time summarizing the plots of the plays or simply describing the scenes in which illusion is particularly important.

If you were asked to evaluate the usefulness of solar energy in home heating, you might begin like this: "Solar energy is potentially useful in home heating, but neither the cost nor the available technology makes it a practical option, at least at this time." With this as an initial main idea, you can go on to develop each point (potential, cost, present technology) in more detail.

The middle section of your answer should expand each of the points mentioned in your brief introduction. Use as many specific details as time and space allow to clarify or defend your main point. Many weak answers are too general: they correctly provide the essentials but fail to support them. Remember that essay tests are not invitations to toss around vague generalities: the more specific the facts and figures you provide, the better will seem your grasp of the issues. But do not think that mere length will impress your instructor. Get to the point quickly and give a concise but reasonably complete response.

Finally, write a brief conclusion. In a short answer, a single sentence will suffice; longer essays will require a short paragraph. Restate your main point clearly and emphatically, returning to the point with which you began (see **14**). Try to reserve a few minutes to check over your answers. Look for unclear statements, omitted words, or errors in punctuation or spelling. You will not attain the type of perfection which more time would make possible, but proofreading can make your presentation much more effective.

Consider the following responses to this essay question:

How did the cases of *Near v. Minnesota* and *New York Times v. U.S.* (the Pentagon Papers case) influence freedom of the press?

1. In both *Near v. Minnesota* and *New York Times v. U.S.*, the U.S. Supreme Court limited the rights of state and federal governments to restrict the press. In *Near v. Minnesota*, the court held that suppression of *The Saturday Press* was unconstitutional censorship. The court acknowledged that, although libelous statements may be punishable, the First Amendment guarantees the freedom to publish news without prior injunctive restraints. *The Saturday Press*, the court ruled, may have been guilty of publishing defamatory articles, but it had the constitutional right to do so.

   New York Times v. U.S. reaffirmed the Supreme Court's reluctance to allow politically controversial material to be suppressed. The court held that the government could not censor publication of the Pentagon Papers by the *New York Times*. The Justice Department argued that publication of some information in the Pentagon Papers could threaten national security. The *Times* replied that the First Amendment protects freedom of the press and that the government had not shown the need for "prior restraint" to halt publication of the papers. The *Times* also argued for the right of Americans to be truthfully informed about their government. Agreeing with the *Times*, the court stated that the government failed to meet the burden of proof showing how the papers endangered national security so as to justify prior restraint. However, the court conceded that the press may be censored in advance by the government in "exceptional cases" or in more urgent circumstances related to national security.

The Supreme Court, in both cases, protected and upheld freedom of the press. The question of libel in *Near v. Minnesota* did not justify prior restraint to halt publication; and, although the court found that national security did not justify censorship in the case of *New York Times v. U.S.*, prior restraint was held to be valid in exceptional situations.

2. Both cases dealt with a particular interpretation of the First Amendment to the Constitution. That amendment states that the government, federal or state, has no right to interfere with freedom of speech, freedom of the press, freedom to follow religious convictions, or the freedom to assemble and criticize the government. The specific and vital issue in *Near v. Minnesota* and *New York Times v. U.S.* concerns the freedom of press. One case had to do with a state government; the other with the federal government.

The Saturday Press, a respectable Minneapolis weekly, published a series of articles accusing the city administrators of corrupt actions. Perhaps out of fear, guilt, or simple revenge, the city officials passed a statute that restricted any newspaper, magazine, or other periodical from publishing an article that was libelous with no good motive. The city officials determined that *The Saturday Press* did not comply with these terms—they had no good motive for publishing the articles. Consequently, the city officials attempted to close down the newspaper.

In 1971 secret government documents describing the early political decisions of the Vietnam War were unlawfully given to the *New York Times*. Prepared by the Secretary of Defense in the Johnson Administration, the Pentagon Papers revealed the clandestine actions of four successive administrations. Military and political decisions were made and executed without the knowledge or agreement of Congress or the people. The *New York Times* began publishing these articles until legal protests from the Justice Department temporarily halted publication.

The question of freedom of the press is particularly

controversial today when government activity demands increasing amounts of security. Various excuses such as internal stability, external threat, or preservation of the national image discourage criticism. However, the Supreme Court continues to uphold the First Amendment and to follow its duty to protect the constitutional rights of Americans to publish the truth.

Note that Answer 1 begins with a clear thesis statement, supports that statement with specific details, and closes with a brief summary. Above all, it answers the question that was asked. By contrast, Answer 2 opens with a vague statement, wanders off into background material, and never addresses the original question. Although it includes as much detail as Answer 1, it is not a satisfactory answer.

81

Keep your abstract as concise as possible, covering only the most important points of the original.

Abstracts come in several varieties: the *descriptive abstract* is nothing more than a few sentences describing the main sections of a document, essentially a detailed table of contents in sentence and paragraph form. Descriptive abstracts are rarely written in college and are best learned by imitating models used by others on your job. *Informational abstracts,* which are much more common and more useful, summarize the main points of a document. The suggestions below will help you to write an effective informational abstract.

Begin by outlining the major points, developing a sentence for each main point. Do not describe the source; condense it. Do not, for instance, make statements such as "The article points out the advantages

Abstract of

"Politics, Commercialism, and the Olympics"

The athletes of the ancient Greek Olympics swore to uphold the rules and the highest ideals of sportsmanship. When Baron de Coubertin revived the games in 1896, he followed the same ideals. Now commercialism and nationalism threaten them. Presentation costs include enormous sums spent on facilities and security by the host nation. Commercial exploitation, aided by worldwide TV coverage, has driven spectator costs to outlandish levels. Even the athletes are exploited commercially by equipment suppliers. The mortal blow is being dealt, however, by political nationalism. Boycotts, protests, and even murders based on racism or religious or ideological bigotry have become almost commonplace. Furthermore, drugs have made many competitors into super-athletes. Five steps must be taken to restore the original ideals: A permanent home should be found for the games. Nations should financially support the athletes. Hostilities should be suspended during the games. No drugs should be permitted. Uniforms, flags, anthems, and national scorekeeping should be prohibited.

and disadvantages of the catalytic converter." Instead say something such as "catalytic converters have the following advantages. . . ." Use no more than one tenth the number of words in the original; some instructors and organizations prefer only one twentieth the original length.

Be generous with the main points, including everything that looks important. The result will be a rough draft that is too long. Edit that draft to the required size: go through it twice, first for coverage, then for conciseness. Delete any points that are less important than the others or that are actually supporting details of other points. Make each sentence lean but substantial; make every word count. The measure of a good abstract is the number of important ideas contained within the allotted number of words.

Do not worry if your abstract lacks smooth transitions or if the sentences are not elegant. Do make them clear and grammatical, however. The model shown here is an abstract of the sample research paper, pages 257–297.

GLOSSARY OF GRAMMATICAL TERMS

Absolute construction   A phrase which qualifies a sentence but is not grammatically related to it: *This being true*, she left.

Active voice   See Voice.

Adjective   A word which describes or limits a noun or pronoun: The *rude* remark. See **15d**, **21**, **52a**.

Adverb   A word modifying a verb (ran *quickly*), an adjective (*very* grateful), or another adverb (*quite* smoothly). See **15d**, **21**, **52b-c**.

Antecedent   A noun to which a pronoun refers: The *men* are coming; here they are. (*They* refers to, or stands for, *men*, the antecedent of *they*.) See **51**.

Appositive   A noun (or equivalent) placed next to another to explain it: Sam, *the teller*, was wrong. See **26b**.

Auxiliary verb   A form of *be, can, could, do, get, have, may, might, must, ought, shall, should, will*, or *would* used in a verb phrase (*had* seen, *will be* going). See **22-24**.

Case The grammatical category of a noun or pronoun that indicates its role in or relationship to other elements in a sentence. The *nominative case* is used for subjects of verbs (*he* is); the *objective case* is used for objects (I hit *him;* beside *me*); and the *possessive case* indicates ownership (*his* arm). See **20**.

Clause A group of words containing a subject and a verb. A main or independent clause can stand alone as a sentence: *He ran his fastest race,* but *he still came in second* (two independent clauses). A subordinate or dependent clause cannot stand alone: *Although he ran his fastest race;* the runner *who came in second.* See **15**, **16**, **45**, **46**.

Collective noun A word such as *class* or *committee* which names a group of persons or things; it may take a singular or a plural verb. See **18**, **19**.

Complement A word or phrase which completes the structure of a predicate. Complements include objects as well as predicate nominatives and predicate adjectives. A *subject* (or *nominative*) *complement* is a word or phrase following a linking verb used to identify the subject:

> Her paper is a *masterpiece.* (predicate nominative)
> Her paper is *excellent.* (predicate adjective)

An objective complement completes the meaning of the object:

> Everyone is calling him a *liar.* (objective complement)
> The jury found the defendant *innocent.* (objective complement)

See **15**, **20**, **21**.

Conjunction A word used to connect parts of a sentence or to relate sentences. Coordinating conjunctions *(and, but, or, nor, for, yet, so)* link equal elements; subordinate conjunctions (such as *because, if, although*) link a dependent clause with a main clause. See **15**, **16**, **17**.

Conjunctive adverb   A word such as *thus, moreover,* or *however* that connects one main clause to another. See **17**.

Coordinating conjunction   See Conjunction.

Dependent clause   A clause that functions as an adjective, an adverb, or a noun. See Clause. See also **16**.

> *Adjective clause:* The senator *who left early* supported the amendment.
> *Adverb clause: Because he left so early,* he missed the crucial vote.
> *Noun clause: That he left so early* is unfortunate.

Direct object   See Object.

Elliptical construction   A phrase or clause in which clearly understood words are omitted: He is taller than you (are tall). Tom is here and Bill is (here) too.

Gerund   The *-ing* form of a verb used as a noun: *Making money* (gerund phrase) is his only concern.

Idiom   A conventionally acceptable but not logically explainable expression *(put up with).* See **59**.

Independent clause   A clause which can stand alone as a sentence. See Clause. See also **15h**, **17**.

Indirect object   See Object.

Infinitive   The uninflected form of a verb (called the stem), usually preceded by *to,* as in *to smoke;* it sometimes functions as a noun: Sally decided *to smoke* (infinitive as direct object). The infinitive can also be used as a modifier: Helen is a woman *to watch.* Occasionally the infinitive appears without *to:* He does nothing but *complain.*

Interjection   A word used as an exclamation: *No!* See **31**.

Linking verb   Forms of the verb *to be* as well as such words as *seem, feel, become,* and *look,* which link the complement to the subject: Jack *is* a hunter. The film *seems* uneven. See **15**, **53**.

Modifier   A word which describes or limits another word or group of words. See **21**.

Mood   Form of a verb which indicates whether the action or condition it expresses is a factual question or statement (indicative mood), a command or request (imperative mood), or a wish or condition contrary to fact (subjunctive mood). See **24**.

Indicative:	*Will* you be there? Adrian *is* there now.
Imperative:	*Be* there at eight o'clock.
Subjunctive:	If I *were* going to be there, I would have left already.

Nonrestrictive   A modifying phrase or clause that does not limit or identify a noun. It is set off with commas. A *restrictive modifier* limits or restricts the noun it modifies. It is not set off with commas. See **26a**.

Restrictive:	People *who overeat* risk early heart attacks.
Nonrestrictive:	Bill Thomas, *who ate twice as much as anyone else I knew,* lived to age 95.

Noun   A word which names something: *lady, squirrel, history, patience, writing* (common nouns). Proper nouns for specific names and places are capitalized: *Mrs. Green, Chicago, University of Illinois.* See **15b**.

Number   Singular or plural: *college, colleges; goose, geese; this, these;* present-tense verbs change form in the third person (he *runs,* they *run*) to indicate the singular. So does *be* in the past (he *was,* they *were*). See **18**, **56b**.

Object   1. A *direct object* usually "receives" the action of the verb: Connors hit *the ball. What* did he hit? 2. An *indirect object* indicates to whom or for whom (or what) something is done: Connors gave *Evert* a kiss. 3. Participles, gerunds, and infinitives take objects to complete their meaning (Turning the *corner,* to win the *election*) as do prepositions (from the *house*). See **15**, **20**.

Participle The *present participle*, which always ends in -*ing*, is used with forms of *be* in verb phrases *(is sinking)* or as a modifier *(sinking ship)*. The *past participle*, which ends in -*ed* for regular verbs (see **23** for irregular verbs), is used as part of a verb phrase *(has sunk, is used)* or as a modifier *(used car)*. See also Verbal. See **15a**, **52f**.

Parts of speech The classes of words determined according to their meaning or to their function in a sentence: nouns, pronouns, adjectives, adverbs, verbs, prepositions, conjunctions, and interjections. See **15**.

Passive voice See Voice.

Person Grammatically, subjects are divided into three *persons*: the person speaking (first person), the person spoken to (second person), and anyone or anything else (third person). Nouns, except those in direct address (*John*, please leave), are always considered third person.

First person:	I am. We are.
Second person:	You are. (singular or plural)
Third person:	He (she, it, the piano) is. They are.

Phrase A group of words which can function as a noun, verb, or modifier and which does not comprise a subject-verb combination. Some examples:

Prepositional phrase:	Henry stood *on the corner.*
Participial phrase:	The man *standing on the corner* is a private investigator.
Gerund phrase:	*Standing here* is a waste of time.
Infinitive phrase:	I hate *to stand around in bars.*
Verb phrase:	Henry *has been standing* there for hours.

Possessive See Case.

Predicate The verb by itself (simple predicate) or the verb with all of its modifiers, complements, and objects (complete predicate). See **15**.

Predicate adjective See Complement.

319

Preposition A word that relates a noun to another word in the sentence: *after, at, before, by, for, from, in, of, on, to, up,* and *with* are some commonly used prepositions. See **15e**.

Principal parts The three basic forms of a verb: infinitive *(to eat)*, past tense *(ate)*, and past participle *(eaten)*. See **15a**, **23**.

Pronoun A part of speech that stands for or refers to a noun. See **15c**, **19**, **20**, **51**.

> The Smiths are here. *I* invited *them* for dinner. *They* are the couple *who* bought our old sailboat.

Proper noun See Noun.

Relative pronoun A pronoun which introduces a subordinate clause: *who, whom, whose, that, which, what, whoever, whomever, whichever, whatever.*

Restrictive See Nonrestrictive.

Subject The word or word group about which the predicate says (or asks) something: The *students* work. See **15**.

Subjunctive See Mood.

Subordinate conjunction See Conjunction.

Tense The time to which a verb refers: present, past, future. See **22**, **23**, **56a**.

Verb A word or word group expressing action, process, or existence: He *is.* They *have shot* him. See also Predicate, Linking verb. See **15a**.

Verbal A word formed from a verb *(laughing)* and used as an adjective, an adverb, or a noun. Gerunds, participles, and infinitives are verbals. See **15a**.

Voice A verb with a direct object is in the *active voice:* Joan *read* the book. When the object *(book)* becomes the subject, the verb is in the *passive voice:* The book *was read* by Joan. See **24**, **48e**, **56a**.

Index

B

Sure, surely, 215
Symbols, pluralized, 121
Synonyms, need for, 151

T

Teach, learn, 215
Television programs,
  bibliography form for,
  254
Tense, 50, 77–82, 320
  avoiding shifts in, 171–72
Tests. *See* Essay
  examinations
Than, then, 215
That, vagueness of, 157
Their, there, they're, 215
Theirselves, 215
There, sentences beginning
  with, 64
Thesis,
  bibliography form for,
  254
  endnote form for, 248
Thesis statement, 11–13,
  44–47, 227–29, 258, 262
  in essay examination
  answers, 309
This, vagueness of, 157
Thusly, 216
Till, until, 216
Time, and use of colon, 109
Time, and verb tense, 77
Time words, 41
Title, of research paper, 262
Title cards, 222
Titles (personal), 99
  in business letters, 300

capitalization of, 125
Titles (of written works),
  capitalization of, 126
  in endnotes, 243–44
  in italics, 118
To, too, two, 216
To be,
  agreement with, 64
  tenses of, 78, 79
  and use of adjectives, 75
Topic, of composition,
  exploring, 9–10
  limiting, 8–9
  selecting, 3, 6–8, 217–19
Topic outlines, 16–18, 19
Topic sentences, 28–30,
  238, 258
  details to support, 31–34
  and other sentences,
  35–38
Trans., 244
Transition, 276–77
  by repetition, 151
Transitional devices, 39–44
Transitional expressions,
  97–98
Transitional paragraphs,
  41–43
Transitional phrases, 106
Transitional sentences,
  41–43
Transitional terms, 40–41
Transitive verbs, 85
Translations,
  bibliography form for,
  252
  endnote form for, 245
Trite expressions, 192–94